CONSUL IN JAPAN, 1903–1941

Oswald White in full-dress uniform in Seoul, 1930

Consul in Japan, 1903–1941

Oswald White's Memoir
'All Ambition Spent'

ဆာ

Edited by

Hugo Read

RENAISSANCE BOOKS

CONSUL IN JAPAN, 1903–1941
OSWALD WHITE'S MEMOIR 'ALL AMBITION SPENT'

First published 2017 by
RENAISSANCE BOOKS
P O Box 219
Folkestone
Kent CT20 2WP

Renaissance Books is an imprint of Global Books Ltd

ISBN 978-1-898823-64-3 Hardback
       978-1-898823-66-7 e-Book

The Publishers, wish to express their thanks to the Great Britain Sasakawa Foundation for their support in the making of this book.

British Library Cataloguing in Publication Data
A catalogue record for this book is available
from the British Library

Set in Garamond 11 on 12.5 pt by Dataworks
Printed and bound in England by CPI Antony Rowe Ltd., Chippenham, Wilts

CONTENTS

ℰↃ

Figures and Plate section face page 110

ACKNOWLEDGEMENTS

AFTER MY GRANDMOTHER died all of the papers belonging to her father, Oswald White, were passed on to our family. The major find in this were two old battered attaché cases containing the handwritten manuscript of his memoirs. My father David Read – White's grandson – and I were very excited with the find and with his encouragement I took on the project of turning the manuscript into a book. It was a much longer process than I envisaged and many thanks are due to a few vital people who have helped the manuscript become the book that you hold today.

First, I would like to thank Oswald White's two grandsons, my father David Read and his brother Tim Read. They and I went through the manuscript in detail, getting the document into a first typed-up version. Thanks are also due to my mother Gill Read who also went through this initial editing process. Following this I owe immeasurable thanks to Jim Hoare, who did a further level of editing on the work and also sorted out, corrected and improved all my footnotes. Following this he also wrote the Foreword to the volume. His unparalleled knowledge of Japan's Treaty Ports at the time, as well as his general enthusiasm and commitment to the project were instrumental in turning it into a book – I can't thank Jim enough. I would also like to thank our publisher Paul Norbury, who has believed in the work and taken it the last vital step, into print.

Finally, my last and biggest thanks go to my great-grandfather Oswald White himself, who was the beloved figurehead of our family. In writing these memoirs he has left us all with an invaluable first-hand account of Japan in the formative years of the twentieth century.

Hugo Read
January 2017

FOREWORD

by

Jim Hoare

℘

TOWARDS THE END of 2014, I became aware of a collection of photographs on the internet relating to John Carey Hall, a member of Britain's Japan Consular Service, whose final post was as Consul-General in Yokohama. Hall, a contemporary of Satow and Aston, was, like them, a good student of Japanese. I had always found him an interesting character, not least because he appeared to be virtually blind and deaf yet had continued at Yokohama until he reached retirement age. I had undertaken to write a short biography of him, which is what had led me to the photographs.

That in turn led me to the person who had posted the pictures, Hugo Read. I had hoped that there would be papers from Hall, but although Hugo was his great-great-grandson, there was little except a newspaper article written for the *Japan Chronicle* in 1918. But what Hugo did reveal was that Hall's son-in-law, Oswald White, had left a memoir. White I also knew. He, too, had been a consul in Japan, serving in Seoul and Manchuria, and had also ended his career as Consul-General. And so I was introduced to 'All Ambition Spent'. It was not, as might be assumed from the low-key title, a record of unfulfilled dreams, but an amusing and informative account of White's career and family, including an affectionate portrait of his father-in-law, together with much rumination about how the exotic Japan of his early career had become the militarist machine of 1941. Thanks to Hugo's preliminary work, it had not only been transferred to typescript but had also undergone some editing. It seemed to me well worth publishing.

Very few first-hand accounts by foreigners in Japan from the opening years of the late 1850s until the Pacific War appear to have survived. We have good archival and press material but the records of individuals are limited in number and most relate to the early years. One can read several accounts by participants in the Perry expedition, a few from the years 1858–1868 but thereafter virtually nothing. So, a first-hand account of living and working in Japan from 1903 to 1941 gives a unique insight into an important period and well-deserves being made more widely available. It is not a contemporary diary but a write-up of notes made towards the end of an eventful career. It thus includes reflective passages on the momentous developments of the later 1930s, as Japan moved onto a war footing in China. As Consul-General in the Chinese treaty port of Tianjin under Japanese occupation, White was in the middle of the growing tenseness between Britain and Japan. His post-war recollections are also valuable as he sought, like others who had lived and worked in Japan, to come to terms with what had happened to the country in which he had spent so much of his adult life. Although some saw him as 'pro-Japanese' (for example, see a report in the *Chicago Herald Tribune*, 28 October 1939), he was well aware of the dangers of Japanese militarism. But he did not merely condemn this; instead, he tried to understand why this had come about. Along the way he provides fascinating vignettes of his colleagues, some well known, others less so, while his service in Seoul, Mukden (now Shenyang) and Tianjin provides fresh material on the Japanese colonial empire. It deserves a wider audience.

INTRODUCTION

by

Hugo Read

ℬ

Oswald White

WHEN MY GRANDMOTHER died in 2000, I was given charge of a variety of her artefacts that had either been in her house or in her son's house. That son was my father. Along with a pile of ancient documents, I found a briefcase containing a manuscript written by my Grandmother's father, Oswald White, which is presented here.

Oswald White[1] was born on 23 September 1884 in Gosforth, Northumberland, the son of James White, a commercial clerk from Newcastle and Annie White, née Fish. He spent his whole career in the Japan Consular Service, serving the last third as a Consul-General, the highest position in the Service. He left his last official post in February 1941, before Pearl Harbor (December 1941) and therefore shortly before Japan, which had been fighting China since 1937, went to war with Britain and the United States. Towards the end of his career in the 1930s, he wrote his memoirs in notebooks, chronicling his time in the Service. These notebooks he subsequently wrote up into a manuscript in 1941 and 1942.

---

1   For a short account of his life and work, see Hugo Read, 'Oswald "Shiro" White (1884–1970): 38 Years in the Japan Consular Service', in Hugh Cortazzi, ed., *Britain and Japan: Biographical Portraits*, vol. X, (Folkestone, Kent: Renaissance Books, 2016), pp. 307–17.

Consequently there is a changing perspective as some of the writing takes place either side of Japan entering the Second World War.

After 1941 Oswald White returned to London, where he finished his career, using his unparalleled knowledge of the Japanese language and culture to help the government in their efforts against Japan. He retired in 1944 when he turned sixty, receiving a warm letter from Anthony Eden, which alluded to 'special services' he had undertaken for the government when back in London during the war:

> ….. The period of your service, which began just before the Russo-Japanese War, has coincided with the rapid growth of Japan and the resultant situation in the Far East which has ended in the present war there. The remarkable knowledge of the Japanese people, language and mental outlook which you acquired and developed through your service has proved of very great value to your country. This knowledge, supported by your gifts of character and ability, has enabled you to render outstanding service at various posts, culminating in your appointments as His Majesty's Consul-General at Seoul and Osaka where, thanks to your energy, tenacity and skill in negotiation, you succeeded to a remarkable degree in protecting British commercial interests in circumstances of great difficulty.
>
> ….
> You will I am sure, be glad that your exceptional knowledge of Japan has enabled you to continue to take a very important part in the struggle against the country. I am fully aware of the outstanding nature of the special services which you are at present rendering to His Majesty's Government. ….

I am not sure exactly what these services were, but with his long experience of the region from a Western perspective, his knowledge and insight must have been invaluable.

Later, in 1952, Shigemitsu Mamoru,[2] the Japanese Foreign Minister who signed the surrender at the end of the Second World

---

[2]   Shigemitsu Mamoru (1887–1957), Japanese diplomat and politician. He was ambassador in London from 1938 to 1941, and was convicted as a war criminal in the Tokyo War Crimes Trials. See Antony Best, 'Shigemitsu Mamoru, 1887–1957: Critical Times in a Long, Ambivalent Career (London 1938–41)', in Ian Nish, ed., *Japanese Envoys in Britain,*

War, published his memoirs. As these were written in Japanese, once again White's assistance was sought. Shortly afterwards, he told his grandson (my father, David Read) that the security services approached him to translate the work, as he was quite probably the West's leading expert on Japanese at the time, plus he had expert knowledge of the Japanese empire. He told my father that the Pentagon and US intelligence services were particularly keen to see a translation of Shigemitsu's work, because it opened a window onto the Japanese mentality that took them into the war. His translation of the work was published in 1958.

As can be readily inferred from these memoirs, White was a very modest man, whose great mind, skills and diplomacy he never bragged about. Even though by the end of his career he was among the leading Western experts on the Japanese language and had profound knowledge of the culture and the region, it would be hard to tell from his own writings.

Following the publication of his translation of Shigemitsu, White, now in his mid-seventies, finally retired for good to his house in Hampstead with his wife Peggy, and not far from his three daughters and two grandsons. After the death of his wife he sold his Hampstead home and lived his last few years in residence at the Leicester Court Hotel, South Kensington. He died on 29 December 1970, at the age of eighty-six.

Before finishing this introduction to his memoirs, it is worthwhile understanding the context of the Japan Consular Service during his time in office.

The Fall of China and The Rise of Japan

Coming into the nineteenth century, China had a very long and proud history as a powerful imperial power through a succession of dynasties. The last of these dynasties, the Qing (or Manchu), started in the seventeenth century and ran until 1912. This multi-cultural empire formed the territorial base for the modern Chinese state. However, by the mid-nineteenth century the

---

1862–1964: A Century of Diplomatic Exchanges. Folkestone, Kent: Global Oriental, 2007, pp. 173–84.

dynasty was in decline. The First Opium War between Britain and China (basically fought on trading rights) started in 1839, which was the start of the 'century of shame' as it is known in China. The decline and weakness continued after the collapse of the Qing and throughout what was called the Republic of China, which lasted from 1912 to 1949. This chapter of Chinese history only finished when the Chinese Communist Party took power in 1949.

At the same time as the Qing dynasty was collapsing, the Japanese Empire, under the Emperor Meiji from 1868 to 1912, was growing rapidly and starting to eclipse China as the main power of the Far East. The first Sino-Japanese War (1894–1895), was won by Japan, resulting in the Japanese increasing their control in Manchuria (Northeastern China) and also replacing China as the main influence in Korea (see Fig.1). Japan subsequently went on to annex Korea in 1910. So from the second half of the nineteenth century and through the twentieth century up to the end of the Second World War, Japan was the pre-eminent power of the Far East.

Treaty Ports

During this Chinese century of shame, the first of what came to be called the Unequal Treaties were signed with Western powers. These treaties were considered unequal in China because they were not negotiated by nations treating each other as equals but were imposed on China after the loss of a war, and because they encroached upon China's sovereign rights, reducing the country to semi-colonial status. In many cases China was effectively forced to pay large amounts of reparations, open up ports for trade, cede or lease territories (such as Hong Kong to Great Britain and Macau to Portugal), and make various other concessions of sovereignty to foreign powers following military defeats.

The first of these treaties, the Treaty of Nanking (Nanjing) was signed in 1842 after the Qing's defeat in the first Opium War. This and subsequent treaties with Britain opened up five ports to foreign trade while also allowing foreign missionaries to reside within China. Foreign residents in the port cities were also put on trial by their own consular authorities instead of the Chinese, a legal system called extraterritoriality. Under the treaties, the UK established a Supreme Court for China and Japan and the United States established the Court for China. Both were based in Shanghai.

Further treaties following the Second Opium War (1856–1860), opened up eleven more ports to Great Britain, France, Russia and the US. Eventually more than eighty treaty ports were established in China, giving extraterritoriality to many foreign powers, including Japan.

In each treaty port, most countries that had signed a treaty gained a concession in the port, which they essentially controlled. These concessions, often newly built on the edges of existing port cities, enjoyed extraterritoriality as stipulated in the treaties. Foreign clubs, racecourses and churches were established in major treaty ports.

So, for example, in the treaty port of Tientsin (Tianjin), the port city for the Chinese capital Beijing, there were separate concessions controlled by Austro-Hungary, Belgium, Britain, France, Germany, Italy, Japan and Russia (see Fig. 2).[3]

Between 1854 and the early 1870s, Japan signed similar treaties. However, in 1899, with the rise of Japanese power, the Japanese 'unequal' treaties were replaced with new treaties that put Japan in a much stronger position. The foreign concession areas still existed in the Japanese ports, but foreigners were now under Japanese jurisdiction and control.

---

3   Tientsin (Tianjin) is one of the five national central cities in China. Lying on the Bohai Gulf portion of the Yellow Sea, it is the largest coastal city in northern China. At the end of the first part of the Second Opium War in June 1858, the Treaties of Tianjin were signed, which opened Tianjin to foreign trade. The treaties were ratified by the Emperor of China in 1860, and Tianjin was formally opened to Great Britain and France, and thus to the outside world. Between 1895 and 1900, Britain and France were joined by Japan, Germany, Russia, Austria-Hungary, Italy and Belgium, in establishing self-contained concessions in Tianjin, each with its own prisons, schools, barracks and hospitals. These nations left many architectural reminders of their rule, notably churches and villas. Today those villas provide an exotic flavour to Tianjin. See Fig. 2 for a map of the Tientsin concessions.

By contrast, the Chinese position was very weak. As well as treaty ports there were also several *leased territories*, which gave the lease-holder not only the right to trade and extraterritoriality over their own subjects, but also effective control over the whole territory – i.e. a *de facto* annexation. One of these was the Kwantung Leased Territory, which made up the southern half of the Liaodong peninsula in Manchuria. The lease was originally held by Russia but was turned over to Japan following the Russo-Japanese War (1904–1905). This included the treaty ports of Port Arthur and Dairen. Also from 1905 Japan obtained extraterritorial rights north of the territory adjacent to the South Manchurian Railway, which extended north of Mukden (now Shenyang) to Changchun.

Extraterritoriality also operated in Korea after 1876, when Japan negotiated that country's first modern treaty, but ended after the Japanese established a protectorate in 1905. The last traces of the old treaties ended with the Japanese annexation of Korea in 1910.

The Japan Consular Service

Britain's Japan Consular Service[4] emerged after the signing of the first British-Japanese treaty in 1858 and operated until 1941, when Japan declared war on Britain. Until 1899, British consular officials exercised extraterritorial jurisdiction over British subjects in Japan, with appeals from consular decisions being made to the British Court for Japan in Yokohama and final appeals going ultimately to the British Supreme Court for China and Japan, based in Shanghai. At the major treaty ports, the consular post would be a consul-general, whereas at the rest it was a consul.

---

[4]   For the work and careers of consuls generally, see D. C. M. Platt, *The Cinderella Service: British Consuls since 1825* (London: Longman, 1971). For the Japan Consular Service, see J. E. Hoare, 'Britain's Japan Consular Service, 1859–1941', in Hugh Cortazzi, ed. *British Envoys in Japan, 1859–1972*, (Folkestone, Kent: Global Oriental, 2004), pp. 260–70, and J. E. Hoare, 'Korea, Taiwan and Manchuria: Britain's Consular Service in the Japanese Empire', in Hugh Cortazzi, ed., *Britain and Japan: Biographical Portraits* vol. VIII, (Leiden, The Netherlands: Brill, 2013), pp. 130–45.

The main treaty ports in Japan were Yokohama, Kobe, Nagasaki and Hakodate. Edo (now Tokyo) and Osaka were designated open cities. Shimoda and Niigata also featured in the treaties but did not develop foreign communities.

As Japan effectively controlled South Manchuria, British concessions in the treaty ports in this region were staffed from the Japan Service. In Korea, there were British consular posts at Seoul and Chemulpo (now Inchon) after 1883. The first consul-general in Korea was W. G. Aston, from the Japanese Service, but from his departure in 1885, Korea was staffed from the China Service. After a brief period from 1900 to 1905, when Korea was treated as an independent country, the posts continued to be staffed from the China Service until the Japanese annexation in 1910. Thereafter, consular staff came from the Japan Service. Chemulpo was closed during the First World War and only Seoul remained a consular post.

Successful entrants into the Japan Consular Service were expected to serve their entire careers in Japan or the Japanese Empire after 1895 and the acquisition of Taiwan. Manila and Honolulu were later added, to improve career prospects. New entrants began as student interpreters whose main task was to learn Japanese, although they were also expected to take a share of other work to prepare them for their future careers. In the first decades of the Service, almost all dealings with Japanese officials were in Japanese and British consular officials had a high standard in the spoken and written language. This declined over time as more Japanese officials learnt English.

It is in this situation that Oswald White entered the Service in 1903. He had finished top of his year in his grammar school (Mercers' School, Holborn) and immediately entered the 1903 *Open Competitive Examination for 4 Situations as Student Interpreter in China, Japan or Siam*. He finished in first place out of the 53 entrants (Sansom and Phipps[5] who finished second and third in the

---

5   G. B. Sansom, later Sir George (1883–1965), was to become not only a successful member of the Consular Service and later of the Diplomatic Service but also one of the greatest twentieth-century scholars of Japan. See Gordon Daniels, 'Sir George Sansom: Pre-eminent Diplomat and Historian, in Cortazzi, *British Envoys in Japan 1859–1972*, pp. 250–9, and Katherine Sansom, *Sir George Sansom and Japan: A Memoir* (Tallahassee, Florida: Diplomatic Press, 1972). Gerald Hastings Phipps

exam respectively, appear in his memoirs) and was duly assigned to the Japan Service as a Student Interpreter in Tokyo. He started in this post later the same year, just shy of nineteen years old. This is where we pick up the memoirs.

Hugo Read
January 2017

Note On Romanisation

Since Oswald White wrote this memoir, there have been major changes in the way words in Chinese and Korean are romanised. His usage has been kept in the text, but the modern equivalent has been added to the footnotes. In addition, he gave many Korean place names in the Japanese reading. Again, this has been kept in the text but the modern Korean way of transliterating such words appears in the footnotes.

(1882–1973) was consul-general at Seoul from 1934 until 1942. He and his family were repatriated in 1942, along with other British diplomatic and consular staff. See 'PHIPPS, Gerald Hastings', *Who Was Who*, A & C Black, an imprint of Bloomsbury Publishing plc, 1920–2016; online edn, Oxford University Press, 2014; online edn, April 2014 [http://www.ukwhoswho.com/view/article/oupww/whowaswho/U158471, accessed 4 July 2016]

LIST OF FIGURES AND PLATES

୫୨

Figures

Plates

PREFACE TO 'ALL AMBITION SPENT'

by

Oswald White

℘

I AM AWARE that the title I have given this book is open to miscon-
struction. It suggests an official, soured by failure, who feels that his
talents have not received due recognition. I hasten to say that this is not
the meaning I wish to give it. The sense in which I use the expression
'all ambition spent' is true of nine out of ten officials who have reached
the end of a longish career. Indeed, it is true of most elderly people
whose constructive years lie behind them. The young man's ambition
is to 'get on' in life, to make a name for himself, to stand out from the
crowd. He realises dimly that it is not an easy task, that if there is really
plenty of room at the top, there is only one top rung of the ladder from
which to step on to the highest floor. But somehow he is going to get
here. At forty, if he has common sense, he knows whether he will or
will not. At sixty he has got there or he is more or less comfortably
installed on a lower floor. But one thing is certain: he has used up or
discarded most of the ambitions with which he had started out. If, as he
should be, he is somewhat of a philosopher, he will be content to have
made the best use of the brains with which nature endowed him and
to have achieved a fair modicum of success. His doings may not have
attracted general attention but what then? So long as he himself feels
that he has done a good job; that is all that is necessary.

For myself, I have no complaints against either providence or
the higher authorities. I look back with pleasure on the thirty-eight
years that I spent in the Consular service and, if I had the opportunity, I would not want them changed.

Chapter 1

THE JAPANESE VIEW

℀

IN MANY WAYS, one of the saddest books on Japan is that subtitled *Japan: An Attempt at Interpretation* by Lafcadio Hearn.[6] Hearn came to Japan in his middle age, liked the country and settled down there for the rest of his life. Eventually he adopted the country as his own and was naturalised as a Japanese. Incidentally, it may be mentioned that the Japanese Government then took the perfectly logical step of reducing his salary to the level of that paid to his Japanese colleagues.

There was much in Japanese manners, their mode of life, their way of thinking, their folk-lore, fables and fairy-tales, their religion, their artistic nature, their attitude towards the problems of life that fascinated Lafcadio Hearn. He proceeded to interpret all these things to the outside world in a series of works written in matchless prose. They present a picture of Japan that is true but to the stranger they are misleading because they show only a portion of the picture. Towards the end of his life Hearn seems to have realised this. His last book spells disillusionment. Side by side with all that he had found so beautiful is much that is ugly. Inside the outer layers that charm the eye is a harder core. His sympathy with the former had blinded his eyes to the latter but in *Japan: An Attempt at Interpretation* he corrects, consciously or unconsciously, his earlier over-enthusiastic estimate of Japan and the Japanese.

---

6   Lafcadio Hearn, *Japan: An Attempt at Interpretation* (New York: Macmillan Company, 1904). For Hearn (1850–1904), see Paul Murray, *Fantastic Journey: The Life and Literature of Lafcadio Hearn* (Folkestone, Kent: Japan Library, 1993).

The reader of this book will detect a more critical attitude developing as the book proceeds. The bulk of the matter was written at odd moments before 1939. My term in Tientsin, from November 1939 to February 1941, if it did not disillusion me, served to strengthen adverse opinions that had been forming in my mind for some years past. Since I am only writing reminiscences, I have left the earlier chapters substantially as I wrote them. They present a true picture of the impressions I formed at successive stages of my career and that is all that I claim for them.

A Japanese friend of mine once begged me to write a book about the Japanese people. He was good enough to say that I understood their way of thinking, their attitude towards the problems of everyday life and towards the outside world and he urged me to write about these things, not glossing over what appeared to one the true facts but setting them all down dispassionately. I am sure he was quite sincere and yet nothing is further from my mind than to attempt the task. Books without number have been written on the subject, the best of which have just failed to hit the mark. Who am I to think I can do better? But, seeing that we are now at war with Japan, to write a book of reminiscences without reference to the causes that led up to that war would seem strange. To deal exhaustively with the subject would demand a book to itself but I propose here to touch briefly on the mental attitude under the prompting of which the Japanese came gradually to regard Great Britain as in her light and as such to be removed at any cost. This, then, is an attempt to answer the question which I may put vulgarly: 'How do the Japanese that way?'

It should scarcely be necessary but, to prevent any possible misunderstanding, I should explain that I am not accepting the Japanese point of view. But I think that, just as the Japanese are apt to deny that the foreigner has any case at all, so the foreigner himself is not innocent of the fault of thinking that the Japanese act out of mere perverseness. Reduced to essentials, these disputes arise out of conflicting interests which cannot be reconciled. None the less, it is generally useful to know what an opponent is thinking. I have come, in recent years, to think that in nothing is there such striking divergence of outlook between the British and the Japanese as in the respective attitude towards rights and duties. An Englishman thinks first and foremost of rights – those of others as well as his own – the Japanese of duties, equally of others as well as his. An Englishman is brought up to be proud of his rights – liberty of person, freedom of thought, the inviolability of his possessions and so forth. Duties are thought of as the responsibility he has to assume in return. A Japanese is brought up to think of his duties – the duty of submission by the subject to his ruler, wife to husband, son to father, younger to elder brother, etc. Less is said of his rights but it is understood that the junior has a claim on the support and protection of the senior. These ideas of course derive from Confucius, whose views were affected by the chaos prevailing in China in his day. His thought seems to have been – give the people good government and see that they are obedient, everything else will follow.

Since, in an ideal state, there can be no right without a corresponding duty and vice versa, it may be thought the two systems should ultimately work out the same way and that the product of the one system should have no difficulty in his intercourse with the product of the other. Actually, the Japanese training does not give him the same respect for the rights of others as the English training gives the Englishman. Equally, the Englishman is apt to think that once he has acquired a right, it is his for all time.

Here, another consideration arises. Prior to the outbreak of the present world war, the Japanese said, in effect though not usually in so many words: 'It is all very well for the British to say that they covet no man's possessions, that they only wish to keep what they have got. The Japanese would say the same if they held half the earth in fee. But the British did not always talk in this way. Time was when they talked of the "white man's burden". What did they mean by that except that Great Britain regarded it as her mission to take over territories that were badly governed and give them good government? What about the scramble for concessions in China itself up to some forty years ago? Great Britain may not have initiated it, but she felt bound to take a hand in order to maintain the balance of power. The Powers had, no doubt, good reasons for their aggression but did China really invite them to come and carve out territory here and concessions there? The spoils then went to the strongest. Now the powers have had a change of heart and wish to maintain the *status quo*. Unfortunately, we have our own ideas as to the best manner of dealing with China and, for good or ill, we propose to try them out. If British interests suffer, that is too bad but it is no concern of ours.'

(I repeat that I have never accepted this attitude as just. I am only trying to explain how this question appeared to a Japanese.)

Thoroughly warmed up to his subject, the Japanese continued: 'What cause have we to be grateful to Great Britain? We were allies for years. We fought in the Great War on the side of the Allies. What happened at the end of the war? At the bidding of America, Great Britain threw away the Alliance like a worn-out glove. It had served its purpose and rather than risk offending America, Great Britain gave us the go-by. We were put in our place at Washington in 1923.[7] We were forced to agree to the 5:5:3 ratios in our navy, we were mortally insulted by America in 1913 over the school question and when our Ambassador slipped up over an English phrase, we were forced to recall him. America and most of the British colonies bar us. Where do you expect us to go?'[8]

'Our action in Manchuria? China lost that to Russia in the Boxer Rising.[9] We wrested the southern half from her and a

---

[7]   White seems to be referring to the 1921–1922 Washington Naval Conference.

[8]   For a brief account of anti-Japanese activities, to which this is a reference, see Mikiso Hane, *Modern Japan: A Historical Survey* (Boulder CO: Westview Press, 2nd ed., 1992).

[9]   The Boxer Rebellion, Boxer Rising or Yihetuan Movement was an anti-imperialist rising that took place in China between 1898 and 1900. The 'boxers' were pro-Nationalist Chinese who opposed foreign imperialism and the associated Christian missionary activity. They were defeated by the Eight Nation Alliance (Austria-Hungry, France, Germany, Italy, Japan, Russia, UK, USA). There is a huge literature on the Boxers – see, for example, Paul Cohen, *History in Three Keys: The Boxers as Event, Experience and Myth* (Columbia NY: Columbia University Press, 1997).

Chinese administration came back and, as it grew stronger, plotted and schemed to nullify our Treaty rights there. Were we to sit down and watch them go by the board? We lost patience and set up a new administration and Great Britain stirred up the League to outlaw us.'

'Great Britain professes sympathy with Chiang Kai Shek.[10] What she is really concerned in is the protection of her vested interests. She is a past-master in the art of placing off one Power against another. She herself risks nothing (remember that this refers to a period prior to 1939) but she eggs on Chiang Kai Shek in the hope that he will be able to keep us in check. If the Powers would stand aside we could smash Chiang Kai Shek but Great Britain keeps the conflict going by creating new avenues of supply, by giving credits, by moving the League to throw whatever influence it may have on the side of Chiang Kai Shek and by setting the US to combine with her against us. Well we have got our back up now. We have finished with the League, the Kellogg Pact,[11] the Nine Power Treaty and all the paraphernalia by which the Western Powers have tried to keep us in leading strings. We are going ahead in our way. If British and other interests suffer, we cannot help it.'

I used to have arguments such as these used to me by Japanese friends many a time. I would explain the British point of view, point out the inconsistencies in the Japanese arguments and the glaring misrepresentations of British policy and strive to make my collocutor see the question for a moment through British eyes. The Japanese friend made an effort, he made an effort, he never really succeeded because, for one thing, the Japanese never understand the other man's point of view and, for another, the Anglo-Japanese Alliance kept obstructing his vision, but when that vexed question had been tactfully put aside, he would

---

[10]   Chiang Kai-shek (Jiang Jieshi 1887–1975) was leader of the Chinese Republic, through the Chinese civil war (1927–1937), the second Sino-Japanese War (1937–1945) and the Civil War 1946–1949. After defeat on the mainland, he fled to Taiwan and ruled there until his death.

[11]   The Kellog-Briand Pact or the Pact of Paris was signed by Germany, France and US in 1928 and most other nations soon afterwards. The signatory states resolved not to use war to solve disputes.

finally say, 'Very well then, suppose we forget our grievances and study the question as it stands today. Why cannot the British be practical? We consider that we have our mission in the Extreme Orient. You cannot really stop us: you can only make it more difficult. Why not concede to us our paramount position and come to an understanding with us? The world is big enough. Even in China there is room for British enterprise. Let us go in there and clean the place up and, if we were friends again, we would see to it that Great Britain did not suffer.'

I would explain then that Great Britain would want guarantees for the fulfilment of this last promise. 'All right, put your cards on the table and say what you need but first make a gesture to prove to us that you want to be friendly. Don't oppose us all along the line and then expect *us* to make overtures.'

There the discussion may well be left. I reproduce it because it is typical of what the Japanese man-in-the-street thought in the years immediately preceding the war. The average civilian did not desire war nor for that matter has he any say in directing his country's policy but his frame of mind made him doubly easy to convince that war was the only possible solution.

To turn to ourselves, though the war clouds began to grow steadily more threatening from the end of 1931 onwards, I am sure that the average British citizen never for a moment thought that war was likely until it was right upon him. As a nation we are not noted for our prescience. We tend rather to ignore portents and hope for the best.

Professor Chamberlain[12] quotes, with approval, a statement that the Japanese are matter-of-fact, the British practical. I have an uneasy feeling that the boot is on the other foot; the Japanese have imagination to spare. They may quote Chinese classics

---

[12]   Basil Hall Chamberlain (1850–1935) was Professor of Japanese and Philology at Tokyo Imperial University. His *Things Japanese*, first published in 1890, has been regularly reprinted. See Richard Bowring, 'An Amused Guest in all: Basil Hall Chamberlain (1850–1935)', in Hugh Cortazzi and Gordon Daniels, eds., *Britain and Japan 1859–1991: Themes and Personalities*, (London: Routledge, 1991), pp. 128–36; Yuzo Ota, *Basil Hall Chamberlain: Portrait of a Japanologist* (Richmond, Surrey: Japan Library, 1998).

when they are explaining their principles but they use them to their own ends. Who that has seen a Japanese landscape garden can say that the Japanese are prosaic and unimaginative? The average foreigner sees large or small trees here and there, a small mound in one place, a tiny stream in another, a string of pebbles, odd rocks strewn about and a pond further on. 'Nothing of the sort,' say the Japanese. 'You are looking at a vast landscape. The mound with a tiny tree is a distant tree-capped hill and there is a stream rising on its flank, growing into a river and expanding into a lake that you can see through the trees.' Who is matter-of-fact, the Japanese or the foreigner?

What nation is more practical than the Japanese? They are ambitious in the extreme. When they have set their heart on a thing, they go all out for it. Obstacles may check them but sooner or later they discover a practical means of overcoming them. And they will be so convinced that they are in the right that they will persuade themselves that theirs is a divine mission but all the time they will keep their eye intently fixed on the goal. Can we British say that we have been quite practical in our methods in the Far East in the last twenty years? It is quite certain that we have, not occasionally, been a little too matter-of-fact. Here is a situation that has been changing constantly under our eyes. Have we always noticed it or have we said, 'Stream? That is a row of pebbles! That a lake? Why it is nothing but a tiny pool! And as for your hill, anyone can see with the naked eye that it is nothing more than an artificial mound of earth!'

The Japanese themselves were wont to say of us that we are *donkan*. A dictionary to which I refer gives the meaning as 'insensible, stolid, dull, thick-headed' to which I would add the meanings, 'heavy, slow, wanting in perception, inanimate, unimaginative', the opposite in fact of the picture the Japanese has of himself.

Chapter 2

STUDENT INTERPRETER IN TOKYO, 1903–1905

ဆ

The Old Type of Competitive Examination

I PASSED MY examination and was appointed to the Japan Service on 28 October 1903. Little of the true Japan was known to the outside world. Numerous books had already been written on the subject but few read the serious works and it was books such as Pierre Loti's *Madame Chrysanthème*[13] that captured the public imagination. To me, as I think to most, Japan was a land of cherry blossoms and charming geisha clad in gorgeous kimonos. As a background there was the two-sworded samurai, the chivalrous warrior who had served his country in more troubled times and whose spirit had survived in the modern Japanese. That the Japanese were a fighting nation must have been known to me as I remember hearing as a school-boy of the China-Japan war. None the less, for some reason I insisted on associating Japan with a mental picture of flowers, temples, fans and tea ceremonies. All these things are there of course but that it is not a complete or true impression of Japan is well-known now to the whole world.

I knew nothing of Japan in fact. There was no harm in that. I had a lifetime to study Japan before me. But, truth to tell, I was not well equipped for service anywhere. At the age of six-

---

13   Pierre Loti was the penname of a French naval officer, Louis Marie-Julien Viaud (1850–1923), who wrote *Madame Chrysanthème* in 1887.

teen my future career was settled by chance. Coales,[14] a former student at my school had just passed into the Consular Service in China and my head-master suggested that I should do the same. At that time, competitive examinations were held at irregular intervals to fill vacancies that had occurred in China, Japan and Siam. The idea appealed to me and, since my father was not in a financial position to do more than give me a good education, I set to work with might and main to qualify for the examination. In those days it was possible to take it at the early age of eighteen so I took the first examination after I had reached that age and, to my great surprise and delight, passed when I had just turned nineteen.

Examination papers then were fairly stereotyped. By taking the papers for a period of, say, ten years and comparing the questions asked, it was possible to guess more or less accurately the range of questions likely to be asked and teachers and coaches for these examinations had reduced their cramming to a fine art. As a crammer, Comyns,[15] who ran the special classes at King's College, was unequalled. I took law from him. The makers of pâté de foie gras could not have taught Comyns anything. He just poured material into you so that you walked into the examination room, picked out the questions of which you had learnt the answers by heart and there you were. By the time I had been two years in Japan, I had forgotten all the law I had learnt and had to teach it to myself again as the need arose. I should not care to say that I approached all the papers with the same confidence but a number of years' experience of school term-end examinations varied by Preceptors, Junior Oxford and Cambridge and London Matric had more or less hardened me for the ordeal. One examination I awaited in fear and trembling and that was

[14]   O. R. Coales joined the China Consular Service aged twenty and died while in service aged forty-five. See P. D. Coates, *The China Consuls*, (Hong Kong: Oxford University Press, 1988), pp. 400, 419–20, 528.
[15]   Probably Arthur James Comyn, called to the Bar at the Middle Temple in 1892 and a lecturer in the Civil Service Department at Kings College London   –   see   http://www.kingscollections.org/catalogues/kclca/collection/k/gb100-kclca-ka-ic/ka-ic-c1-135?id=20204&asId=as1&search=Comyn&sub.x=0&sub.y=0&sub=Search (accessed 28 August 2016).

German Viva-Voce, which was one of the compulsory subjects. Languages have never come easy to me. If I have attained proficiency in Japanese, it has been as a result of sheer hard work. German I had had no opportunity of talking. After ten minutes stumbling and floundering on my part, the examiner asked me, 'How old are you?' 'Nearly nineteen? Ah well, you have plenty of time in which to pass this examination haven't you?' and I slunk out convinced that I was ploughed. But that examiner must have been kind-hearted for he gave me the minimum marks so that I was not ploughed on German Viva-Voce. And so I found myself starting out in November 1903, the 13th and a Friday at that.

Examinations now are conducted on stricter lines. The miracle is that under the old system, the men who got in turned out so well. As regards myself, I am conceited enough to think that the good material was present but it was entirely undeveloped – how should it be otherwise when I had done nothing beyond cramming for the previous three years – and I am afraid I was callow, uncouth, ignorant of all outside text books and ill-mannered. Small wonder that my first years out were not particularly happy. I have a great debt to Mr Hobart-Hampden,[16] then Vice-Consul at Yokohama, whither I was drafted towards the end of my second year out. Mr Hampden it was to whom I owed my first grounding in Consular work and I could not have had a better teacher. I marvel at the monumental patience he displayed over the foolish mistakes I made. One I particularly remember was telegraphing to the Foreign Office a return that should have been posted. It had to go into the accounts and, mirabile dictu, no 'snorter' came out to enquire why we were wasting public money in this absurd fashion.

---

[16]   Ernest Miles Hobart-Hampden (1864–1949) a son of the sixth Earl of Buckinghamshire; one of his sons by his second marriage is the tenth (and current) Earl. He joined the China Consular Service in 1888 but transferred to the Japan Service in 1889. He was White's first chief when at Yokohama. Soon after, he became the Japanese Secretary in Tokyo, retiring in 1919. See *Foreign Office List* 1921; Cracroft's Peerage (on line) at http://www.cracroftspeerage.co.uk/online/content/buckinghamshire1746.htm (accessed 5 July 2016).

Consular Pay

When I joined the service it was badly paid. It was not so much that the salary was small: a careful man could just keep within it and one member of the service who had a reputation for parsimony actually saved on it. But allowances for home leave were utterly inadequate. The Consular Officer departing on leave received one half of his passage money and a third of his family's and he received a reduced salary while on leave. The result was that instead of having a good time at home he had to pinch and starve to eke out his pay. If he was rash enough to marry young, he returned from leave in debt. If, like Micawber, he trusted to something turning up, he remained perpetually in debt. Otherwise he pinched and starved once more until he got straight.

In the meantime, the struggling junior looked round him and saw his contemporaries in banks and leading business houses earning twice his salary and living, as it seemed to him, in the lap of luxury. Promotion, except for a lucky few, was slow and discontent was rife.

Matters were vastly improved by the Steel-Maitland reforms.[17] Salaries and allowances are higher and leave arrangements more generous. If, as in my case, a Consular Officer continued to return from leave temporarily 'broke', that is because there is no sense in coming to the old country after years abroad and not savouring a few of its delights. A Consul nowadays will never become rich out of what he earns but he will be paid an adequate salary during his service and he will have enough to live on when he retires.

The drawback to the service is that there are too few 'plums' and those not sufficiently well paid to compensate for the extra responsibility and value of the work done. In one's jaundiced moments one envies the merchant or banker of ability who earns far more. But in more philosophic mood one notes the failures

---

[17]   Sir Arthur Steel-Maitland (1876–1935) was a conservative politician who held a number of minor posts. In 1919, he chaired a committee that recommended changes in salaries and career prospects for consular officers. See Platt, *Cinderella Service*, pp. 83–4.

and reflects that, provided a Consul behaves himself, he is settled for life. In my own experience I have found that my colleagues who attained to high posts never made money out of them but they themselves rarely complained of the money side of the question. I imagine that they found sufficient cause for satisfaction in the secret knowledge that they were holding down a hard job and doing it well.

Record of the Japan Service

The Japan Service, which I joined, has a record of which it may be proud. Side by side with men of mediocre talent, it has produced men of conspicuous ability. To attempt to list them would be an invidious task but two may be mentioned who rose to high position in other spheres. The one was Sir Ernest Satow,[18] who served his country as Minister to Bangkok, Monte Video and Morocco in turn, came back to Japan as Envoy, transferred to Peking when he retired in 1906 after forty-five years' active service. The other is Sir E. F. Crowe[19] who also started as Student Interpreter in Japan, became the first Commercial Attaché there and later Commercial Counsellor, was transferred to the Department of Overseas Trade and rose to be Comptroller-General, retiring in 1938 on reaching the age limit after forty-one years' service, but only to take up other activities. The service has reason also to be proud

---

[18]   Sir Ernest Satow (1843–1929) is certainly the most famous of many highly-talented men who worked for the Japan Service. He was an exceptional linguist, a traveller, a writer of travel guidebooks, a dictionary compiler, a mountaineer and a major collector of Japanese books and manuscripts, before the Japanese themselves began to do so. His main legacy is his diaries, comprising forty-seven volumes. In retirement, he compiled *A Guide to Diplomatic Practice* (London, Longman, Green, 1917); a seventh revised edition will appear in December 2016. See Peter Kornicki, 'Ernest Mason Satow (1843–1929)' in Cortazzi and Daniels, eds., *Britain and Japan, 1859–1991*, pp. 76–85; Ian Ruxton. 'Sir Earnest Satow: Minister to Japan, 1895–1900' in Cortazzi, ed., *British Envoys in Japan*, pp. 78–88.

[19]   For a brief account of Crowe, see J. E. Hoare, 'Sir Edward Crowe (1877–1960): Forgotten Star of the Japanese Service', in Cortazzi, ed., *Britain & Japan: Biographical Portraits*, vol. X (Folkestone, 2016 pp. 303–307).

of its succession of Japanese scholars – Satow, Aston,[20] Gubbins,[21] Hall,[22] Hobart-Hampden, Parlett,[23] Sansom – whose names are associated with the publication of dictionaries of the language and essays and books on the literature, history and life of the Japanese. It is not given to the rest of us to leave our mark on the hall of fame but I think I can fairly say that the general average

[20]   William George Aston (1841–1911) entered the Japan Service in 1884, serving in Tokyo, Kobe and Nagasaki. In 1884, he became the first consul-general in Seoul. An expert in the language and culture of Japan and Korea, to whom Satow deferred as a scholar, he would have become Japan Secretary but Seoul ruined his health and he retired early. With Satow he undertook in-depth research into Japanese, which formed a basis for future Western scholars. In 1912, Cambridge University Library acquired 10,000 rare Japanese volumes from the collections of Aston and Satow which formed the starting point of the Library's collection. See Peter Kornicki, 'William George Aston (1841–1911)', in Cortazzi and Daniels, eds., *Britain and Japan, 1859–1991*, pp. 64–75.

[21]   John Harington Gubbins (1852–1929) entered the Japan Service in 1871 and rose to be Japan Secretary. He also undertook diplomatic work, as the main British negotiator for the Treaty of 1894, which ended the unequal treaties, and as chargé d'affaires in Seoul in 1900. He retired in 1908 and turned to scholarship. At Lord Curzon's prompting, he became lecturer in Japanese at the University of Oxford, although he had no university degree. He was an excellent linguist and translator, publishing several works. In the First World War, he worked as a censor and was also responsible for press monitoring. He and Satow were close friends. See Ian Nish, 'John Harrington Gubbins: An "Old Japan Hand", 1871–1908', in Cortazzi, ed., *British Envoys in Japan, 1859–1972*, pp. 241–9.

[22]   John Carey Hall (1844–1921) entered the Japan Service in 1868 and became fluent in Japanese. His last position was as British consul-general in Yokohama when White was assistant at the same office. White, who married one of Hall's daughters, refers to him in the chapter on Yokohama. See J. E. Hoare, 'John Carey Hall (1864–1926 – *sic,* correct dates 1844–1921): A Career in the Japan Consular Service' in Cortazzi, ed., *Britain & Japan: Biographical Portraits*, vol. X, (Folkestone, pp. 278–91.

[23]   Sir Harold Parlett (1869–1945) was another distinguished Japan Secretary, who retired in 1927. He wrote on diplomatic developments in Manchuria, translated the tenth-century Japanese story *Sumiyoshi Monogatari*, and, with colleagues, produced a new edition of Satow's English-Japanese dictionary. In the Second World War, he worked at Bletchley Park. See *Foreign Office List* 1929 for his official career.

is a high one.[24] I, at least, am proud of having belonged to the Japan Service and I own to a feeling of sentimental regret that it is passing. Formerly, just as in the Levant, the China and the Siam Services, unless special talents led to transfer to higher posts elsewhere, the youngster who joined the Japan Service stayed in it until he retired. Some years before the present war, arrangements were made to merge it into the General Service so that if any officer showed no particular aptitude for work in Japan, he might be drafted to other parts of the world and, equally, officers might be brought in from outside. (I am speaking, of course, of peace conditions.) On balance, I am sure that the alteration is a wise one.

The service has a colourful past. Like the diplomats, Consular Officers in the early days carried their lives in their hands, as may be read in a score of books recording the history of those times. By comparison, present day life is humdrum. But if a Consul is no longer vitally concerned in the safety of the person of the British subject, he is at least concerned in the safety of his interests. A Consul's duties in Japan and her dependencies nowadays are mainly associated, in peace times, with British trade which, most of the time, looks like being strangled to death. The Consul cannot make trade. He can only try to ensure that the British trader is given a fair opportunity. He sits on the corner of the ring, patching up and encouraging his man between rounds and appealing to the referee against, what seems to him, foul blows. But it is all too often the referee who appears to be favouring the other man. And then the fight is stopped for a time while the Consul argues the matter out with the referee (the local or higher officials), usually with poor success since the Japanese official's sympathies are with the Japanese trades and he approaches the problem from a different angle from that of the British Consul and the British trader. If, then, the life of the Consul is not an exciting one, it still has its interests.

---

[24]   White says modestly that 'it is not given to the rest of us to leave our mark on the hall of fame', yet towards the end of his career, when he was writing these memoirs, his mastery of Japanese language and his knowledge of the culture was matched by few in the West.

Appointment to Japan

The examination at which I passed in 1903 was for four vacancies – three in Japan and one in Siam. Sansom, Phipps and I took Japan which left Siam to Brenan. The latter, however, shortly afterwards got himself transferred to China, became in due course Consul-General at Shanghai and was later, as Sir John Brenan KCMG, attached to the Foreign Office.[25] Sansom succeeded to Sir E. F. Crowe as Commercial Counsellor at Tokyo in 1925, a post at which he rendered brilliant service, retiring from it in 1940; he is now Sir George Sansom KCMG. Phipps was Consul-General at Seoul, Corea.[26]

The Foreign Office booked our passages out in the P & O *Himalaya*. The P & O of those days was not over-popular with Far Eastern people. There was no direct first-class service. Passengers were transferred at Colombo to old tubs running from Bombay to Shanghai. The ships' staff were autocratic and cavalier. They forgot that passengers paid for their accommodation and treated them as unwelcome guests. Other companies charged less and gave better treatment and, in consequence, Consular Officers in Japan travelled for the most part in Japanese, German or French ships according to their predilections and only by P & O if they could not help themselves.

The P & O underwent a change of heart after the First European War, stimulated no doubt by the bid of their competitors for the passenger trade and, maybe in some quarters, the old prejudice against the P & O survives. I for one think that when all the difficulties of competing with subsidised lines of other flags are considered, there is nowadays little room for complaint.

---

[25] Sir John Fitzgerald Brenan (1883–1953) had wanted to join the China Service, of which his uncle was a member. As there were no vacancies, he joined the Siam Service instead but in 1905 was able to transfer. His father was a commissioner in the Imperial Chinese Customs Service. Brenan's half brother was also in the China Service. Brenan retired at sixty but was then engaged in war work. See *Foreign Office List* 1938 and Coates, *China Consuls*, pp. 468, 477–82, 530.

[26] Before the Second World War, British usage was often, though not invariably, Corea. After 1945, Korea became more common. Both usages have a long history.

Arrived in Japan we were attached to the British Legation at Tokyo as Student Interpreters. This curious title might seem to indicate that we were training to become interpreters. Actually it meant that it was our duty to acquire the thoroughgoing knowledge of Japanese that was then essential to the making of a good Consul. Our studies were under the supervision of the Japanese Secretary, J. H. Gubbins, who examined our proficiency at the end of the first and second years and gave us a final examination whenever we were ready to take it. (The system is still in force.) To anticipate a little, all three of us were very keen and successfully took our finals early in the fourth year.

On Learning Japanese

The Japanese language is a lifelong study. Apart from those who were born in the country, the number of foreign students who can speak it 'like a native' is surprisingly small. Probably the missionary living in the interior and speaks Japanese constantly does better than most. The scholar who is interested in their literature can, and does, attain a thorough knowledge of their written language. British scholars delved into their early records and their few outstanding classics and gave them to the world accurately translated and brilliantly annotated. But to speak it like a Japanese is another matter. The Japanese themselves are fond of complimenting a foreigner on his Japanese. He soon learns to discount this appreciation. In his heart he is only too conscious that what he has acquired is only a working knowledge of spoken Japanese. With practice he learns to use the little that he knows accurately and can even deliver a prepared speech in Japanese. But, with rare exceptions, he will never talk idiomatic Japanese and will be wise not to attempt it. This at least is the view of one who has spent thirty-eight years in service in Japan and its dependencies and has passed the greater part of them at posts where he has been thrown into fairly close contact with the Japanese.

I would go a step further and say that the scholar does not generally make the best speaker of Japanese. Gubbins, who compiled what was, in his day, an invaluable dictionary of Chinese words in the Japanese language,[27] was followed with difficulty by the Japanese when speaking because he used learned terms that were rarely used in colloquial Japanese and the same was true of a number of other scholars. Bonar,[28] on the other hand, Consul-General at Kobe and later at Seoul, was not a scholar but he spoke Japanese fluently. I was frequently present some years later when he was entertaining or interviewing Japanese and I came to the conclusion that he had only a small Japanese vocabulary but the words he used were accurate and his intonation was that of a Japanese. This I believe to be the secret of speaking good Japanese for all but the favoured few who have a flair for language. It is not necessary to remember on the spur of the moment the Japanese term for, say, aircraft carrier, alternating current or unitarianism. What is necessary is to have a vade-mecum of current phrases turned in Japanese fashion. It is no discredit to introduce an English word occasionally; the Japanese themselves do it constantly and when they are talking together you will frequently hear such a word as 'interest' or even 'enjoy' (there is no exact translation in Japanese of 'I have enjoyed myself'). What is fatal is consciously to translate English into Japanese. It then becomes Anglicised Japanese. So my advice to the beginner would be this – if you have a natural flair for the language, well and good. No doubt, in time, you will speak Japanese just like a native. If not, do not attempt to fly: be content to walk well and train your ear to act as your watch-dog when you are talking Japanese. One would be inclined to think that many men are tone deaf from the obstinacy with which they speak Japanese in the manner of

---

[27]   John Harington Gubbins – *A dictionary of Chinese-Japanese words in the Japanese language* (1889)

[28]   Henry A. C. Bonar (1861–1935) joined the Japan Consular Service in 1880. He served in most consular posts and was also assistant judge in British Court for Japan. He was the consul-general in Seoul at the time of the Japanese annexation of Korea in 1910. He retired in 1912, and, like Gubbins, worked in the Censorship Department in the First World War. See *Foreign Office List* 1921.

Stratford-atte-Bowe.[29] But Horne,[30] who was an accomplished musician, was a sinner in this respect. One could only conclude that his ear transmitted, not a telephone message, but merely a telegram of the meaning conveyed and that he never actually heard the voice of either himself or his *vis-à-vis*.

One of my chiefs, whose Japanese would have made a cat laugh, once said to me, 'It is an excellent thing to talk to officials in Japanese, even if they understand English. They like it.' 'I don't pretend to be a scholar,' he added modestly, 'but I can hold my end up in conversation.' The same official, being unreasonably annoyed at not being called upon to make a few remarks at a Japanese banquet, said to me, 'I had my little speech all ready but, under the circumstances, I decided not to make it.' Altogether a very wise decision.

My Own Experience

Sansom, Phipps and I arrived in Tokyo 4 January 1904. A month later the war with Russia broke out. Following the usual custom we had to put in a certain time working in the Chancery but as there were also two senior students, Horne and Royds,[31] the work was not over strenuous. Work in a Chancery in war-time sounds interesting but actually it was not. A great part of the time was occupied in taking down or reading out the figures of cypher telegrams, the contents of which the Head of the Chancery kept to himself. We only knew what was happening when the time came to copy the despatches on the subject days later.

---

29   Chaucer's *Canterbury Tales* refers to his Prioress speaking the French of 'Stratford atte Bowe' rather than that of Paris, which she did not know. The phrase has come to mean speaking a foreign language in the manner the foreign person knows without ability or attempt to speak more like a local.

30   Hugh Archibald Fisher Horne (1878–1923) joined the Japan Consular Service in 1902. He served in various parts of Japan and its empire, and at Manila. He was killed in the 1923 earthquake. *Foreign Office List* 1921.

31   William Massey Royds (1879–1951) also joined in 1902. He was consul-general in Kobe and at Seoul, from where he retired in 1934. *Foreign Office List* 1936.

At that time, typewriters had just made their appearance in the Chancery and for a month or two we copied out despatches in longhand. Presently we taught ourselves one finger typing and it is surprising how fast it is possible to type by this method.

Work in the Chancery, except on bag-days, only took a small part of our time which was mainly occupied in learning Japanese. I exchanged teachers with another student. I have no idea what method the Japanese Secretary employed in selecting teachers for the students but I do know that the two whose services I enjoyed had no idea of teaching. All they did was to correct my mistakes and I had to teach myself. One was a doddering old man who found it difficult to keep awake. I would find him in my study, when I came in from breakfast, fast asleep. He would doze off again at intervals. Winter was a bad time as he found the blazing fire conducive to slumber and summer was bad because the natural heat sent him to sleep. For the rest, he was an amiable old gentleman whose joy in life was to compose thirty-one syllable poems. When all else failed, I could galvanize him into mental activity by asking him for his last effort.

The other teacher was not a gentleman but a rogue. I went up country with him in my second year. I suspected him of taking a 'rake-off' on all expenditure and I was convinced of the fact when he left me to return to Tokyo for my own bills dropped immediately by 50%. He was attached to a newspaper, I believe in the capacity of 'prison editor'. Newspapers that fell foul of the authorities did not pay the fine but put up a scapegoat who expiated their crime by going to prison; hence the title.

I had a little grudge against this man. There are subtle differences in the English and Japanese pronunciation of certain consonants. The 'r' for instance is, roughly speaking, half way between our 'r' and 'd'. I tried for weeks and weeks to copy my teacher's pronunciation and I found it impossible to correct myself with the other because he had a curious lisp. It was only after I had given up the effort in despair that I discovered that he was a native of a part of Japan with a pronunciation peculiar to itself. As a matter of fact, the difference between the English and the Japanese 'r' is not so great as to be of supreme importance though, to this day, I confess to inability to pronounce the diphthong 'rys' as a Japanese pronounces it.

To continue this record of learning the language, the second year was the hardest as we had to read through a collection of official despatches. These had evidently been collected years earlier since they made use of terms that had long since passed into disuse. The worst was a portentously long and involved discussion of an out-of-date currency question. I never found anyone, Japanese or English, who could understand its meaning. Through this and other similar despatches, students had to plough their way until the Japanese Secretary had the bright idea to replace them with a modern set, the study of which was of value to the student.

As an adjunct to the second year's examination, students had to write a report on some useful subject. Casting round for a subject, I studied Rein's classic work *Japan, Travels and Researches* (1884)[32] and selected that of Japanese paper-making. I felt that Rein knew far more about the subject than I was ever likely to know so I 'mugged' up all he had to say, travelled round checking up his facts and noting changes that had occurred in the interval and wrote a report which was much appreciated and I am sure has never been of the slightest use to anyone since.

The final examination was a matter of slogging away at the language with might and main. Having arrived out together, Sansom, Phipps and I agreed to take it together. My chief at the time was constantly urging me to take it as early as possible. We were shorthanded at the time and I suspect that he was worried by doubts as to whether I could cope with the office work in the busy time that he saw approaching. Finally, we took the examination in the spring of 1907. Having a shrewd suspicion that the others had passed me in the race, I made herculean efforts and at the finish was employing three teachers a day. As a result, I headed the colloquial test but was well beaten in the other subjects and finished third. And that, thank Heaven, is the last examination I have had to pass.

---

[32]   Rein, J. J. (Johann Justus), *Japan: Travels and Researches Undertaken at the Cost of the Prussian Government*, (London: Hodder & Stoughton, 1889).

Chapter 3

TOKYO IN 1904 AND 1905

ℰⒹ

Russo-Japanese War

MY RECOLLECTIONS OF the war with Russia are rather hazy.[33] We followed the victories of our allies with sympathy and admiration. The system of propaganda with which one became so familiar in the 'Great War' was already well developed. With the aim of sustaining the morale of the nation, successes were magnified and reverses concealed or minimised, sometimes with disconcerting results. The Russian fleet in Port Arthur was reduced to scrap iron more than once and, each time, reassembled itself in surprising fashion. When Port Arthur was invaded the public, instead of being warned that it was a hard nut to crack, was told that its reduction was a matter of a week or two. Informed that the Vladivostock fleet dared not show its nose out of harbour, the public failed to understand how it could make raids on shipping even at the entrance to Tokyo Bay and set Admiral Kamimura's[34] house on fire as a protest.

---

33   The Russo-Japanese War, February 1904 to September 1905 was the first major war of the twentieth century. It was fought over parts of Southern Manchuria and Korea. The Japanese victory shocked the West since this was the first war in modern times to be won by an Asian nation over a European one. The result was various islands and the town of Port Arthur and other parts of Southern Manchuria were ceded to the Japanese. See J. N. Westwood, *Russia against Japan, 1904–05*. (Ithaca, N.Y: State University of New York Press, 1986).

34   Kamimura Hikonjo (1849–1916) was a samurai from Kagoshima who became one of the first cadets in the Japanese Imperial Naval Academy. Commissioned as a naval ensign, he fought in the Sino-Japanese War.

Finally, when they had been given to understand that Russia was beaten to the dust, the supposed moderation of the peace terms roused the ire of the public to fever heat; serious rioting occurred and the envoys, who had made a wise peace for their country and brought back substantial gains, had to be guarded on their return from the US.

Possibly one is too prone to judge the value of propaganda from its effect on the cities and towns. Crude methods are suitable enough no doubt, to a population whose patriotism is not calculated and who do not weigh facts, when they are disclosed, against previous government announcements. Nor is the war brought home to the townspeople to the same degree as it is to the country-people, amongst whom war losses leave a gap in the community perceptible to all. The knowledge that their sons have died for the country and, in doing so, have enabled the country to march gloriously from triumph to triumph, is no doubt a source of pride which might be damped if it were known, for instance, that the form of attack adopted at Port Arthur in the early stages, had been wasteful in the extreme.

During the 'China incident',[35] foreign observers commented on the calmness of the Japanese people when face to face with a crisis in the country's fate. The same might have been said of them at the time of the war with Russia. No doubts were entertained as to the outcome and, except when stung to action by the occasional contrast between Government statements and actual facts, the public read the news of the latest victory and, satisfied that all was well, went about 'business as usual'. The principal battles were signalised by well organised lantern processions but otherwise there were few signs of excitement observable to the foreigner. Alone, the progress of the Baltic Fleet to the Far East was followed with palpable anxiety and the frenzy of joy that broke out when it

---

Later victories in the Russo-Japanese War improved his reputation with the public. He became a full admiral in 1910.

[35] The usual Japanese term for the war with China that began with the Marco Polo Bridge incident outside Beijing in 1937.

was finally eliminated in the Battle of the Sea of Japan may readily be imagined.

Tokyo in the early part of 1904 was full of official observers and war correspondents who chafed and fumed at the restraint under which they were kept. The General Staff were evidently anxious that no inkling of their plans should come out so they gave vague promises for the future and withheld permission to go to the front for the time being. Finally, the storm of protest that arose caused them to give way but there is no doubt that the army regarded observers and correspondents as Public Nuisance No. 1.

I caught but fleeting glimpses of the British observers, famous then and afterwards, who came and went in Tokyo at the time. Of two only have I a mental picture – (Admiral) Troubridge,[36] the incarnation of the popular idea of the bluff sea-dog and (Admiral) Pakenham,[37] suave and immaculate. The main impression that lingers in my mind is of the tone in which the despatches and books of most of the military and naval experts were written. There was unstinted appreciation of the essential soundness of Japanese strategy and tactics and admiration for the steadiness and bravery of the Japanese fighter. But there was also a hint of complacency, a suggestion that a little more dash here, a trifle more originality there, more boldness on the part of this commanding officer and more initiative on the part of that, would have converted any of the successive defeats of the Russian army into a knock-out blow, that, in a word, genius could have smashed the Russians instead of merely pushing them from pillar to post.

---

[36]   Sir Edward Thomas Troubridge (1862–1926). Naval officer, later admiral. As naval attaché in Tokyo 1902–1904, he covered the early stages of the Russo-Japanese War. See Paul G. Halpern, 'Troubridge, Sir Ernest Charles Thomas (1862–1926)', *Oxford Dictionary of National Biography* (Oxford University Press, 2004; online edn, January 2013). http://www.oxforddnb.com/view/article/36563 (accessed 6 July 2016)

[37]   Sir William Christopher Pakenham (1861–1933). Naval officer, later admiral. Promoted commander in 1904, when he was a member of the Naval Intelligence Department. Succeeded Commander Troubridge as naval attaché in Tokyo in 1904 and covered the Russo-Japanese War. See V. W. Baddeley, 'Pakenham, Sir William Christopher (1861–1933)', rev. *Oxford Dictionary of National Biography* (Oxford University Press, 2004). http://www.oxforddnb.com/view/article/35364 (accessed 6 July 2016)

These writings would have made sad reading during the course of the Great War. Very few reputations for brilliancy survived that test. Criticisms of Japanese conduct of their war with Russia may have been justified but Japan could not afford to take chances. The Russian Empire was big enough to stand defeat but it was a matter of life and death to Japan. Her army and navy gained the lead in the early stages and maintained it throughout but the margin of safety was never very great. One false step might have proved costly.

The British Legation

I do not know whether conditions have altered since but, in my time, the student interpreter in Tokyo was a 'very small potato'. If he was of a nature to put on airs, he could act as though he were a budding diplomat but he was only temporarily attached to the Legation; his true home was a Consulate and, of course, he was just at the very bottom of the ladder. Only Horne, the senior student at that time, was taken into the inner diplomatic circle. His musical talent, in a day when radio was unknown and the gramophone merely tinned music, and his fine, open character that no favours could spoil, made him justly popular wherever he went.

To digress for a moment and to discuss a personality that I intensely admired, at first from a distance and, later, on more intimate terms. Horne's Japanese studies while he was in Tokyo suffered from his social activities. Good resolutions went by the board. Free evenings that were to have been devoted to study were interrupted by a summons from No. 1[38] or from one or other of his great friends, to come along to dinner and a quiet evening's music. Nor was there anything snobbish about Horne. His heart was in his music and his talents were at the disposal of any genuine lover of that art. And, even when he got a free moment, the temptation to go to his beloved piano, bang out a few crashing chords and light-heartedly carol his favourite songs, was usually too great.

He just scraped through his final examination at the same time as Sansom, Phipps and myself but subsequently, though

---

[38]   The ambassador.

never really proficient at Japanese, he made good a great part of
the leeway he had lost. He proved his true worth as Vice-Consul
at Kobe from 1914 to 1917. It is not allowable for me to enter
into details of our duties at that time. It must suffice to say that
our main aim was to obstruct German trade by every legitimate
means. I was Vice-Consul in the neighbouring city of Osaka at
the time and I know how brilliant was Horne's work at a time
when his chief was not one of the world's workers himself.

He was always a man of tremendous force and driving power.
While putting in the work of two men in the office, he still
had sufficient energy to act as the musical leader of the foreign
community. A born conductor, he organized a private orches-
tra which gave us first-class musical evenings from time to time.
At intervals he put on oratorios, no light task when most of the
singers were entirely untrained.

Horne was also good at sports. At golf, it was characteristic
of the man that he was best with the irons. He had tremendous
strength in his wrists and would hit the ball as if it was his worst
enemy. In competitions, his temperament was against him.
On his off-day he became so disgusted with himself that his play
went to pieces at once. None the less he was essentially a good
loser. His annoyance was entirely with himself and the moment
it was pointed out to him that his conduct was disconcerting to
his opponent, he would be full of contrition.

At the end of the war, he became No. 2 in the Commercial
Counsellor's office and would no doubt have made his mark in due
course but he was killed in the Great Earthquake of 1923. I offer
his memory this little tribute. To me he was 'one of God's own'.

Our Minister in Tokyo was Sir Claude MacDonald[39] who was
too well-known to need description here. As a chief he was kindly

---

[39] Sir Claude MacDonald (1852–1915) was a former army officer who
became minister in Beijing in 1895. During the siege of the legations
in 1900, he was asked to assume command of the foreign troops and
volunteers who defended the Legation Quarter. At the end of that
experience it was thought he needed a rest and he replaced Sir Ernest
Satow in Tokyo. During his time in Tokyo, 1900–1912, the Anglo–
Japanese Alliance was agreed and the legation became an embassy,

and affable on the rare occasions when, as a student or later as an assistant at Yokohama, I came in contact with him. He had a way of looking at you appraisingly from behind his bushy eyebrows which made you feel rather small and insignificant if you were a junior but one soon noted that there was a kindly twinkle which gave the lie to his otherwise fierce demeanour. I believe that he was well liked by the Japanese. He had been through the Siege of the Legations in Peking during the Boxer Rising and had then exchanged posts with Satow. The change worked out well for him since, at the close of the Russo-Japanese War, the Legation in Tokyo was elevated to an Embassy and he became the first Ambassador to Japan. Lady MacDonald was justly beloved of all.

Barclay,[40] the First Secretary of Legation and later Counsellor, and Hohler,[41] the Second Secretary, were poles apart in character. The latter was in charge of the Chancery and I am afraid we looked upon him in those days as a slave-driver. No doubt we needed driving. I cannot remember that he was ever unjust and if he had a rough edge to his tongue, I imagine we tried his patience sorely on occasion. He certainly saw to it that the work was done. Barclay was easy-going and slow to find fault. We were not directly under his wing and so I cannot speak from first-hand knowledge but I imagine him to have been capable and efficient since both he and Hohler had distinguished careers later. He was somewhat of a bon vivant and kept a good table. One of my most vivid recollections of him was a dramatic telephone conversation with a Secretary of the US Legation. In those days the Chancery was housed in a small office with only one telephone and conversations were plainly audible throughout the building.

---

with MacDonald as the first ambassador. See Ian Nish, 'Sir Claude MacDonald, Minister and First Ambassador to Japan, 1900–12', in Cortazzi, ed., *British Envoys in Japan, 1859–1972* pp. 94–102, which also contains information on Lady MacDonald.

[40]   George Head Barclay (later Sir George, 1862–1921). Joined the Diplomatic Service in 1886. In Tokyo 1902–1906. He was later minister in Iran and Bucharest. He retired in 1919. *Foreign Office List* 1921.

[41]   Thomas Beaumont Hohler (later Sir Thomas, 1871–1946). Joined the Diplomatic Service 1895. In Tokyo 1902–1905. Later served as minister to Turkey, Hungary, Chile and Denmark. *Foreign Office List* 1934.

When we heard him calling up the other Legation, we made sure that something important had happened and, I confess, I listened with bated breath. What we heard was this: 'What vegetables are you getting these days?' – pause – 'Oh, my cook says there is a shortage and has been producing nothing but etc.' I hate to spoil a good story but it is only fair to add that Barclay was in ill-health at the time and had been condemned by his doctor to a diet of vegetables.

Gubbins, the Japanese Secretary, to whom it fell to supervise our studies, was inclined to be peppery and it was not advisable to argue with him. But provided you did not tread on his corns, he was kind and helpful and really took an interest in the students.

It remains to mention one other important person – 'Pet' Peacock, the office constable. Peacock and Hodges,[42] the then Shipping Clerk at Yokohama, had come out originally to the Legation Guard at a time when the Minister needed a body-guard. He was in charge of the office servants and acted as messenger to Yokohama when mail-bags were received or despatched. Unassuming and obliging, he was a great favourite, hence the abbreviation of his Christian name. One story is recorded of him. Stamp collectors were interested in the £5 stamps on the incoming mail-bag but by the time the bag came into the office, the stamps had generally disappeared. On one occasion, a Secretary remarked that this was very strange. At that moment Peacock stumbled over the bag and fell full length on the floor. 'Oh, I have found the stamp sir,' he said as he got up, 'here it is.'

Japan in Retrospect

The Tokyo at which we arrived at the beginning of 1904 was rapidly changing. Horse-drawn trams had just been taken off the streets and were being replaced by electric trams. The motor-

---

[42]   For Peacock, who died in 1906, and Hodges (died 1916), see J. E. Hoare, *Embassies in the East: The Story of the British and their Embassies in China, Japan and Korea from 1859 to the Present* (Richmond, Surrey: Curzon Press, 1999), p. 114.

car was not yet in use. For the most part, people went about in rickshaws, at that time equipped with hard tyres. Apart from government departments, legations, leading offices and a few foreign houses, Tokyo as seen from a height was a sea of low wooden houses. The principal residential districts had a rural atmosphere about them. Trees were abundant and one walked or rode down what might have been country lanes.

A few years were to bring great changes. Roads were widened and presently asphalted. Cars began to appear and then taxis to drive the rickshaws off the streets. As business expanded, merchants abandoned their picturesque Japanese style offices and put up first stucco and then ferro-concrete buildings and Tokyo lost its old-fashioned, provincial appearance. The 1923 earthquake swept away the vestiges of the old Tokyo and opened the way to the modern Tokyo, a more up-to-date, but, in the eyes of many, an uglier city.

Japan, though she was Great Britain's ally and was shortly to defeat Russia, was, in 1904, still a second-class Power and English newspapers in reporting the course of the war spoke somewhat condescendingly of the 'gallant little Japs'. In the next thirty years Japan, by the exercise of courage, determination and pertinacity, won for herself the rank of a first-class Power. And yet one may question whether her people have gained anything thereby. Life for the average Japanese has always been one of hard toil with scanty returns but he has, at the same time, enjoyed one of the greatest of natural blessings – the ability to be content and happy with little. Now his life is not his own, he is disciplined and regimented, told that he must subject not only his conduct but his every thought to the good of the State. His country is over-running China, demanding that the whole of Asia east of Singapore be managed according to her dictation and causing constant headaches to the statesman of the Western powers but the people are impoverished, finances are in queer street, taxes are rising, the cost of living has soared, commodities are becoming ever scarcer, the whole life of the people is subjected to the juggernaut of success. For what? In order that Japan should control the Far East and establish a new order in Asia.

Well. *Tu l'as voulu Dandin* ['Tis your own fault, Dandin]. It is not for the alien to tell Japan what is good for her. But to one who likes the Japanese people for themselves though detesting the course on which Japan has set herself, it seems a tragedy that the Japanese, who in many ways had achieved true philosophy – the art of happiness, not that of mere pleasure-seeking but of working hard and yet extracting a maximum of joy from simple pleasures, should have flung this priceless gift away for battleships, armies, industrialism, totalitarianism, glory, a divine mission to dominate and control Asia.[43]

---

[43]   This section was written before the outbreak of the Second World War

Chapter 4

ASSISTANT AT YOKOHAMA, 1905–1908

∞

Duties of a Consul

AT THE CLOSE of the Russian war I was transferred to the Consulate General at Yokohama and began, for the first time, to learn something of Consular work. Vice-Consul Hampden used to complain good-humouredly that the task usually fell to him of licking raw assistants into shape and, whether it was intentional or not, the first move from Tokyo was usually to Yokohama. Possibly it was felt that it was better to let a student down gently rather than to fling him out to a distant Consulate but, more probably, it was just chance. In any case the move was a fortunate one for me since Mr Hampden was a most efficient and fast worker and I flatter myself that under his guidance I soon developed from an unlicked cub into the semblance of a Consular Officer.

The duties of a Consul were, at that time, in a state of transition. Up to 1898 they had been mainly judicial. British subjects were under the jurisdiction of the British Government. Important cases were tried by His Majesty's Judge at Yokohama but misdemeanours were tried by the Consul acting as magistrate. The questions he had to discuss with the Japanese authorities had mainly to do with the maintenance of law and order. When extra-territoriality was given up, these functions ceased but other ones gradually took their place. In the interim he was kept busy straightening out the confusion naturally caused by the change. In particular, the main question that engaged his attention was the famous dispute over the House Tax. This is no place for an elaborate discussion of this vexed question but, briefly, the Japanese Government claimed that they were entitled to collect house tax from the holders of perpetual leases in the foreign settlements and the Powers maintained that they were not. The Hague Award in 1904 was in favour of the Powers but, unfortunately, the award was vaguely worded and the local authorities then began to impose other taxes which were merely the house tax under a different name. Perpetual lease holders on their side were apt to push their just case too far and claim exemption from all taxation. One important duty of the Consul then was to assist encroachments on our rights under the Hague Award while withholding protection in cases when the leaseholder appeared to be going too far. The dispute remained as a chronic cause of bad feeling between the foreign communities in Japan and the authorities until a settlement was reached years later in 1936 when Sir Robert Clive,[44] KCMG, was Ambassador, but its acuteness died down after a few years and ceased to occupy the main attention of the Consuls. Thereafter, apart from general routine, the task of furthering British trade – or trying to do so – gradually became the most important of the Consul's duties.

Relations with the Community

Relations between the Yokohama Consulate and the merchant community were, at the time, a trifle curious. The community rightly respected the Consul-General, Mr Hall, and the Vice-Consul, Mr Hampden. They brought their troubles to the Consulate where they knew they were assured of a sympathetic hearing and all possible assistance. And yet there was an ill-defined undercurrent of resentment, almost hostility, against the Consulate as such. It was as though the community were saying

---

[44]   Sir Robert Clive (1877–1948) was ambassador 1934–1937. He had joined the Diplomatic Service in 1903, and served as third secretary in Tokyo from 1905 to 1909. His time as ambassador was marked by deteriorating relations between Britain and Japan. Anthony Best, 'Sir Robert Clive Ambassador to Japan, 1934–37' in Cortazzi, ed., *British Envoys in Japan, 1859–1972* pp. 140–4.

to themselves that Consuls were well-meaning enough but you could not trust them not to let you down in an emergency.

Similar conditions prevailed in Kobe when, a few years earlier, a silly little episode occurred. Owing to a misunderstanding the Committee of the Kobe Club were under the impression that the officers of one of HM Ships had not settled their bar chits and 'posted' them. When the Consul remonstrated, they became so rude that the Consul had no option but to resign from the Club in protest. Subsequently when they discovered that they themselves had made a mistake, the Committee asked the Consul to resume his membership, which he did. Alas for the unfortunate members of his staff who also had resigned out of loyalty. They had to be re-elected and pay their entrance subscription a second time!

The only importance of this storm in a tea-cup lay in the evidence it afforded that relations were not as they should have been. The resentment apparently dated from the abandonment of extra-territoriality. Many merchants considered that the Powers had been in too much of a hurry to give up the right. It is too much to expect of human nature to suppose that a community can regard, dispassionately, any question in which it is vitally interested. That the action of Great Britain and the other Powers was statesmanlike and wise cannot be doubted. But the merchants did not think so. They resented their Government's action and unconsciously took it out on the Consul who, a year or two earlier, had exercised judicial powers, possibly at their expense.

By the time I went to Yokohama the feeling had almost disappeared and only showed itself in a tendency to have sly digs at the Consuls and an occasional habit of putting him 'in his place'. But some years later, a friend, subject to sudden flashes of temper, told me that it was time Consuls realised that they were not God Almighty. To which, if I had thought of it in time, I should have replied that the community should be careful not to act like a black beetle.

To me, the leading members of the Yokohama community showed every kindness. Those were formal days. The bachelor was expected to call on the leading ladies on their At Home days.

To walk into a room full of strangers was an ordeal to a nervous person but was no doubt an excellent training. Occasionally the results were ludicrous as, for instance, when having been told to call on a certain lady, I looked up her apparent address. I omitted to note that there were two ladies of the same name in the directory and, of course, called on the wrong one.

Trade Assistance

In the early years of the century, the average Consul in Japan knew little or nothing about trade. For the most part the merchant was able to carry on his business 'without any assistance from the Consul, thank you'. Home mails would bring in two or three letters from firms in the UK wanting to open up trade with Japan and asking to be put in touch with the right firms locally. It was obvious that most of these letters were of the hit or miss type, copies of letters scattered broadcast in likely countries in the hope of hitting the target somewhere. Others were of the coals to Newcastle type. But if there seemed any possible chance of trade being done, the Consul would send the enquiry round to a suitable firm and, if the reply were favourable, would give the name to the home firm. I suspect that business did not often result since we frequently got plaintive letters out saying that so and so had ignored communications sent to them. I fancy that all too often the Japan firm said, 'Oh, look at this! Another letter from the Consul. What is it about? Loofahs? Well, buzz it in the waste-paper basket and tell the Consul we will write direct.'

Once a year the Consulate would stir into activity over trade and that was when the annual trade report had to be compiled. The Consul had to take the statistics of trade for the year at his post and write a report explaining them and, if possible, pointing out opportunities for trade. It was a thankless task and the average Consul regarded the annual trade report with loathing. He knew that the local merchant was, or should be, on the look out for openings of trade and secretly he doubted the value of the reports under the method, or lack of method, then in vogue. Each Consulate sent an independent report on his district – Yokohama, Kobe, Nagasaki, Hakodate, Shimonoseki, etc. though the general factors governing trade were similar at each. This absurd system dated from the early days when communications were undeveloped and the trade of each post was really independent. However, the Consul had to write a report and he wrote it, well or ill according to his temperament and the attitude he adopted towards the distasteful thing.

When I first went to Yokohama, the subject was a fruitful cause of discussion once a year between Mr Hall and Mr Hampden. The latter considered that, as the former had plenty of spare time since he himself took over all the ordinary routine work and could handle most of the other work under the Consul-General's supervision, it was up to the Consul-General to write the trade report. Mr Hall firstly agreed in principle and would promise to write the trade report 'this year'. But his heart was not in the job and he would put off the evil day. Presently it would become a matter of urgent necessity that the report should be written immediately and Mr Hall would, with profuse apologies, ask Mr Hampden to write it.

I vividly remember the trade report for 1904. Mr Hall was due to go on home leave in April 1905 and faithfully promised to write the report this time. As the annual Customs returns were always slow in appearing, I was set to compile the statistics from the monthly returns. I set to work to add up the monthly figures for eleven months from January to November and was seconded from ordinary work for the purpose. It proved to be an endless task. Day by day I added up figures until my brain reeled. Eventually I had the figures complete up to the end of November and sat down to wait for the December figures. To my horror, the Customs that month adopted a new system of classification and the figures had to be gone over again. Eventually I handed the complete figures in triumph to Mr Hall.

The effort was entirely wasted. You may take a horse to water but you cannot make him drink. Mr Hall once more adopted Fabian tactics. He became surprisingly active over everything but the trade report and departed on leave in April with the report untouched. Mr Hampden wrote it from the ordinary annual Customs returns.

The annual report stood some Consuls in good stead. One Consul at an outpost who notoriously never did a stroke of work was asked why his trade report was long overdue. He replied that as he was single-handed he had no time and actually got an assistant as a result of this outrageous falsehood.

The method of writing a trade report was simple enough. Knowing nothing about the subject himself, the Consul appealed to merchant firms to supply him notes on the lines they handled. In due course they did so. Many of these notes were very carefully written and were suitable for incorporation as they stood. Others were scrappy or wandered into innumerable by-paths. The conscientious Consul then edited the notes and wove them in his text in a readable narrative. The careless Consul simply flung the notes into the body of his statistics where they stuck like badly made porridge.

If the Consul did not wish to perpetrate schoolboy howlers, he took his draft to a friendly merchant whom he got to glance it over. This at least is what I did. But occasionally time did not allow of this precaution. I remember to have reported solemnly on one occasion that there was an opening for Indian cotton which Japanese mills would buy if only India would bring her prices down, or words to that effect. The Mercantile Guardian took an unholy joy in printing gems culled from Consular trade reports, framed in caustic comment. Needless to say, the system has been long scrapped and such reports are now written by the Commercial Counsellor who calls on the Consuls to supply him with such local information as he requires.

My First Chiefs

I am scarcely competent to speak of Mr Hall's career since I only knew him from 1905 onwards. He joined the service as Student Interpreter in 1867 and eventually retired from the post of CG at Yokohama on January 22nd 1914 after forty-seven years of active service. He had a natural leaning towards judicial work. As early as 1881 he served on the Japanese Prisons Commission. He was called to the bar in 1881, was Acting Registrar and Interpreter at Yokohama Court in 1886 and Acting Assistant Judge of the Supreme Court for China and Japan at Shanghai in 1888–1889, but never attained to the position of Judge for which his judicial bent and his encyclopaedic brain seemed to entitle him. It was, I believe, one of the disappointments of his career.

Personally, I think he was better fitted to be an advocate than a judge. He had a genuine love of humanity, hated wrong but was mild in his judgement of others and was a master of language. In all these aspects he would have made an ideal judge. But his very chivalrous nature, his sympathy with the under-dog and his passionate desire to right a wrong, on occasion obscured his judgement. Once he had made up his mind, no fresh argument could make him change it. He would fight for his point of view till his last gasp. Unassuming where his own interests were concerned, he was a doughty champion of the rights of others. I have often thought that he could have made a name for himself as a barrister, that his sincerity, his eloquence and his enthusiasm for his client's cause would have swayed the balance in many a hard-fought case. But I have my doubts as to whether he would have made a perfect judge.

One of his best pieces of work was the preparation, as Senior Member of the Commission, of the house-tax case laid before the Hague Tribunal, a case decided, as stated elsewhere, in favour of the Powers. In such work he had no equal. He was the traditional bookworm; he lived in the society of his books. Dusty records that appal the average reader had no terrors for him and he could browse happily amongst them, digesting and assimilating what was useful and rejecting the remainder.

Circumstances enforced his love of learning. As a student in Dublin he fell a great height from a building.[45] Miraculously, he escaped with his life but he suffered ever afterwards from hardness of hearing. His sight also was very bad and in later years he was dependent on his devoted daughters for reading but if left to himself was always to be found dipping into one or other favourite volume.

---

[45]   Hall was never a student in Dublin. He attended university in Belfast. White may have confused the two Irish towns.

In the course of his career he served at most of the ports in Japan and, when I joined, occupied the senior post in the service at Yokohama, a post which he continued to hold to his retirement in 1914. In many ways he was the Grand Old Man of the service and was universally beloved and respected.

His wife was the daughter of Judge Goodwin.[46] She was witty and accomplished but from the time I knew her was already in ill-health. They were a remarkably devoted couple and the family as a whole the most loyal and united family I have ever come across. There were two sons. I think it was a disappointment to Mr Hall that neither of them inherited his great brain power. Both served in the Great War: one was killed and the other is now living in South Africa. There were four daughters, all talented in their own way. I married the second – Kathleen Elizabeth – in 1908.

In some respects Mr Hall would have been happier in the China Consular Service for he had a deep love and reverence for the Chinese classics. He turned away from the light, almost effeminate, touch of the few Japanese works that have found favour in western eyes, to the philosophy, the aphorisms and the teachings of the Chinese sages. That their language was cryptic and the meaning doubtful only stimulated his interest and he should have been a Chinese rather than a Japanese scholar.

His deafness and his poor sight debarred him from mixing with the outside world. He spent all his time out of office hours at home in his family and with his beloved books. But there was nothing aloof about him. He would show the same old-world courtesy to the rawest youngster as to his contemporaries. By nature the mildest of men, he could only be roused to anger by the sight of wrong or by the incitement of his family.

---

[46]   Charles Wycliffe Godwin (1817–1878). Egyptologist turned lawyer. Appointed assistant judge for the Supreme Court of China and Japan at Shanghai in 1865 and worked occasionally at Yokohama. See Francis Espinasse, 'Goodwin, Charles Wycliffe (1817–1878)', rev. Josef L. Altholz, *Oxford Dictionary of National Biography*, Oxford University Press, 2004. http://www.oxforddnb.com/view/article/10988 (accessed 6 July 2016)

Meal hours were a movable feast as time meant nothing to him when immersed in literature. Eventually, when the dinner was cold or burnt, he would be dragged from the library murmuring that time was made for slaves. No doubt as a result, it was difficult to keep the cook up to scratch and periodically his wife would insist on his reprimanding him. Mr Hall hated this job. He would contentedly eat whatever was put before him. But eventually he would send for the cook and then deliberately work himself up to a temper which was alien to his nature. After a recital of the cook's sins, the conversation would proceed on these lines: '*Do in wake de?*' (this simply means 'What is the reason why?') accompanied by a mild bang on the table. The cook then apologized and edged towards the door. But Mr Hall, having made up his mind to give a scolding, was determined to do the thing properly. '*Do in wake de?*' in a fierce voice with a smart bang on the table. The cook would then apologize more profoundly and edge a little nearer the door. Then one final '*Do in wake de?*' in a roar with a ferocious bang on the table that rattled the plates and spilt the glasses and the cook, bowing his head off but now close to the door, would turn tail and fly.

I once came in for similar treatment. One holiday Mr and Mrs Hall were to have gone up to the Embassy to a garden party but as the day set in for rain, Mrs Hall wrote down to me to telephone that they were not going. I was busy at Japanese and since the telephone was in the office and it would take half an hour to get through, I imprudently entrusted the message to the office boy who, of course, bungled it. The following day Mr Hall came quietly into my room in the office and told me that my failure to transmit the message myself had caused inconvenience, both to the Ambassador and himself. I naturally apologized for my shortcoming and Mr Hall said no more. One minute later he was back again and this time he spoke crossly. 'I hope I shall not have occasion to reprimand you again.' I assured Mr Hall that he would not and he left once more but two minutes later he literally dashed into the room, flinging the door open and shouting at me. 'If I have any more trouble with you, I shall report you to the Ambassador and ask him to punish you severely.' By this time I was reduced almost to tears but half an hour later, when I had occasion to go to him, Mr Hall was his old sweet self and had obviously forgotten the incident. When I got to know him better, I realised that he had felt it his duty to pull me up and, hating the task, had had to work himself up into a rage. It was quite clear that he had no idea he had somewhat overdone the lecture particularly since, though I would gladly have done any-thing for him or his family, it was not strictly part of my duty to act as messenger boy regarding his social engagements.

In April 1906, Mr Hall went on home leave, Mr Hampden was left in charge and I duplicated the positions of Acting Vice-Consul and Assistant. I hate to say it but Mr Hall's absence made little difference in the work. Many Consul-Generals at that time, of whom Mr Hall was one, took their office work very easily. I should say that on average he put in slightly more than two hours a day in the office. No inconvenience resulted since Mr Hampden was thoroughly competent and we were not busy at that time but in the course of a few years a Consul-General who delegates tasks that he should be doing himself gets slack and shirks away from work when it is thrust at him. Mr Hall was no exception. Papers laid before him had a habit of disappearing into a drawer where they were lost amongst a pile of unimport-ant odds and ends. Periodically it was my duty to go in and clean out the Aegean stables, rescuing papers that required attention. None the less Mr Hall had a very active brain and when roused could display great energy.

Hampden on the contrary hated to leave over until tomorrow work that could be done today. A quick worker, he made the office hum when we were busy but I rarely had to work over-time when serving under him. In the spring of 1907 he also went on home leave and Hall's leave, having been extended, Wileman,[47] Consul at Taiwan, Formosa, was brought up to act. Crowe had

---

[47]   Alfred Ernest Wileman (1860–1929). Joined the Japan Service in 1882. Was assistant Japan secretary and later acting Japan secretary in the 1890s. Held a variety of posts and was and finally consul-general at Manila. Retired 1914. He established a reputation as an entomologist. His collection of specimens from Japan and Taiwan is held by the Natural

recently been appointed to the new post of Commercial Attaché and had taken up his quarters in the Consulate while Harrington had also been drafted to Yokohama as Acting, and later as substantive, Vice-Consul so the office was again fully staffed.

This happy state of affairs was interrupted when Crowe fell seriously ill and was compelled to take extended sick-leave. During one hectic week, Mr Wileman was absent for some reason that I forget – probably he also was ill – and Hodges, the Shipping Clerk, was away on a local holiday. For that week Harrington was Acting Commercial Attaché and Acting Consul-General and I was Acting Vice-Consul, Assistant and Shipping Clerk – somewhat of a record.

Wileman, nicknamed the Wild Man of Borneo, proved a very pleasant chief. Long residence in the wilds of Formosa had made him somewhat eccentric in his habits and his health was not too good. It was necessary, therefore, to listen to a catalogue of his symptoms – usually buzzing in the ears – every morning before discussing the work. But there was no question of his competency and he was kindness itself to his staff. His great hobby was the collection of butterflies and there is a story of him that when he was a junior, his chief had occasion to go into the office one night and, that being the era before electric light was introduced, groped round for matches. He found a box all right but on opening it got the shock of his life for it contained not matches but caterpillars!

In the autumn of 1907 Hall returned from leave and, Hampden having become Japanese Secretary in Tokyo, Harrington[48] became Vice-Consul. I had, in the meantime, reverted to assistant.

History Museum in London. *Foreign Office List* 1921. http://discovery.nationalarchives.gov.uk/details/r/C11138687 (accessed 6 July 2016).

[48]   *sic* – Thomas Joseph Harrington (1873–1953.) Joined the Japan service in 1896. Served in a wide variety of posts, and ended his career as consul-general in Manilla, where he and his wife were detained in 1941. See *Foreign Office List* 1920. http://www.meiji-portraits.de/meiji_portraits_h.html#20090527093325890_1_2_3_28_1 (accessed 6 July 2016).

Chapter 5

STRAY NOTES ON LANGUAGE

℘

Yokohama Dialect

WITH RARE EXCEPTIONS the foreigners at the ports never learn Japanese. On the whole they are probably wise. It is not a language that can be picked up easily and a smattering would be worse than useless in their business. As a result, their transactions are conducted through the medium of a *bantō*[49] or head Japanese.

Servants and tradespeople soon acquire sufficient English to meet their needs. In earlier days when foreigners were new to the country, it was evidently necessary to learn a little every-day Japanese and a curious local dialect grew up, a few words from which still persisted when I first went to Yokohama. My servants used to call Sunday *Dontag* and Saturday *Handon* (Han means 'half' so that Handon meant *half dontag*). A walk or an outing was *marumaru* (literally 'round-round') and food was *tabero* (literally 'will eat'), a foreign dog a *Kameeru* ('come here') and so on.

In course of time the foreigner picked up an odd word here and there such as *ic* (no), *yoroshii* (good), *warni* (bad), *kakai* (dear), *yasni* (cheap), *atarashii* (new), *furni* (old), *kaimono* (purchases), *so des'ka* (is that so?), *kirei* (clean, beautiful), *takusan* (plenty), *arimasu* (is), *arimasenu* (is not), which the ladies, in particular, used with telling effect. By extending the meaning of these words a little they were able to carry on animated conversations with their servants

---

49   A *bantō* was a head clerk or manager in a Japanese house or business, running the business in the absence of the owner. In a larger house there could be several *bantō*, who would report to the Head of the House

and shop-keepers, who made it their business to learn foreign-Japanese. I used to have a copy of a delightful book of colloquial Japanese written by the entirely apocryphal Bishop of Honmoku[50] but I have unfortunately lost it and I doubt if there are any copies now left in existence. Conversations in it ran something like this:

Amah:	Okusan Kirei (you *do* look smart, madam)
Mistress:	Ic, furni (don't be silly, amah, it's a fearfully old dress: I am almost ashamed to go out in it.)
Amah:	Okusan, marumaru? (is madam going out for an outing?)
Mistress:	Ic, kaimono (no I have some shopping to do.)
Amah:	Yoroshii (well, please look after yourself.)

At the shop:

Lady:	Shapo (chapeau) arimasu-ka? (This obviously does not mean 'have you any hats?' as it is a hat shop and is stocked with hats from top to bottom. The shop-keeper therefore understands the question to mean 'I am thinking of buying a hat, if you have got anything that takes my fancy')
Shop-keeper:	Kore (this) atarashii (new): (Why, yes. You have come at the right time. I have just got in a supply of the latest models from Paris. What do you think of this madam? It would suit you admirably.)
Lady:	Ic (no), furni (old). (Stuff and nonsense. You know you have had that hat in stock for a twelve month. I wouldn't dare to be seen wearing it. It is utterly démodé.)

---

50   Merchants made no real attempt to learn Japanese and got by with a few basic phrases. This Pidgin Japanese or the 'Yokohama dialect' was satirised in the *Revised and Enlarged Edition of Exercises in the Yokohama Dialect* by the Bishop of Homoco (i.e. Honmoku in Yokohama). A facsimile edition was published by Charles E. Tuttle and Co. (Rutland VT and Tokyo), in 1953.

	Shopkeeper is stung into expostulations and talks fluently in Japanese for five minutes while the lady looks round the shop and finds a hat more to her liking.
Lady:	Ikura? ('How much?' spoken in a tone carefully devoid of eagerness) (Well, I don't see much in your shop that I care about but I might put up with this one if it were reasonably cheap.)
Shopkeeper:	(airing his English) Five yen.
Lady:	Takai (dear). (Do you mean to tell me you want to charge me five yen for a little bit of straw and ribbon like this? Be reasonable.)
Shopkeeper:	Ic (no) asui (cheap). (But my dear madam, you must remember that I have my overhead to consider and though you think that a hat like this costs nothing, you won't find another shop in Yokohama that will sell you a hat like it so cheaply.)
Lady:	Four yen.
Shopkeeper:	Yoroshii (good). (Well madam, you may have it for that price but I shall go bankrupt.)
	Lady takes the hat and departs while the shopkeeper says to his assistant, 'Now, Yame, when that lady comes to buy a hat, remember she will want the price knocked down so be careful to add on 25% beforehand.'

At lunch:

Husband:	Been shopping?
Wife:	Yes, I bought a dinky little hat for four yen. Ridiculously cheap. I had to talk to the shopkeeper ten minutes before he would let me have it for that.
Husband:	Beats me how you can talk the lingo.
Wife:	I wish you would learn the language George. It is a lot of trouble, I know, but it is well worth while.

I knew one man who got along perfectly with a single word of Japanese: *daijobu* (which, for the purpose of this story, we may translate 'ok'.)

'A' comes out of his office and climbs into a rikisha which has previously been ordered.

Presently, as the rikisha man puffs and pants up an incline:

A: daijobu (stick to it, old man, you can do it.)

ARRIVED AT THE HOUSE:

A: daijobu (you're certainly a smart runner), handing him his fare, daijobu (that's the right amount so don't you pretend it isn't).

ENTERS THE HOUSE AND CALLS THE BOY WHO SPEAKS ENGLISH:

gin daijobu (get me a gin quickly: I want it badly.) Boy brings it and presently comes in to say the rikisha man wants twenty sen more.

A: *in an outraged voice*: Daijobu (why? I gave him more than the correct fare.)
       After a pause, Daijobu, handing twenty sen to boy (it's not worth worrying about, he can have it.)

BOY COMES BACK A FEW MINUTES TO SAY THE RIKISHA MAN WOULD LIKE TO TAKE 'A' REGULARLY TO AND FROM OFFICE.

A: Daijobu? (Can I rely on him do you think?)
Boy: (who has been promised a commission). berry good rikisha man.
A: Daijobu (all right, I'll give him a trial.)

Another friend of mine in Kobe was a positive genius in his use of the word *sayonara* (goodbye). He had a yacht and spent all his spare time sailing. Behold him starting out on a trip:

X: (*to his boatmen*) Anchor sayonara (pull up the anchor.)

TRIP PROCEEDS FOR A WHILE. PRESENTLY WIND SHIFTS.

X: Spinnaker? (I think we shall get the wind aft in a few minutes. What do you think?) Boatman nods and puts out spinnaker and so trip goes on until destination is reached.

X: Anchor sayonara (let go the anchor.)

X: Gin.

(INTERVAL)

X: Gin sayonara. (clear away these glasses and bring the lunch)

(INTERVAL)

X: Sayonara (clear away all this débris and we'll get going again.)

But 'X' found that, useful as this word is, it is not entirely sufficient so he took another word, slightly adapted and had a complete vocabulary. This word is *poochi-poochi*. You will not find it in the dictionary, but you must understand it to mean 'just a little'. Behold 'X' racing:

X: Main sheet poochi-poochi. (Slacken that main sheet a little will you?)

A SECOND LATER:

X: (*indignantly*), Poochi-poochi! (I didn't tell you to let it out like that you oaf. Where's your common sense? I only wanted it slackened a trifle.)

PRESENTLY:

X: (*sniffing the wind from seaward*). Poochi-poochi (I think we shall get more wind if we stand out a little. What do you say?)

BOATMAN NODS AND THEY STAND OUT. TEN MINUTES LATER:

X: (*with satisfaction*) Poochi-poochi (what did I tell you? I bet those others are kicking themselves for keeping in shore. We gained quite a lot on that leg.)

AFTER AN INTERVAL:

X: Main-sheet poochi-poochi (I think you had better tighten up that main-sheet again.)

AFTER THE RACE:

> X: Poochi-poochi. Poochi-poochi. (Well, that was a good
> race and we showed the others how to sail.)

TWO MORE ANECDOTES AND I HAVE FINISHED THIS TALE OF
FOREIGN-JAPANESE:

> Scene: A club bar. Newcomer joins the crowd.
> Newcomer: Whisky!
> Boy: Asks how he wants it.
> Newcomer: Foots, foots (intended for futsu – supposed to
> mean 'the same as usual')
> Friend: (somewhat sardonically). How well you speak
> Japanese.
> Newcomer: (modestly) Boots, boots (intended for botsu:
> botsu to be translated apparently 'slightly')
>
> Scene: Nagasaki. A lady, known at all the ports for
> her delightfully funny Yokohama dialect,
> steps ashore from the boat just in from Shang-
> hai and remarks to a friend, 'My dear, you
> have no idea what a joy it is to come back to
> a country where you can speak the language.'

I hope that this good-natured ridicule will not be taken in ill part.
If the main purpose of language be to communicate thought,
it must be admitted that this Yokohama dialect can claim success. And before those of us who profess to speak the language
become 'superior', we should reflect on the numerous occasions
when our own supposed command of the language has broken
down. The following anecdote was related to me by a man who
had studied Japanese in England under a Japanese professor
before coming out to Japan and had got so far with language as
to translate an anthology of Japanese poetry.

Staying at an inn, he told the maid in the morning that he
wanted hot water (to drink). He noticed that the maid showed
surprise but attached no importance to the fact. An interminable
delay ensued. Eventually the maid came and reported that the
hot water was ready. 'Where is it?' 'Downstairs.' 'Well, bring it

here.' It was now the maid's turn to look bewildered. Eventually she decided that he was joking and, smiling politely, begged him to come downstairs. Grumbling to himself he did so and was conducted to the bathroom where he found that a hot bath had been prepared! It should be explained that the Japanese custom is to take the bath in the evening and not in the morning. My friend had omitted to explain that he wanted the hot water to drink and since the 'bath' is, in ordinary conversation as often as not called simply 'hot water', the maid had concluded naturally enough that he wanted a bath.

To my shame I remember attending a military review at Osaka years ago in Consular uniform. The Emperor was reviewing the troops and I foolishly jumped to the conclusion that it was to be regarded as a State occasion. What I had overlooked was that there are two Japanese words for uniform – one for the uniform worn by an officer when on duty; the other for full dress uniform. The instruction on this occasion was for the former and I found myself on the parade ground decked up in my Consular uniform amongst a sea of civil servants in frock-coats. My first instinct was flight but that was out of the question since no one could leave before His Imperial Majesty. What I looked like I cannot imagine: my feelings of discomfiture I shall never forget.

Japanese Borrowings of English

The Japanese have a genius for imitation and in the last century they have borrowed generously from the west in their progress towards the status of a first-class power. It is perhaps a tribute to the universality of the English language that they are constantly adopting new English words. In one edition of a Japanese newspaper published in Mukden I counted fifty recent importations.

On the whole it is a wise practice. The Japanese language has a very small vocabulary. Faced with the necessity of incorporating ideas that were new to the country, the Japanese first followed the Chinese practice of manufacturing new words – e.g. *musendenshin*, meaning no-wire electric communication (for wireless telegraphic), but evidently found it simpler after a time to adopt

the English word with the idea. Why go to the trouble of invent-
ing a word for 'radio' when it is so easy just to take the word?
Similarly, when traffic lights came into use, it saved no end of
bother just to call them '*Go-stop*'. Indeed, the vocabulary has
been enriched, for now you can say of a man who blunders on
careless of all warnings that he ignores the go-stop signals. When
Japan took to erecting several-storey buildings in foreign style
it was natural to call them buildings, taking the foreign word,
for example the Asahi Building, the Osaka Building, etc. and,
since building is a clumsy word, to cut it down and call it a
buil. Unfortunately, the Japanese cannot easily pronounce an 'l'
so it becomes a *birru* (pronounced half-way between *birru* and
beeru according to taste). A railway platform becomes a *homu*, a
department store a *depa(r)to*, an apartment an *apa(r)to*, a punc-
ture a *panko* and a diagram or a diamond (baseball) a *dia*.

There are two objections. One is that owing to the absence of
certain foreign sounds in the Japanese language, the foreign word
when adopted tends to become clumsy and ugly. It is all very well
to adopt the word 'sentimental' but to a Japanese 'senchimen-
taru' is a terrible mouthful.

The second objection is that there is a marked tendency to
'show off' and use a foreign word in place of a perfectly good Japanese word to hand. In the edition of which I spoke just now I
noted the words *credit, agreeman* (agreement), *condishionu* (condition), *puranu* (plan), *panfuretto* (pamphlet), *smaruto* (smart)
and others for all of which purely-Japanese words could have
been used.

It is high time that the Japanese Government appointed a censor of foreign words. I fear, however, it would become intensely
nationalistic and bar anything foreign and then the Japanese
would lose such handy words as *taku* (taxi), *Rhine* (any river
scenery that they think is like that of the Rhine), *ideo* (ideology),
mogu (modern girl), not to speak of *homu, panko* and *dia*.

A maid at an inn once tried to learn a little English from me.
After asking me for the English of beer, sauce, knife, fork, she
exclaimed, 'What a poor language English must be to borrow all
these words from us,' and gave it up as a bad job.

Romanised Japanese

For many years, a battle raged as to the best manner of writing Japanese in Romanised letters. Foreign scholars evolved the Hepburn system by which consonants are to be pronounced as in English and vowels as in French. The system has its drawbacks. There is nothing to indicate, for instance, how the consonants and vowels are to be pronounced and foreigners are apt to murder Japanese place names when they see them in roman for the first time but then many continue to mispronounce them after ten years in the country! But I think a majority of opinion holds that the Hepburn is so good a system as it is possible to find. Many Japanese however, for some obscure reason, disliked it, I suspect because it was foreign. Nationalism has, in recent years, come to their support and Japan has adopted a system which is entirely logical and has but one objection: it is entirely impractical.

Most languages have certain irregularities in pronunciation. In Japanese a 't' becomes 'ch (as in church)', before the vowel 'i (ee)', and 'ts' before 'u (oo)'. Hepburn, being a practical man therefore, wrote the syllables 'chi' and 'tsu'. But the Japanese like to have everything in patterns and a syllabary running 'ta, chi, tsu, te, to' offends their eyes. They prefer to write it 'ta, ti, tu, te, to'. They write the name of one of their crack ships 'Titibu Maru' which the foreigner, not unnaturally, pronounces 'Tittyboo Maru'. Actually the pronunciation is 'Chichibu Maru'. Another ship is the 'Tatuta Maru' which the foreigner cheerfully proceeds to call the 'Tatooter Maru' instead of 'Tatsuta Maru'. Their principal mountain known all over the world as 'Fuji (Foojee)', has become 'Hugi' and the principal port of Corea 'Fusan'[51] has become 'Husan'. But diphthongs are the hardest nut to crack. What is the foreigner to make of 'sin, tiyan, siyan'? How is he to know they are pronounced 'shu, cho, sho'? Well, it is their language and if the Japanese prefer to write it that way, it is, to use a vulgarism, their funeral.

---

[51]   Pusan or Busan, the principal port of Korea.

Chapter 6

ASSISTANT IN COREA, 1908–1910

ℰℴ

First Impressions

IN 1908 I did one of the wisest things I have ever done. I married Kathleen, second daughter of Mr Hall, my helpmate, companion and counsellor for nearly thirty years. At the same time I was transferred to Seoul, the capital of Corea.

We landed in Corea towards the end of February 1908. It was like coming into a different world. Viewed from a train, the countryside in Japan is charming, beautiful at times, dull at others, but nearly always pleasing to the eye. The hillsides are clothed in trees, the towns and villages look neat and everything that denotes man's handiwork reveals a people that is orderly and tidy. First impressions of Corea in 1908 were exactly the reverse, the white costumes worn by the poorer classes showed up their grubbiness, the villages looked miserably poor and unkempt, the hills were bare of trees and scored with ravines, heaped up with rocks and boulders. The main impression of our first journey from Fusan to Seoul was of a poverty-stricken country.

First appearances are often deceptive. Nor is the winter the best time to judge a country in northern latitudes. For that matter, many of the villages in Japan that look so neat and tidy from a distance are less pleasing at close quarters. In later years, when I came to travel all over Corea, I found it to be a beautiful country and in the intervening twenty years, the Japanese had made valiant efforts to plant the bare hills with trees. But much of my first impression was correct. Years of corrupt and inefficient government had impoverished the country.

The capital, Seoul, told the same story. Its setting is picturesque in the extreme. It is almost completely encircled by hills,
round which runs a wall, complete in 1908 but since taken down
at vital points in order to allow traffic to pass. Considerable areas
were, and are, taken up by what were popularly known as the
North and East Palaces. The former had been abandoned since
the murder of the Queen in 1895.[52] The latter was still the residence of the Corean King. Looked at from a height, Seoul made
a striking picture. For the greater part of the year the climate is
dry and sunny, the rocky ridge that forms the northern rampart
of the city is coloured purple against the clear blue sky. The Palace grounds and the northern slopes are clothed in trees and the
crowded and residential section is relieved of drabness by the
strong sunlight.

A walk through the city destroyed this pleasing impression
and told of poverty and squalor. There were one or two broad
main roads, elsewhere there were narrow, winding lanes along
the centre of which ran a ditch into which the residents poured
slops, garbage and sewage. Everything was insanitary in the
extreme but apparently the populace had gained immunity from
living generation after generation amidst this filth and seemed
to thrive on it. The strong sun no doubt should take its share of
the credit and the thousands of crows and magpies were efficient
scavengers. I imagine also that the death-rate was high.

The Corean in those days loved finery. On holidays the men
and children were decked out in all the colours of the rainbow,
somewhat crude for the most part but toned down in the bright
sunlight. The women had a quaint habit of wearing a short green
coat thrown over the head. The cause of this custom had long
been forgotten but probably the original intent was to shroud

---

[52]   The Eulmi Incident of October 1895, in which the Korean Empress
        Myeongseong, often still known as Queen Min, was killed at her private
        residence within Gyeongbok Palace by Japanese agents. See Andrew C.
        Nahm, *A History of the Korean People: Korea Tradition & Transformation*
        (Elizabeth, NJ: Hollym, 2nd ed. 1996), pp. 182–4. For Seoul's palaces, see
        Edward B. Adams, *Palaces of Seoul: Yi Dynasty Palaces in Korea's Capital,
        Seoul* (Seoul: Taewon, 1972).

the face when meeting strangers. Corean women were kept in seclusion and ladies went abroad only in closed sedan-chairs. The women-folk of the poorer classes, however, had tasks that took them out-of-doors. What more natural then than to throw a jacket over the head to screen them from the inquisitive gaze of others? This, however, is only guess-work for at the time of which I am speaking, the women still wore the jacket over their heads but only as an ornament or covering.

In later years, when I went back to Corea, the Coreans had abandoned their bright colours entirely and wore nothing but white and that, frequently enough, was dirty and greyish. It was said that they had gone into mourning for the loss of their independence.

The men wore their hair tied up in a top-knot, covered in a gauze hat which, in turn, was covered in rainy weather with a small hat made of oil-paper just like a tiny umbrella perched on their heads. The average Corean was quick-tempered. One would come on a couple of them arguing by the way-side. They would abuse each other, their voices rising rapidly, until it seemed that a fight to the death must ensue. But suddenly having said all that they could think of for the moment, they would separate and go their ways – the quarrel was ended. At times, one would seize the top-knot of the other and shake him vigorously but the watching crowd would rush in and pull them apart.

Two sections of the city were comparatively clean. The Japanese government offices, shops and residences were grouped on the lower slopes of Namsan[53] (Southern Hill) and several of the Consulates were together in the western corner of the city interspersed with a number of foreign houses. This section was popularly known as Legation Street. At its Eastern end was the British Consulate General, next was the American, followed by the Russian and French, standing in large compounds and forming together an oasis of peace and comfort.

The foreign Consulates had been raised to Legations in 1898 when the King of Corea had assumed the title of Emperor.

---

[53]   Namsan ('South Mountain') is a 262m peak in the Jung-gu district of south central Seoul

As such they remained for only eight years since at the end of 1905 Japan established a Protectorate over Corea and the Legations lapsed into Consulates General early the following year. In 1907 the Emperor abdicated in favour of his son and came to live in a detached palace adjoining the British Consulate General. The house in which I lived overlooked a tiny section of the compound and at one time the question was raised of moving the site of this house but shortly afterwards the ex-Emperor died and the question solved itself. I do not think the suggestion had ever been meant very seriously. Apart from the fact that the upper floor of my house was higher than the wall of the compound, there was no question of the privacy of the ex-Emperor being endangered and I never saw either him or any member of his entourage.

The Corean Character

It was difficult to feel respect for the Corean. For the loss of independence the country had only its own misrule to thank. It was true Corea had had hard luck in the past. It had been frequently overrun and devastated by foreign armies – twice in the sixteenth century, first by the Manchus and second by the Japanese.[54] They had been subject to Chinese suzerainty but China had not interfered unduly in the internal administration of the country and Corea had had ample time to set her house in order.

In the past Corea had, at times, shown promise of greatness. Civilisation and the arts had flourished in the eighth century in the south where the rock-temple[55] and other works of art at Keishu are of remarkable beauty. The Corean had also proved a sturdy fighter. They had turned on the invader and given a good

---

[54]   White has got mixed up here. The Japanese under Hideyoshi invaded Korea twice in the 1590s, in what are known as the Imjin Wars. The Manchu invasion came in the late 1620s. Ki-baik Lee, trans. Edward W. Wagner and Edward J. Shultz, *A new history of Korea* (Seoul: Ilchokak, 1984) pp. 209–17.

[55]   The Seokguram Grotto and Bulguksa Temple were established in the eighth century on the slopes of Mount Toham, near Gyeongju (Kyongju – Keishu in Japanese), South Korea.

account of themselves. The celebrated Admiral Yi Sun[56] had given a sound beating to the Japanese fleet and thereby forced the army of invasion to withdraw.

But something seemed to have gone out of the Corean character. The officials were hopelessly corrupt and the people generally utterly unreliable. The missionary had every reason to sympathise with his convert and dislike the harsh methods of the alien ruler but it was a missionary who told me that when the Coreans formed any financial organisation amongst themselves they had to appoint a Japanese manager of accounts because they could not trust one of themselves not to rifle the till.

When Japan began to turn longing eyes on the so-called Hermit Kingdom, Corea's fate was sealed. She leaned in turn on China, on Japan and on Russia. Probably she could have done nothing else. With the foreigner hammering at her gates, she was bewildered. She turned helplessly from one Power to another and found in turn that the aims of each were selfish. Whichever side won out, Corea was bound to lose. The pitiable tragedy ended when the Japanese established a Protectorate in 1905 and the separate status of Corea ended for good and all when she was forced to sign away her independence in 1910. If Japan had not taken the country, Russia would have done so and, however much one may sympathise with the unfortunate Corean, I myself do not see how Japan could have acted otherwise. She had too much at stake.

The Corean aristocracy, the yangban,[57] merited a little sympathy. They had been brought up to rely on patronage, to regard themselves as a class apart and the common people as beasts of burden. The only occupation they had ever learnt was to intrigue for the spoils of office. In 1908 they were living in the memory

---

[56] Admiral Yi Sun-sin (1545–1598) is regarded as Korea's greatest hero, with many statues and shrines dedicated to his memory. See Yi Sun-sin, *Nanjung Ilgi: War Diary of Admiral Yi Sun-sin*, trans. Ha Tae-hung, ed. Sohn Pow-key (Seoul: Yonsei University Press, 1977).

[57] The yangban were the traditional ruling class or nobles of dynastic Korea during the Joseon (Chosun) Dynasty, which ruled Korea from 1392 to 1910.

of their past greatness. When they went abroad, they had their retainers, some of whom went ahead and cleared a path down which they strutted as though they did the earth an honour to tread on it. At the few state occasions they appeared in magnificent robes which dazzled the eye, the melancholy vestiges of an order that was passing away.

The Corean scholar merited more pity. His eyes were turned towards China on whose classics he had been nurtured. Nothing that came out of any other country could have good in it. He lived in a past, an illusory past, the illusion of which had been masked by the centuries of his country's seclusion.

The educated younger Corean merited still more pity. He was not responsible for his country's misfortunes. And he had not the experience to know how he could use his talents to the good of his country. If he was weak, he simply withdrew from the unequal contest. If he had backbone, he wasted his energies in plots against his Japanese overlord that were doomed to failure from the start. No self-respecting Corean would co-operate with the Japanese and the shadow government that pretended to rule the country under Japanese tutelage was composed mainly of unscrupulous self-seekers who were willing to sell their name.

The Administration

I think the Coreans lost an opportunity in the early days of the Protectorate. The resident general, Prince Ito,[58] was one of Japan's greatest statesmen. He held the balance for a time between the Coreans and the Japanese military, who were impatient to 'clean up the mess'. What was possible to help the Corean he did but the Corean would not, or could not, help himself and it was obvious that half measures were failing. A foolish Corean killed

---

[58]   Prince Itō Hirobumi (1841–1909) was a samurai of Chōshū domain, Japanese statesman, four time Prime Minister of Japan (the 1st, 5th, 7th and 10th), genrō (elder statesman) and Resident-General of Korea. Itō was assassinated at Harbin station by the Korean nationalist An Jung-geun when Korea was on the verge of annexation by Japan. See *Hamada Kengi*, Prince Ito, (London: George Allen and Unwin, 1936).

Prince Ito at Harbin whither he had gone on a special mission and presently the civil administration was replaced by a military whose rule bore still more harshly on the hapless Corean but could not quite crush him. It was left to Viscount Saito,[59] a navy man but first and foremost a great administrator, to bring peace to the unfortunate country years later.

In the years 1908–1910 the so-called Corean ministers went in fear of their lives. They used to dash along the narrow streets in rikishas with pushmen and extra pullers attached by rope to the shafts. Gunmen proceeded and followed them. Even so, the Premier, Yi Wan Yong,[60] was caught and all but killed owing to a piece of incredible carelessness. A requiem mass for King Leopold of Belgium was held at the Roman Catholic Cathedral in 1910 [sic – December 1909]. The compound in which the cathedral stood had two or three steps down to the road so that the Premier had to alight from his rikisha and walk into the Cathedral. By the gate was a harmless-looking Corean peddler with a stock of oranges. Just as the Premier was stepping into his rikisha, the Corean leapt on him and stabbed him with a knife.

My chief and I had already left and were walking away when we heard a cry of pain. We hurried back to see the rikisha being drawn off at full speed with the Premier huddled in it. In the ditch by the side of the road was the Corean, face down, with three gendarmes sitting on his back and carefully trussing him up with rope. The Premier lingered for a long time on the verge

---

[59]   Admiral Saito Makato (1858–1936). Naval officer and later politician. He became governor-general in Korea after the March First Uprising of 1919 until 1927, and again from 1929 to 1931. Prime Minister from 1932 to 1934 and then Lord Privy Seal. He was assassinated in the attempted officers' coup of 1936. Janet Hunter, *Concise dictionary of modern Japanese history* (Berkeley, CA: University of California Press, 1984), p. 186.

[60]   Yi Wanyong (1858–1926). Prime minister of Korea 1907–1910. He was a reformer, who took a pro-Japanese stand and who signed the Japan-Korea Annexation Treaty in 1910. He has been condemned as a traitor ever since. Richard Rutt and Keith Pratt, *Korea: A Historical and Cultural Dictionary* (Richmond Surrey: Curzon Press, 1999), p. 525.

of death but was eventually nursed back to life. The Corean, of course, paid the death penalty.

For the rank and file of the Coreans one could not but feel the utmost sympathy. Law and order throughout the country were maintained by Japanese gendarmerie who knew no half measures. I fancy the idea was that it was necessary to cow the Coreans and certainly kindness would not have won over the insurgents who roamed round the country in bands harassing the administration. But the same methods were used towards the peaceful Coreans and were imitated by subordinate officials. To give one instance, the average Corean did not understand that when he wished to take a train at the station, he had to line up in a queue. His idea was to go straight to the barrier and insinuate his way in. The method of the railway official was short and sharp. He kicked the Corean back to his right position in the queue.

In later years, when the majority of the Coreans had learnt that Japan had come to stay and that it was no good kicking against the pricks, it was Viscount Saito who saw that the time had come for milder methods. The gendarmerie were replaced by police and unnecessary harshness disappeared from the administration. In travelling round the country in the years 1928–1930 I saw no traces of physical savagery. Japanese officials meted out justice without favour and if, as missionaries thought, their firmness might have been softened by a little more understanding, the impatience of an efficient race at the apparent fecklessness of the average Corean is a very natural one. I have seen a Japanese policeman cuff an ignorant cartman who did not understand the rule of the road but then I have more than once seen a policeman in Japan do the same to one of his own nationals who, whether wilfully or unintentionally, ignored the 'go-stop' signals.

I regard the Coreans as a whole with mingled feelings. Sympathy with them in their troubles was always being undermined by irritation at their lack of practicality. I admit that my knowledge of the Corean is gained mainly at second hand since I had few contacts with them outside my office staff and servants but I have studied the views of those whose work brought them into close contact.

Mentally the intelligent Corean is extremely alert. He learns languages with facility – speaks them accurately and fluently. He acquires book-learning quickly. He absorbs theories with surprising rapidity and quotes them glibly. But he does not assimilate them to the hard facts of life from which indeed he shies away. The Corean could well spare a little of his learning for an ounce of common sense. In a perfect world where justice prevailed and eloquence and enthusiasm were better than powder and shot, the Corean would be happy but he is out of place in the present world.

A Digression – Independence Movement of 1919

One of the minor tragedies of history was the Corean Independence Movement of 1919.[61] Wilson's doctrine of self-determination was eagerly swallowed by the Corean and a movement to acquire independence by peaceful method spread like wildfire throughout the country. The Coreans, in their hundreds, mainly scholars and students, men and women, youths and girls, marched unarmed to the local government offices and demanded independence. The outside world would arise at this sight and back their demands. Alas for the poor deluded Corean. The world is only too ready to proclaim from the house-tops the sacredness of principles and liberties but fight for them, no! The Japanese, taken by surprise and thoroughly alarmed, broke up the meetings, threw the demonstrators into prison where they were treated like criminals and generally used the harsh methods that are appropriate enough in the case of armed rebellion. In one way only the movement brought forward good. Opinion in Japan was stirred and the way was paved for Saito's milder administration so that the victims of self-determination did not suffer entirely in vain.

Missionary Influence

Most missionaries love the Coreans. Their own training and outlook makes them tolerant of the weaknesses of their converts so

---

[61]   Known as the *Samil Undon* or March First Movement, and one of the few events marked in both North and South Korea.

long as their heart is in the right place. But I could never resist a suspicion that the devotion of the Christian convert was partly calculated. A great missionary friend, who came comparatively late in life to the field, shared this suspicion. It was his view that the number of converts who did not enjoy any *material* benefit from their adherence was extremely small. During my second term of office in Corea I was struck by the growing intransigence of the Corean Christians. Very few of the native churches were self-supporting but while expecting the missions to continue to provide the funds, the clergy and their flock were impatient of all restraint. The missionary naturally wished to see the members of the church stand on their own feet before they tried to run and until they showed an ability to govern themselves, the missionaries wished to supervise their activities. But discipline is a word that the Corean intensely dislikes. At heart, he thinks that the family system should be brought into his religion. The faults of members of the family should be condoned and much should be forgiven them for their faith.

The spiritual message of the Christian religion finds a ready response in the heart of the Corean but it is the sentimental side of its teaching rather than the practical that appeals to his nature. His faith is great but, with many striking exceptions, he finds it difficult to translate his devotion into the more prosaic duty of healing himself. His family instincts war against the need of dealing firmly with the black sheep and punishing the idle shepherd.[62]

The Corean now enjoys an orderly and, on the whole, just government. One serious handicap still remains. In business he is no match for the Japanese whose knowledge, energy and application leave him streets behind. In official life only the lower ranks are open to him. No doubt the Japanese are loath to entrust responsible positions to those whose sense of duty is apt to be clouded by the desire to help his family and friends.

---

[62]   Few would now share this negative judgement of Korean Christians. For a recent and more sympathetic account of Christianity in this period see Sebastian C. H. Kim and Kirsteen Kim, *A History of Korean Christianity* (New York: Cambridge University Press, 2015), pp. 107–56.

But it is difficult to see how the vein of weakness that runs through the Corean character can be eliminated so long as he is kept in a subordinate position.

Corea Living in the Past

But I have wandered far from the subject of my early years in Corea and return to it with apologies for the digression. Arriving in Corea was like stepping back into the past. When we went to call at the Palace on the Emperor's birthday, we were carried in palanquins, the office *kisno* (messengers) togged up in their fineries and filled with a sense of reflected glory, strutting in front and ordering the pedestrians out of the way. The street scenes were those of another world. One had an impression, no doubt erroneous, that the men-folk did little work. They strolled about looking comical in their funny little hats that reminded me of the Welsh bonnet or squatted about by the side of the road smoking their long slender pipes. At intervals one came across *yangban* strolling down the centre of the road regardless of traffic and looking important. Only the women walked as if they had an objective, carrying loads on their heads. By water-courses one came on them laundering their husband's clothes, washing them in the dirty water and then pounding them with batons on stone. But I forget the Corean coolies who certainly worked hard. I have seen them carrying gigantic wardrobes on their backs. Then there were the water-carriers who supplied households with well-water that they carried in old kerosene tins.

At the Consulate we still used kerosene for lighting. Milk we got from cows kept by Huntley,[63] the Consulate constable. Huntley had also another source of income. He kept what amounted to a Corean chest store. The Coreans used to make very serviceable chests with brass fittings that foreigners were eager to buy. I suppose Huntley had originally kept a few to sell to Consuls' wives and their friends but it had gradually grown into a business which was a source of embarrassment to the office since strangers

---

[63]   Shadrach T. Huntley was constable at Seoul until 1914.

would come in and ask to see the shop or complain that they had been overcharged.

Seoul was a happy hunting ground for the curio-hunter in those days and many treasures were picked up by the diligent seeker in the market popularly known as the Thieves Market. The screens were a joy. The paintings were crude and the artists cheerfully ignored perspective but what they may have lacked in technique was compensated in the liveliness of the detail in pictures of court and hunting scenes and of the arrival of foreign envoys. The latter were quite untrue to history. It was Corea that was the vassal and China the suzerain but the artists allowed their fancy to run riot and depicted Chinese envoys bringing tribute to Corea, including the weirdest of wild animals evidently supposed to be elephants and lions. (One wild animal that the artist could depict faithfully was the tiger for here he did not need to draw on his imagination since the Corean tiger is one of the finest specimens of his species.) Besides the chests and the screens there were Corean embroideries and silks and brass-ware. There was one trap for the newcomer. One of the commonest objects to be seen in the shops was a round pot that, well polished, looked quite decorative on the table in the drawing room, particularly as a flower-pot and in their first enthusiasm the newcomer frequently so used it until he or she learnt of its more prosaic use by the Corean as a chamber-pot.

Chapter 7

COREA IN 1909 AND 1910

∞

Mr Cockburn

My FIRST CHIEF in Seoul was Henry Cockburn, CB.[64]
He was, I believe, highly thought of at the Foreign Office;
the fact that he had a CB was indirect proof of the fact.
(A KCMG is common enough in the Consular service but a
CB is rare.) In the office we regarded him with respect and
admiration. He worked his staff hard but since he was a hard
worker himself, there was no question of complaint on this
score. He had one habit which I imagine was a good one but
which added to the rush of work. In those days our despatches
were sent at regular intervals to catch the Foreign Office bag
from Tokyo. Cockburn would allow his despatches to sim-
mer in his brain until the last minute, would then be galva-
nized into activity and pour his drafts in an unending stream
on the office. I used to type and type them until my brain
reeled. His despatches were beautifully phrased and written
in a style that was lucid and incisive but I always thought
they were too long. No doubt I was prejudiced!

---

[64] Henry Cockburn CB (1859–1927). Joined the China Consular
Service 1880, becoming Chinese Secretary. Appointed chargé
d'affaires in Korea 1906, and then consul-general. His son was the
journalist Claud Cockburn, and his grandsons are also journalists.
Foreign Office List 1921. Patrick Cockburn, 'How My Grandfather's
Brave Stand for Justice Cost Him His Career', *CounterPunch*,
Vol. 24, no. 3.

Cockburn's appointment to Seoul was the tragedy of his career. He came from the China service in which he had held the post of Chinese Secretary with distinction. He was appointed Chargé d'Affaires at the then British Legation in Seoul towards the end of 1905 and it was obviously the intention to appoint him Minister. Unfortunately, just at that moment, Japan established its Protectorate over Corea and he became, instead, Consul-General. In place of the Corean Government, he had the Japanese Residency-General to deal with.

From every point of view except that of his own interests, the appointment was an ideal one. The affairs of the late government were in a hopeless mess and the question of protecting British rights was a ticklish one. Under a corrupt administration the title to foreign concessions for mining and utilities was rarely clearly established and, in particular, there was a constant crop of disputes with the Residency-General over mining rights held by British subjects. In all these Cockburn held a just balance between equitable and inequitable claims and fought on the side of the former with great firmness and success. By 1908 most of these claims had been adjusted.

The Affair of the Korean Daily News

One thorn in the flesh of the Consul-General remained. This was a daily newspaper published in English and Corean by an Englishman whom I will call 'X'.[65] Since Great Britain at that time still retained extra-territorial jurisdiction, X was subject, not

---

[65] It is not clear why White was so coy about naming the person concerned, Ernest Thomas Bethell, since the case was widely reported in the foreign press in Japan and China, and noted in Britain. Bethell (1872–1909) came to Korea as a correspondent covering the Russo-Japanese War. Shocked by the behaviour of the Japanese towards Koreans. He founded two newspapers, one in English, *Korea Daily News*, and *Daehan Maeil Shinbo* in Korean. See Chong Chin-sok, *The Korean problem in Anglo-Japanese relations 1904–1910: Ernest Thomas Bethell and his newspapers: The Daehan Maeil Shinbo and the Korea Daily News*, (Seoul: Naman, 1987). Bethell is buried in Seoul Foreign Cemetery, where an annual ceremony is held in his honour.

to the Corean Courts but to the British authorities. The paper was anti-Japanese in its policy and attacked the Japanese administration in season and out of season. So long as it confined itself to fair criticism, it could not be touched, distasteful as it was to see a British subject shielding himself behind extra-territoriality to harass the administration.

Rendered bold by his immunity, X overstepped the mark and published articles inciting to a breach of the peace. Cockburn acted promptly, summoned him to the British Court and bound him over. A nice little question of legal procedure was involved. X's conduct was calculated to cause a serious breach of the peace but it was the peace of Corea that was endangered and not the Peace of the Realm and there were no special Orders in Council that covered the case. Cockburn could only proceed against him, therefore, on the complaint of an aggrieved party and this was the Japanese administration. But the latter, while pressing Cockburn to take action, were not willing to sue in a British Court. The matter was urgent as the Japanese Crown Prince was due on a visit. Cockburn cut the Gordian Knot by instructing his assistant, Mr Holmes,[66] to lay the complaint. Technically, therefore, Cockburn was trying a case that he, or rather his assistant acting under his orders, had brought. This, of course, is against British ideas of fair play. His superiors drew his attention to the irregularity and I think Cockburn rather felt that their remarks concentrated on this point and showed little appreciation of the fact that his criticised action had prevented an irresponsible British firm being the cause of bloodshed. In due course, the necessary Order in Council was promulgated. All this had happened before I came to Corea but I give it as part of the whole story.

X did not remain quiescent for long. In the spring of 1908 his Corean paper began to publish accounts of successful historical risings. I do not remember all the instances quoted but the theme of each was the same – the oppression of the tyrant, the sufferings of the oppressed, their final revolt and the over-

66   Ernest Hamilton Holmes (1876–1957). Joined the Japan Consular Service 1897. Served in Seoul on various occasions and retired in 1936 as consul-general at Yokohama. *Foreign Office List 1937.*

throw of the tyrant. The implication was obvious and the British authorities were once more forced to take action. This time there was a 'full-dress parade'. A judge and the crown advocate came over from Shanghai, X was tried, found guilty and sentenced to imprisonment which he underwent in Shanghai. The main problem was therefore satisfactorily dealt with but out of it arose a very unfortunate episode.

Arrest of Corean Editor

X had judged it necessary to call his Corean editor, Yang Ki Tak, as a witness for the defence. Since he was likely to say hard things about the Japanese, it was thought that they might wish to get 'their own back' later on and Cockburn sought out, and obtained, immunity for him. What was the meaning of this pledge? Obviously it did not mean simply that the Japanese would not trump up a charge against Yang Ki Tak. It must mean something more. It certainly meant also that no evidence given by Yang Ki Tak and no facts that emerged as to his conduct of the paper would be used against him subsequently. Even so, it was, in practice, difficult to make a nice distinction between actual facts and ideas suggested by the evidence of lines that might be followed up in the hope of finding a stick with which to beat Yang Ki Tak. Cockburn interpreted the pledge to mean that the slate would be wiped clean and that no action whatever, based on Yang Ki Tak's past conduct of the paper, would be taken by the Japanese authorities. As events proved, the latter were not prepared to go so far as this.

Some weeks later, the Japanese arrested Yang Ki Tak and threw him into prison. Cockburn protested vigorously and was informed that the charge against Yang Ki Tak had nothing to do with the X case. The newspaper had, for some time past, been running an anti-smoking campaign. The money saved by this self-denial was sent to the newspaper which put it into a fund to be used to redress their grievances, in plain English, to free the country from the hated Japanese yoke. The Japanese maintained that Yang Ki Tak had embezzled part of these moneys.

A furious controversy then arose, Cockburn maintaining that the Japanese had been guilty of a breach of faith and were merely using the charge as a means of getting Yang Ki Tak into their power. Meanwhile Yang Ki Tak languished in prison and, prison conditions being far from humane, soon fell very ill. On Cockburn's urgent insistence, he was put into hospital, where he recovered. Then a mistake occurred which would have been amusing but for the circumstances. The authorities issued orders that Yang Ki Tak should be put back in prison to await his trial. Someone blundered and he was, instead, turned loose. He made use of his temporary liberty to double back to the newspaper office, which being British property, could not be entered by the Japanese police except under warrant from the British Consul General.

Before handing Yang Ki Tak back, Cockburn demanded guarantees that Yang Ki Tak should be humanely treated in prison while waiting his trial. These the Japanese would not give. They declined to discuss his treatment which they maintained was beside the point. Yang Ki Tak was a fugitive from justice and should be handed over immediately. The Japanese Residence of Seoul, who was conducting the negotiations, tried bluffing. He said that the case must be tried on a particular day and if Yang Ki Tak were not present, it would be the worse for him. The day came and the trial was postponed. Eventually Yang Ki Tak was handed over without specific guarantees. Later, the case was, I believe, dropped on the score of insufficient evidence.

Mr Cockburn's Actions

Looking back on the dispute after thirty years, I should say that honours were about even. If Cockburn had not gained all the points he wished, he gained many, he had shown that British ideas of justice could not be brushed aside as irrelevant and he had shown that if it came to a fight in shirt-sleeves, he could give as well as take punishment. Unfortunately he then took a step which nullified the good effect of his firmness. It was perhaps natural that the case had caused misgivings to his superiors and, while the Ambassador at Tokyo had given his support and the Foreign Office its approval of his views and action, they were not prepared to go quite so far as Cockburn wished in pushing certain of the demands he had made. (He had, for instance, demanded that the case should be taken out of the hands of the Japanese Resident whom he accused of lying. Actually, in my opinion, the offence of which the Resident had been guilty came more under the heading of bluffing – a double-edged tool.) Cockburn took this to heart and the moment the case was ended, he left for England on home leave. He kept the date of his departure secret. I think he was, to use the colloquialism, 'fed-up'. He had had a strenuous three years culminating in a dispute which frayed the tempers of both sides. He only wished to get away. Unfortunately, his action gave the impression that the Foreign Office disapproved of his conduct of the case and had recalled him, an impression which was strengthened when he retired some months later.

It was a tragic sacrifice of a brilliant career. I am convinced that the Foreign Office still thought as highly of him as ever and that, with a little patience, he could have obtained a transfer to a higher and more congenial post.

Comment on the Case

As to the merits of the case, both sides were right according to their own standards! British ideas of fair play demanded that Yang Ki Tak should not be lulled into false security and then trapped when he was off his guard and elementary prudence suggested that the Japanese should be circumspect in their action in order to avoid suspicion that they were not playing the game. They could have urged Cockburn to use his influence to have the tobacco campaign stopped and if he declined they could then have made it clear that their promise of immunity could not cover such a case.

Unfortunately, it is the invariable Japanese rule in judicial matters to act with the greatest secrecy and pounce on the suspect before there is any possibility of his escaping or destroying evidence. The tobacco campaign was a pernicious one because it unsettled the Coreans and encouraged them to think the Japanese rule could be overthrown. Nor had it any connection with the X trial other than that it was the same paper that published the articles preaching sedition and also ran the tobacco campaign. Finally the Coreans, as I have suggested elsewhere, could not be trusted in money matters and the odds were that, if the money was not being embezzled, it was being squandered. The campaign was almost certainly a ramp.

X, the cause of all this trouble, was by way of being a 'character'. On one occasion he wrote to Cockburn somewhat on the following lines: 'I have captured a Japanese soldier stealing fruit in my garden. What shall I do with him?' I was sent round post-haste to find that X had given the soldier a bottle of beer and sent him away, the best of friends! That, at all events, was the version he gave me.

X died about a year later of heart failure and the paper then became the property of his widow. Bonar, who had by that time, become Consul-General, prevailed on the Japanese authorities to buy it in order to get rid of a source of annoyance and, since the paper at that time was not paying, this was a happy solution for both sides.

Mr Lay

After Cockburn's departure, Lay,[67] the Consul at Chemulpo[68] took charge for the best part of a year. He was a quiet, unassuming man and, neither side having any further desire for fighting,

---

[67]　Arthur Hyde Lay (1865–1934) joined the Japan Consular Service in 1887, and ended his career as consul-general in Seoul 1914–1927. He came of a family with wide connections in China and Japan. As well as qualifying in Japanese, he was the only member of the Japan Consular Service to qualify in Korean as well. A. C. Hyde Lay, *Four Generations in China, Japan and Korea*, (Edinburgh and London: Oliver & Boyd, 1922).

[68]　Chemulpo is now part of Incheon, the port city for Seoul in Gyeonggi (Kyonggi) Province. The Battle of Chemulpo Bay, where the first shots of the Russo-Japanese War were fired in 1904, took place nearby.

relations speedily became normal once more. At a later stage he was appointed Consul-General and held the post until his retirement in 1927.

I never met anyone half so cautious as Mr Lay. I am sure that he never gave a wrong opinion for he was careful not to express any opinion at all. On one occasion I drafted a reply to a commercial enquiry quoting facts and drawing conclusions as to the possibilities of trade. Mr Lay carefully eliminated the conclusions, leaving only the facts. To my remonstrance that the firm had asked for our opinion, Mr Lay replied, 'That is just what he is not going to get.' His despatches were masterpieces. They consisted of extracts from the local government organ prefaced by 'it is reported in the Seoul Press that...' My wife told me that I sat up on bed one night, while sound asleep, and shouted, 'I won't type another word of this dammed tripe.'!

Mr Bonar

Bonar, who was the next Consul-General, was not especially liked by the other members of the service but he always treated me justly and I had a great respect for his ability. He was not of the same calibre as Cockburn but he understood the Japanese and he could get results from them with a minimum of fuss. He wrote few despatches to them but he made personal contacts with the officials and when any business was on the tapis, discussed it with them informally at first, gradually working up to his objective. With patience he usually got what he wanted in the end.

I learnt a great deal from Bonar whose methods I have copied. The average Japanese official is ultra-cautious when it comes to committing ideas to paper. His instinct is to 'watch his step' and avoid giving anything away. But in easy conversation, when he realises that every word he uses is not going to be quoted in evidence against him, he is far more open. None the less, I cannot remember any instance where a Japanese official has gone back on a verbal promise made to me.

In September 1950, the Incheon landing was a major turning point in the Korean War.

Years later I was engaged in protecting the interests of a British merchant who was suing a big corporation for damages. The case had gone on for years. He had apparently a good moral case but the legal rights were a trifle doubtful. I had frequently to discuss, not the actual merits of the case, but the need for a decision with the judge. The latter was in agreement but the corporation was a powerful one and determined to fight the case to the last ditch. Finally, the judge suggested to me that we should try and compromise the case and, the plaintiff being willing, we called on a leading director. The director was most emphatic in disclaiming any liability but on the judge recommending that the corporation should pay as an act of grace, without prejudice to its legal stand, he promised to think it over. A few days later the corporation paid the plaintiff a handsome sum with which he was more than satisfied. The amour-propre of the corporation was preserved, the plaintiff got his money and the judge was more than pleased to see the last of a troublesome case. I hate to have to add it but the Japanese Counsel for the plaintiff thought that there was dirty work afoot and offered me what he considered my share of the swag.

Chapter 8

VICE-CONSUL AT YOKOHAMA, 1911–1913

ॐ

Random Recollections

In THE SUMMER of 1910 I took my first home leave just before Corea 'voluntarily' signed away her independence. Returning to the Far East in the autumn of 1911, I was appointed Acting Vice-Consul at Yokohama, a post which I filled until the spring of 1913.

I find that I recollect little of the work of these years. No doubt the more stirring events of the years to come – 1914 onwards – drove the events of those years out of mind and, since I have never kept a diary, I cannot fill the gap. I take the opportunity however, to indulge in a few random observations on matters of interest to the Consular Service, particularly the Service in Japan.

Age of Retirement

My father-in-law, Mr Hall, was still Consul-General in 1911 and did not retire till 1914 when he was seventy. Nowadays the retiring age is sixty and many 'wangle' their retirement earlier on the plea of ill-health. It is recorded of one Consul-General at Shanghai that his medical certificate stated that his health had suffered from long residence in a paludal atmosphere. A hundred years ago Shanghai was a swamp: so were most of the treaty-ports, the truth being that the Chinese Government set apart areas which they had never had the energy to make habitable but which the enterprising foreigner proceeded to drain and build-up until they were ten times healthier than the surrounding areas. This, however, is beside the point, but I mention it because the fact is often lost sight of when the Chinese, and the Japanese too, accuse the foreigner of seizing the best sites and stealing their country's birthright.

To return to the question of early retirement on the score of ill-health, the tendency to retire round about the age of fifty-five is one which has the cordial support of juniors in the service. Promotion[69] by seniority is a matter of luck. Hobart-Hampden had to wait many years for promotion to Vice-Consul and this was only one of many similar cases. I myself was helped by deaths and early retirements and became Vice-Consul in nine-and-a-half years, Consul in rather more than sixteen and Consul-General in twenty-four years. A colleague who joined at the same time had to wait six years more before his final promotion. It was not a question of merit for he was promoted as soon as there was a vacancy. There is something to be said for a system which would allow a Consul to be promoted to the higher rank *and pay* after a certain number of years' service even if there is not a post vacant at the moment but no doubt the Treasury would object.

Consular Residences

In Yokohama I occupied the Vice-Consul's quarters which were above the office. Rumour had it that the architect who built the premises forgot the staircases. However that may be, the staircase occupied a built-in part of the back verandah and access to the assistant's quarters – also above the office – was obtained by an outside staircase exposed to the elements. The quarters were comfortable but the building was an old one and always gave the impression of being on the verge of falling down. It did so

---

69   There is much discussion of this difficult issue in Platt, *Cinderella Service* and in Coates, *China Consuls*. Slow rates of promotion in the specialized services was one reason behind the decisions in the 1930s and 1940s to move first to towards a unified consular service, and then to the unification of the diplomatic and consular branches.

unfortunately in the great earthquake of 1923 when Horne and Haigh[70] lost their lives.

The Office of Works is possibly not to blame since the Treasury in those days was notoriously niggardly in its disbursements for Consular buildings. The old Consulate in Kobe was another decrepit building and a Consul, who had applied in vain for repairs, created a good deal of local amusement by putting up a notice that the building was dangerous. In those days the Consuls and the Office of Works regarded each other as natural enemies. In 1929 I had a spirited argument with the Office which I dropped when I had gained my main point. The ambassador, who had had his own quarrel with them and had, so to speak, cheered me on, wrote and chided me for not pressing home my advantage!

Japanese Staff

In 1911 the office in Yokohama still employed boatmen. That is to say they were described in the quarterly accounts as such and at regular intervals the cost of their uniforms would appear. Clad in their navy-blue tunics, they were a pleasing anachronism. In the early days, access to ships in the harbour was, no doubt, by sampan manned by Consular boatmen, but, for many a year, they had been nothing more than messengers. No one had bothered to tell the Foreign Office that conditions had altered and to get the men entered on the payroll in their real capacity. No doubt this was on the principle that it is better to let sleeping dogs lie; the Finance Department has an awkward habit of enquiring into the numbers, scale of pay, etc., if their attention is aroused whereas, if nothing is said, the same rote is passed and no questions are asked. When I went to Nagasaki in 1920, I found a Consular sampan reposing in the compound and since it was getting no better year by year, just drawn up on dry land, I got sanction for its sale.

---

[70]   William Haigh (1891–1923). Joined the Japan Consular Service in 1913. He was vice-consul at Yokohama when he was killed in the earthquake.

Japanese Writers

Another slight anachronism is the employment of Japanese 'writers' at the Consulates. Originally, they had indicted despatches in Japanese under the direction of the Consul. Nowadays these are sent out in English and most of those received are also in English. But the writer remains. He does little or no 'writing' but he carries out more responsible duties. He acts as Japanese secretary and I wish to record my gratitude to the many who have served under me at my different posts. His position is a delicate one. He is, first and foremost, a patriotic Japanese subject and it is only fair to him to entrust him with no secrets that would be of interest to his own government and not to ask him to obtain confidential information. But, knowing his own people, he can advise his foreign master as to the way in which a problem would appear to them. I have always leaned heavily on my Japanese writers and, within the necessary limits of their duties, have received nothing but loyal service from them. Some have been scholars and some have been rather rough diamonds but not one of them ever let me down and I am sure that, by their advice, they have saved me from many a mistake. It is the oriental method to approach a problem cautiously. The system makes for delays but avoids head-on collisions. Instead of principals meeting at the outset, their seconds frequently meet in the first place. From their report, the principals get a fairly clear idea of each other's views and can shape their course accordingly. Often enough, by the time the principals meet, agreement has been reached and all that is required is confirmation. In such indirect negotiations I have always found my Japanese writers extremely useful and I could not have wished for better service than I received. It is a thousand pities that the embitterment of relations between Japan and Great Britain has led misguided Japanese agitators to attack these writers and to tell them that it is their duty, as patriotic Japanese, to leave foreign employ. Their role at some posts has been thereby rendered unhappy but secure in the knowledge that the work they are doing is not to their country's disadvantage but actually to its good, they have hitherto stood to their guns.[71]

---

[71]   White added an asterisk after this point and wrote in the margin: 'written before the outbreak of war'.

I think with affection, therefore, of the writers who have served under me. I hope they feel the same towards me. One can never be absolutely certain and once, when I heard an expression of opinion, it was adverse. In Osaka, a writer left me to join a newspaper. Shortly afterwards a friend of mine met him and disingenuously steered the conversation round to the subject of myself. 'Yes,' said the former writer, 'he is a nice man and I liked him but it is a pity he is so short-tempered.' I fancy he meant that I was impatient. The foreigner in his first years in Japan frets and fumes at the time it takes to get things done. It is not the delay so much as the fact that the Japanese are too polite to tell the foreigner that he is asking the impossible when he expects a thing to be done immediately. But, then, the alien always wants a thing done in his own way and rarely makes allowances for difficulties. It was an American lady on a bus held up on a traffic jam near Trafalgar Square, who said, 'Take your time. Take your time. That's the British motto.'

Japanese Servants

I add a word about Japanese servants. In my opinion they are hard to beat. They are hard-working and, decently treated, are thoroughly loyal. At the time of the great Yokohama earthquake they stood by their employers, risking their lives to guard their well-being and their property. No doubt there were exceptions but I heard many instances of their devotion and not one of desertion of duty. During the whole of my life in Japan I do not recollect ever having dismissed a servant. The only time we changed them was when we were transferred to another place. On the whole it is better to have women servants. A mixture does not work well unless it be husband and wife. The best cook I ever had had one failing. Sooner or later he turned lustful eyes on the maids. But he was absolutely loyal to our interests and extremely resourceful. Called upon to produce a dinner for guests at short notice and asked if he had sufficient supplies, he would stand silent for a moment with his eyes closed. They he would begin slowly to carve up the joint or chicken in imagination, tracing the cuts with one finger over his body! Then he would open his eyes and say triumphantly that he could manage and he always did. The same man took over all the arrangements whenever the family had to make a trip, bought the tickets, looked after the luggage and invariably saw the whole thing through without a hitch. One of the most loyal servants was an *eta*[72] (member of the pariah class). He was tremendously proud of the Consular flag and once, when ordered to take it down – I forget the occasion – refused. It had always flown day by day in his experience and had never been taken down except at sunset. When his master ordered him to take it down, during the day, he decided that the master had taken leave of his senses and was not going to let the Consulate down by obeying such a foolish order.

---

[72]   *Eta* ('unpure') also known as *Burakumin* ('hamlet people'/'village people') are an outcast group at the bottom of the Japanese social order, who are the victims of severe discrimination and ostracism. They were originally members of outcast communities in the Japanese feudal era, composed of those with occupations considered impure or tainted by death (such as executioners, undertakers, workers in slaughterhouses, butchers or tanners), which have severe social stigmas of *kegare* (defilement) attached to them. Traditionally, they lived in their own hamlets or ghettos. See Louis Frédéric, trans. Käthe Roth, *Japan Encyclopedia* (Cambridge, MA: Belknap Press, 2002), pp. 93–4.

Chapter 9

VICE-CONSUL AT OSAKA, 1913–1919

℘

I WAS APPOINTED Acting Vice-Consul at Osaka in 1913 and subsequently Vice-Consul, a post I held till 1919. In those days it was a Vice-Consulate under the control of the Kobe Consulate General. I came back in 1931 when it had become an independent Consulate-General and was in charge till 1937 so that, altogether, I have served twelve years at Osaka.

Life in Osaka

I always had a little grudge against my first chief in 1913. Some time earlier he had decided that the Vice-Consul at Osaka should live in Osaka and not outside. In theory, the opinion was irreproachable; in practice, it was not. The work at Osaka has always been almost entirely commercial. Since ninety per cent of the leading merchants, Japanese and foreign, live outside Osaka, there was really no need for the Vice-Consul to be at his post out of office hours. During the four years I lived in Osaka, on no occasion was I called on to do any work out of office hours that could not perfectly well have waited over.

However, the Consul-General had decided that the Vice-Consul should live in Osaka and a tiny lot had been acquired in the old foreign concession. A Vice-Consulate and residence combined was later built and my family and I moved in at the beginning of 1915.

At first, living conditions were not too bad. It was true the building fronted on a main road down which trams rumbled for eighteen hours out of the twenty-four. The dust was bad and the smoke from the river, fifty yards off, where small steamers were arriving and leaving at all hours of the day and night, was troublesome. A far more serious matter was that two factories on the other side of the river were stirred into great activity by the Great War and commenced to pour sulphuric acid fumes into the air which, with the prevailing wind in summer, settled down in our quarter.

I once tried to get this nuisance abated. First, I called on the zinc refinery, which was one of the culprits. The director I saw was most sympathetic. It was an outrage that the air should be polluted in this way. 'But,' he added, 'why do you come to us? The fumes you complain of come from the Steel Works next door.' I went next door. Again, the director was most sympathetic. 'I am glad you have brought the matter up. We have complained to the refinery more than once and I shall be only too glad to back up any complaints you make. Why don't you go and see them yourself?' I gave in and, for the most of our life in Osaka, we suffered from the sulphuric acid fumes, the smoke, the dust and the noise.

When I was leaving Osaka in 1919, I recommended to the Embassy that the site and building should be sold. I think I must have been in bad odour with the embassy at the time for I got a 'wigging' for my pains but when I came back from leave eight months later, I found that the site and building had been sold and, ever since, office accommodation has been rented and the Consul has lived outside Osaka.

When we moved into Osaka the old foreign concession at Kawaguchi was still intact, though long since merged in the city administration. It was a tiny little settlement of some thirty or forty houses, of which half a dozen were occupied by business firms and the rest by missionaries. The front, which faced the main road was dirty and noisy but, behind that, the settlement was neat and tidy. Owing to the war, however, land values increased rapidly and, one by one, the missions sold their lots and the missionaries moved out to the outskirts of the city. We were left marooned. There was a miniature garden at the back in which the Office of Works had kindly planted a microscopic lawn and a few fir trees. But the grass and the trees soon gave up the unequal struggle against dust and fumes and we abandoned the pretence of a garden.

I am afraid I am rather piling on the agony. My wife, fortunately, was gifted with a happy disposition and a genius for making the best of things. When the average woman would have gone melancholy mad, she looked round and found things to do. There were first our three little girls, the eldest aged six in 1915. We had a nurse to look after them who was efficient and trustworthy but fiercely jealous of any encroachment on her duties. Good-natured to a fault, my wife did not interfere unduly but on one thing she insisted and that was to teach the children their lessons. Both in Osaka and in Nagasaki, whither I was transferred in 1920, there were no foreign schools and from 1920 I appointed myself head master and between ourselves we educated our children until the eldest was fourteen and the youngest was nearly nine. It sounds like conceit but I honestly do not think the children suffered.

Simple lessons to the children could not, however, occupy my wife more than a few hours in the morning. Of social life there was little. The missionary community was friendly but, for the most part, narrow-minded. One Christmas we had a little party with crackers but one little girl, who had evidently been carefully brought up, refused to wear the imitation jewellery that came out from the crackers because she said that God would not like her to adorn herself. If I may be allowed to digress for a moment, wherever I was stationed, my wife and I made it our business to get to know the missionary community which we always found friendly and well-disposed towards us but inclined to look askance at our liberal views on religion. On one occasion a dear lady sent my wife a copy of the new Testament with passages specially marked (I was evidently past praying for) and when we were leaving Osaka, another missionary wrote to my wife, who was justly noted for her social work, and after a few nice remarks about her goodness, stated that it had been a source of grief to her that my wife was not a Christian but added that she would never cease to pray for her!

While we were occasionally taken aback by the extreme narrowness of so many missionaries, their lack of sense of proportion afforded us a good deal of quiet amusement. In Seoul, when we first went there, there was a group to which we belonged which met at intervals for a little reading or music. The meetings were opened with prayer and the first evening we listened awestruck while a missionary opened with 'Oh, God! We thank Thee for Thy interest in the Social Circle.'

In Osaka we were delighted to find one 'human' couple, Mr and Mrs Rawlings, with whom we became life-long friends. But they unfortunately lived outside Osaka about one hour's journey away by tram. One way and another, social activities were circumscribed. Fortunately, my wife had one source of amusement that never palled. She was fond of curios and, whenever she was free, she went to a famous curio-street and spent long hours with the dealers. She rarely bought anything but it is a pleasing trait of the dealer that when he realises that a visitor genuinely loves beautiful objects, he will show his treasures and discuss them even when he knows the visitor has not the money to buy them. Meanwhile, I went along to the Japanese Club. At this time of day it was deserted, since between six and eight, the average Japanese is at home, taking his bath and dining, or he is at a 'tea-house'. But I amused myself playing billiards with the marker and for two or three years this was my recreation for five nights out of seven. So much for social life. It is time to speak of Consular work.

Effect of the War on Osaka

I was stationed at Osaka throughout the Great War and watched the city grow from a manufacturing centre of secondary importance to one of the leading centres in the world. It had already become known as the principal cotton spinning and weaving centre. Not that all the mills were placed there – Tokyo, Nagoya and Kobe had a number of mills and a tendency, which afterwards became more pronounced, to place new mills in country centres where labour was plentiful, was already observable.

But Osaka has always been the business centre of the industry. It had also the nucleus of the heavy industries which afterwards became so important – there was a big shipbuilding yard, the Sumitomo firm had steel works, there was an important factory of railway rolling-stock and so on. But Osaka was also noted as the principal manufacturing centre of the miscellaneous cheap goods, which are turned out in such quantity by hundreds of small factories employing twenty to fifty workers.

When the first European war broke out, Osaka soon woke up to its opportunity. If Osaka had a good fairy which watched over its destiny with benevolent eye, Osaka must have said to her, 'Send us a nice big war in Europe and please make it last as long as possible.' At first it was thought that the war was too good to be true. It must come to an end in a year or, at the outside, in two years. The more cautious Japanese made their little pile and drew out. It was the more adventurous spirits, who held on and on, that reaped the golden harvest. And presently the Japanese threw caution to the winds and acted as if the war would go on for ever. Ships passed hands at seven hundred yen a ton and even a thousand yen (£100 at that time). There was a crash at the end and a large proportion of the profits were lost over night but in the meantime the manufacturing capacity of Osaka and the centres which it controls had grown out of all recognition and, after a period of adjustment, Osaka took its place as one of the manufacturing centres of the world.

Growth of Japanese Trade Competition

Among the many enterprises that benefited from the war, shipping was one of the principal. The NYK (Nippon Yusen Kaisha) had been steadily growing. When I first went out it already maintained a European combined passenger and freight line, the principal merit of which was its cheapness. Most of the skippers and engineers were foreign, mainly British. Before the war these had been replaced and modern vessels put on the run but it was the enormous profits made during the war that enabled the company to branch out as one of the leading shipping companies in the world. Its rival, the OSK (Osaka Shosen Kaisha) had merely run coasting services with a host of small vessels that were a convenient, but not particularly comfortable, means of transport. The Company also rose to the occasion. Its fleet has been built up since the war but it was during the war that the assets were laid by that gave it the opportunity to start its over-seas services.

But in 1915, this was in the lap of the gods. In world trade Osaka was merely the supplier of goods whose only merit was their cheapness and the British manufacturers could look on complacently at the puny Japanese efforts to compete with him in textiles and machinery. Osaka had built itself a harbour but it was quite inadequate and it was only when, some years later, it was all made over again on a much larger scale that ocean-going vessels began to make use of it. In the meantime, its wooden pier was the favourite haunt of the amateur fisherman who sat on it and angled by the hour. It is three or four miles from the main business centre of Osaka to the harbour and, in those days, half of the distance was marshy ground overgrown with reeds and intersected by muddy creeks.

I believe, myself, that Osaka would have grown to its present importance in any case but it would have been a long and hard struggle. The war was her heaven-sent opportunity and she should raise a temple to the God of (Other Peoples') Wars.

Cotton Industry

In cotton spinning and weaving, Japan was then in the transition stage. One of two of the leading manufacturers had realised that it pays to study the health and the happiness of the operatives and Kanegafuchi at Kobe had a mill of which they were justly proud. They were only too pleased to show visitors round the dormitories, the dispensary, the play-ground and they would also take them through the mill itself to show how spick and span it was but the conductor discouraged any attempt to linger and take it all in. I was always rather amused and inclined to be a little irritated at this. It needs an expert to take in details and a Consul is certainly not an expert on spinning and weaving.

Attitude of British Manufacturers to Consuls

But I cannot blame the Japanese manufacturer. Years later (in 1931) I wished to learn something about the British rayon industry in order to be competent to report Japanese developments. With a little difficulty, I got permission to visit a British mill and an expert very courteously and painstakingly took me round and explained the various processes, but he had had particular orders not to show me one section in which I was particularly interested. Since I cannot imagine that the management doubted my integrity, I could only imagine they distrusted my discretion. It is not for me to question their judgement: the manufacturer knows his own business best: but after I arrived in Osaka, the same company frequently applied to me for information which could only be answered by one who had some knowledge, however slight, of the processes involved.

While on this subject, I may as well go on to say that when I was coming back to Osaka in 1931, I made a point of visiting manufacturing centres whose industries were being injured by Japanese competition and, on the whole, I found the manufacturer only too anxious to instruct me but there were exceptions. One leading manufacturing company, on being applied to through the proper channels, replied that it had its own representative in the Far East and that there was no point in my visiting their works. I had hardly installed myself in my office in Osaka before the said representative walked in and asked for my advice and assistance!

On this same tour I called on a leading producer of cotton textiles in Manchester. Having made rather a study of Japanese methods I had imagined that he would take the opportunity of learning what little I could tell him. Instead, I listened for an hour to his explanation of the superiority of Lancashire's methods. There is a story of a native shown an elephant for the first time who simply refused to believe it. In 1931 there was still a type of Manchester merchant who simply could not believe that the Osaka bogy existed.

Profits of Japanese Companies

To revert to Osaka in 1913–1919, the average British visitor who applied to me to get him or her permission to visit a cotton mill was interested, not in the skill of the Japanese spinner, but in the social conditions in the mills. They asked to be shown a 'bad' mill. There were a number of them in Osaka – old type mills, floors dirty and air full of cotton dust, dirty dormitories in which the operatives on one shift turned straight into the 'futon' (quilts that take the place of bed-clothes in Japan) just vacated by the first shift. As far as I know, these old mills have been swept away and companies have learnt the lesson that expenditure on the health and well-being of the operatives pays.

The spinning companies were enabled to put their house in order by the enormous profits they made during the European War. At the end of the war they were paying, in some cases, fifty per cent dividends and more and actually were turning their capital over in the year, putting by huge reserves by the simple means of writing down their stocks far below the market price.

In turn, all industries benefited and money poured in. Shares jumped up and up and, for once, the 'bears' got the worst of it. Tokyo Stock Exchange fifty yen shares went to seven hundred yen and were 'talked up' to a thousand yen. Periodically there was a shake-out and those who had sold at the top made a fortune – on paper. But the drop would be so severe that few could have paid up. So the exchange directors stopped transactions and arranged a mean price (in a double sense) and the losers were let off lightly.

The Narikin (Parvenu)

A new class of being came into existence, known as the narikin (one who had made money overnight, a parvenu). These were men who earlier had, for the most part, lived on the smell of herring and now had so much money they did not know what to do with it. One narikin arranged a tiger hunt in Corea on the scale of a polar expedition. Many of the narikin spent money like water, built themselves 'palaces', chartered steamers and special trains when they travelled and would spend as much on an evening's entertainment as would keep the average Japanese in comfort for a year. But these were the antics of the few. Most of the successful men were too engrossed in the game of making money to be interested in the problem of spending it. Those who were cultured indulged their passion for collecting works of art. Well-to-do Japanese have always taken a delight in selective buying of rare works of old Chinese and Japanese masters and are willing to pay amazing prices for them. During the war years they were enabled to add considerably to their collections. The big business houses paid large bonuses to their employees and distributed handsome presents to their clients at the New Year. One beautiful little work of art went backwards and forwards from my office with polite expressions of regret on my part at my inability to accept it. Ultimately I learnt that the giver had had several hundred of them made and was distributing them widely. There could therefore be no suggestion that it was payment for favours received or to be received and I finally accepted it.

Japanese Disparagement of the British Army

As the war progressed, the Japanese came to the conclusion that Japan had put its money on the wrong horse. Whether this belief caused concern to the Japanese Government I do not know. It certainly did not worry the Osaka business man who cared little which side won so long as the war lasted as long as possible, though what did cause him sleepless nights was the peace rumours that periodically sent a shiver of apprehension through the markets. But considerable academic interest was shown and opinion was overwhelmingly unfavourable to the Allies.

The local Japanese thought of warfare in terms of the Russo-Japanese War; when one side – Japan – advanced, the other – Russia – retreated. The trench stalemate on the Western Front was totally incomprehensible to them. Here was Germany, encamped in the heart of the French. Why did not the British and French push them out? An unfortunate story, which was generally accepted, supplied an answer to the satisfaction of the Osaka Japanese. The story was that, during the siege of Tsingtao,[73] the general in command of the British troops had complained that the trench or trenches occupied by them were too advanced and had withdrawn his men, whereupon the Japanese commander had not only occupied the line, but pushed it forward. Obviously, therefore, the British had no real stomach for fighting and if the British troops in France did not advance, it was because they weren't brave enough to attack the enemy and push him back.

The Japanese used to commiserate with me on the lack of success of the Allies. I used stoutly to maintain that war was decided by the last battle and tell them to 'wait and see'. But I knew they were not convinced and those who had been trained in Germany – scientists, doctors, etc. – used to hold forth, so I was told, on the inevitability of a German victory. The swift change that occurred in the summer of 1918 took the Japanese by surprise and they simply could not believe, till the last moment, that the Allies were winning at long last.

It would scarcely be right to accuse the business men of callousness in their attitude towards Great Britain – the ally of their country. The war was altogether too remote to catch their imagination and the issues at stake meant nothing to them so that they were not really interested in either side. The Osaka business

---

73   Tsingtao (Qingdao in the pinyin translation system now used in China) is a major city on the Shandong Peninsula, looking out onto the Yellow Sea. The peninsula was a German concession in China from 1898 to 1914. The Siege of Tsingtao lasted from 31 October to 7 November 1914 and was fought by Japan and the United Kingdom against Imperial Germany. The siege was the first encounter between Japanese and German forces and also the first Anglo-Japanese operation during the war. The German garrison held out for nearly two months but was eventually overrun. The German dead were buried at Qingdao, while the remainder were transported to prisoner of war camps in Japan, where they remained until the formal signature of the Versailles Peace Treaty in 1919. See Jonathan Fenby, *The Siege of Tsingtao* (Melbourne, Australia: Penguin Group, 2015). Many buildings from the German period remain, while the German-style 'Tsingtao Beer' is widely regarded as one of the best produced in China. Many of the vineyards in the peninsula, revived and modernised in the 1980s, produce German-style wines.

man has little, one might say no, voice in the determination of his country's foreign policy. He takes his cue from the government and accepts its decisions. In the case of the Great War, he might be pardoned for thinking his own government was indifferent since he was allowed to trade freely with the enemy. I have a suspicion that, at heart, he dislikes wars and would, for instance, prefer a less aggressive policy towards China. We used to be called a nation of shop-keepers. Something similar might be said of the Osaka business man who only wants to trade and knows that his business is going to suffer from war. Given time and treated with copious propaganda, he can be brought into the 'right' frame of mind but, left to himself, I think he would be all on the side of peace.

Attitude towards the US

When the US came into the Great War, a curious change in the Japanese attitude towards them took place. As the US woke into warlike activity, so the Japanese became critical of American growing military and naval strength. This was curious since Japan also was an ally and should have welcomed a further ally against the Germans. Instead, they displayed growing concern at the expansion of the US Navy. Some prophetic insight seemed to warn them that they would find the US ranged against them in the years to come.

Combating Enemy Trading

The war revolutionised Consular work for the time being. One of our many duties was to prevent, as far as possible, supplies of materials from British territories going into the hands of Japanese who were trading with the enemy. The Japanese importer could not get his supplies unless he had obtained a certificate from the British Consul that he had been satisfied they were not to pass ultimately into the hands of the enemy. The system was not, of course, water-tight as the Consul had no control over the materials once they passed into the hands of the importer.

He had to rely mainly on his knowledge of the character of the importer and, no doubt, was bamboozled often enough.

On one occasion, a leading importer came to get a certificate to cover an import of castor-oil from India. This article has many uses other than medicinal. It is, for instance, a valuable lubricant. The importer wanted the oil, so he told me, to sell to a soap manufacturer. I expressed a desire to meet the latter and was duly taken to a soap-works. It proved to be a comparatively small factory. Presently, I asked the proprietor how much castor-oil he used monthly. He looked at me in surprise and, after a pause, replied that it was a trade secret. I dropped the subject at once.

The importer evidently sensed that things had gone wrong for, when we left, he suggested lunch. I declined but, as he was very insistent, I finally accepted rather than be rude. I should explain that the foreign meals one get in Osaka in those days were very 'scratch' and there was no question of expansive entertainment. At the end of lunch, the importer said, 'Do I get my certificate?'. The answer was in the negative. He had made two blunders. In the first place, he had taken me to a small works which, in any case, would not be likely to use such an expensive oil except in minute quantity. And he had neglected to prime the manufacturer.

I forget why I had been especially suspicious in this instance. Normally there was nothing to be gained by meeting the alleged consumer. If the importer's story was plausible and there was no reason to doubt his bona-fides, he got his certificate. Deception was all too easy but then the whole story did not end there. If he were really trading with the enemy, his activities would, sooner or later, be uncovered elsewhere.

Many Japanese resented, I believe, the British Consul's interference but on the whole I think they found that it paid to co-operate with him since he could assist them in what we considered legitimate business at a time when the Allies were subjecting foreign trade to control wherever possible. It is, I presume, an open secret that the British Government had its secret list of firms who were known to be trading with the enemy. Japanese merchants used to come to my office and ask if it was 'safe' to trade with so and so in a foreign market. They were never told 'yes' or 'no' but something in the nature of 'I should imagine there is no reason why you shouldn't' or 'I am sorry but I cannot tell you anything about this firm' from which they were at liberty to draw their own conclusions. On one occasion, however, an unfortunate mistake occurred which might have been serious.

By an incredible oversight a printed list had been sent to my office through the ordinary post in a newspaper wrapper, from the ends of which the booklet projected. That day, I was away from my office and by an evil chance, a Japanese came in to ask if it was safe to trade with X (an American firm in the USA). My Japanese clerk had seen me refer to similar booklets and, concluding that a booklet sent through the post in this open manner could not be particularly secret, in all good faith opened it up. Sure enough the name of X was down on the list. Not only did he so inform the merchant but he naively showed him the entry. The merchant, probably maliciously, informed X that he could not trade with him because he was on the black list and then the fat was in the fire. X, of course, went to the State Department in Washington and protested. That was bad enough but what was worse was that it was just the time of the Presidential election in 1916 when Wilson was running for a second time on a platform of neutrality. Needless to say, the State Department was not going to submit to a British Consul in Osaka butting in on trade between Japan and the US, least of all at such a moment.

I was blissfully unconscious of the gathering storm, until one fine day, I received a peremptory telegram. The wires had been busy. The State Department had taken the matter up with the British Ambassador at Washington who had telegraphed to the Foreign Office who had telegraphed to the British Ambassador in Tokyo who had telegraphed to a trembling little Vice-Consul in Osaka for an immediate explanation.

To go back, my Japanese writer had brought me the list the following day and I had explained to him that he was not to open any mail whatever. But he had not thought fit to tell me he had shown it to the merchant. He now made a clean breast of it and there was nothing for it but to communicate the whole story to the British Ambassador. Exactly what explanation was given to the State Department I do not know for I heard no more of the incident.

British Volunteers from Japan

A task of a different nature, which I cordially disliked, became necessary in 1917. This was to round up British subjects of military age and ask them 'voluntarily' to place themselves in my hands. One British subject demurred. He said that he was convinced that he was serving his country better by remaining in charge of his company's branch in Osaka. If I ordered him to go home and fight, he would go but he had no desire to 'volunteer'. I explained that the question of what use should be made of his services came later. What I wanted at the moment was that he should express his willingness to accept, in advance, the decision of the British authorities.

We argued the matter round and round in circles. The truth is that there was a good deal of bunk about the whole business. The British Government could either order British subjects abroad to submit (or take the consequences) or it could issue an appeal. It did neither. As the instructions came to us at the Consulates, we were to coerce British subjects into volunteering – a contradiction in terms. Anyway, this British subject demanded orders and, in their absence, declined to put himself in my hands. The absurd thing was that, though I could not tell him so in advance, I had already made up my mind to exempt him as being of more use to his country at his post, which was one of importance.

When I reported the facts to the Embassy, I received, by return, a very angry letter. Every other Consulate in Japan had reported complete submission from all the British subjects in the district. And here was one black sheep in Osaka spoiling the whole record. Once more I sent for the unfortunate man and, this time, bullied him into submission. The ranks were now complete. British manhood had responded to the call and all was well. A day or two later, I exempted that British subject.

As a matter of fact, the record of the British community in Japan was a good one. A large proportion of the young men joined up at the outset. The British in Japan retain their fondness for outdoor sports and keep themselves fit with football, cricket, golf, tennis, etc. and the volunteers from Japan were a fine body of men. One sportsman, who was well known to be over the age-limit, was such a good all-round athlete that he had no difficulty in knocking off several years of his age. The roll of honour for Japan is, considering the size of the community, a large one. By 1917 there were very few young British in Japan who one could say ought to go to the front. The only value of this campaign of which I have just spoken was to demonstrate the solidarity of the British community.

A Relic of the Days of Sailing Ships

To turn from the war, my principal bugbear during my first years in Osaka was a British ship which made periodic visits laden with timber from Canada. The skipper was a prize rogue. He made money on the side by shipping Canadians 'wanted' by the Police. On the return voyage he took Japanese who paid him a premium for being allowed to desert. No doubt there was an organisation to smuggle them into Canada. Seeing that it was an open secret I could never make out why the Canadian authorities were unable to catch him out. But that was no business of mine.

His crew was somewhat of a mixed bag. Defaulting bank clerks are scarcely likely to be much good on board a sailing ship and even the sturdy ruffians would need some knocking into shape. The regular seamen were a tough bunch: no self-respecting seaman would have shipped on the old tub if he could help himself. The skipper used to boast – when he was on shore – that it was as much as his life was worth not to go round fully armed but I suspect that his real protection was that he was the only man on board who could be trusted to bring the ship into port.

When she did come in, then the trouble began. In the intervals of coming to me to lay complaints against the captain, the crew would spend the time getting blind-drunk in grog-shops and being run in by the police. When not fighting all and sundry on shore, they fought each other on the ship. One free-for-all ended in several having to go to hospital. Perhaps the Canadian authorities did, after all, catch the captain out as, after two years, the ship suddenly ceased coming to Osaka.

Chapter 10

CONSUL AT NAGASAKI, 1920–1925

ℰↃ

IN 1920 I was promoted to be Consul at Nagasaki, a post I held till 1925. They were five quiet, uneventful years. There was never much work to do and, at times, nothing at all.

Former Importance of Nagasaki

Nagasaki was engaged in foreign trade when Kobe and Yokohama were non-existent. While the country was closed to foreign intercourse, the Dutch were allowed to maintain a 'factory' at Nagasaki on Deshima,[74] a tiny little island separated by a channel from Nagasaki itself. Their doings were carefully watched and, for the most part, they were confined to the island. I fancy, however, that in quiet times they were allowed more freedom. To this day, the children in the country around call out '*Orandajin*' (Dutchman) whenever they see a foreigner.

In 1920 there were still many relics of the Dutch to be found. Screens depicting the 'black ships' (the term for foreign ships) were to be found in the curio shops and Dutch decanters and glasses, the value of which was historical rather than artistic.

---

[74] Dejima was a small fan-shaped artificial island built in the bay of Nagasaki in 1634 by local merchants. This island, which was formed by digging a canal through a small peninsula, remained as the single place of direct trade and exchange between Japan and the outside world during the Edo period. Originally built to house Portuguese traders, it was used by the Dutch as a trading post from 1641 until 1853; Frédéric, *Japan Encyclopedia*, p. 152.

When Western persistence won the day and Japan was opened to foreign trade, Nagasaki was the first to benefit and a Consul was appointed there in 1858, two years before Kanagawa[75] (Yokohama) and ten years before Hiogo[76] (Kobe). It had one substantial advantage in its land-locked harbours whereas Kanagawa and Hiogo were open road-steads. Shortly afterwards, another asset was discovered in the excellent coal to be mined in two small islands off the entrance to the harbour. It has one fatal defect that has proved its undoing. It is situated near the tip of a hilly peninsula and it is cut off from sources of supply and from buying centres. As the only port of Kyushu, the south-westerly of the four main islands of the Japanese Archipelago, Nagasaki held its own for a time but presently, when communications were developed, Nagasaki found itself on the end of a branch-line, the upstart, Moji at the northern end of the island took what foreign trade was going and Nagasaki went to sleep.

Decline of Nagasaki

This may seem an exaggeration since Mitsubishi has a magnificent ship-building yard there, but somehow the Mitsubishi works never seemed a part of Nagasaki, certainly not of Nagasaki as a trade port. In 1920 and 1921, the yards on the western shore of the bay were a scene of thriving activity. The tap-tap-tap of riveting never ceased day or night: Mitsubishi were doing their share

---

[75]   Japan is divided in forty-seven prefectures which form the country's first jurisdiction and administrative division levels. Kanagawa is a prefecture located in the southern Kantō region of Japan, in the Greater Tokyo Area. The capital of the prefecture is Yokohama. Although the 1858 treaty named Kanagawa as the foreign settlement, the Japanese decided it was too near the main road, the Tokaido, and erected buildings for the foreigners at the nearby village of Yokohama. Diplomatic and consular protests proved no match for the foreign merchants who took the Japanese buildings. But it was not until the 1880s that British consular despatches were dated from Yokohama and not Kanagawa.

[76]   Hyōgo Prefecture is in the Kansai region on Honshu island. The capital is Kobe. Again, the city of Hyogo was named in the treaty but the foreign settlement was at the nearby village of Kobe.

in the big naval expansion that started when America joined the Allies in the European War. Nagasaki City itself, just opposite on the eastern shore of the bay, was a sleepy, provincial town. Mitsubishi owned the coal-mines and had its own trading organisation, which handled all orders. The local Nagasaki merchants merely got the crumbs that fell from the rich man's table, quite substantial in their own way but not requiring any great effort to secure. The Osaka merchant is noted for his shrewdness in business. He has always had to struggle hard against keen competition and there is no more astute trader. The Nagasaki merchant has had his humble meal served to him on a platter. He is – or was in the years I knew him from 1920 to 1925 – an old-world gentleman, quiet, placid, easy-going and polite. My wife found the courtly manners of the tradespeople a constant source of pleasure.

The fates have been kind to Nagasaki only to be cruel. Nature gave it a perfect harbour – and no hinterland. The coal-mines attracted shipping for a number of years – and then became exhausted. Foreign fleets, and particularly the Russian, that brought prosperity to the merchants and tradespeople of Nagasaki, ceased to use it as an anchorage after the war between Japan and Russia.

The Washington conference of 1922 dealt a shrewd blow to the Mitsubishi Shipbuilding Yard and so, indirectly, to Nagasaki City. Just before the signing of the treaty, I attended a melancholy function – the launching of the battleship *Mutsu*, over the building of which the company had been so proud but which everyone knew was to be scrapped. 1922 to 1925 were years of depression. The main passenger steamship lines gradually ceased to call and Nagasaki relapsed into slumber.

Smuggling on a Small Scale

The cessation of the calls of the passenger liners (other than the two smaller Empresses) came rather as a blow to the foreign ladies of Nagasaki. They used to flock off to the ships when they were in and, curious to relate, would come ashore looking much stouter than when they went off. This was not due to food-absorption. The stewardesses on the American ships

would execute orders for clothing when the ship was in San
Francisco and when it came into Nagasaki, the ladies went on
board, put on the new clothes under the old and walked ashore.
I fancy the Japanese Customs were well aware of the practice
but did not interfere since the total duty on the clothes brought
ashore by a handful of foreign ladies would not have amounted
to very much. And since the public consider a government fair
game, the foreign ladies were proud of their exploits in bringing ashore bathing-suits, corsets, slips, knickers, dresses and
even furs. The men were satisfied with a modest tin of cigarettes
or, if they were bolder, a box of cigars.

And that reminds me of a story which has the merit of being
true. At another port, the manager of a foreign bank was partial to a
certain brand of cigar not sold by the Japanese Monopoly. He used
to have these sent a few at a time in bank envelopes. One day the
Director of Customs invited him to dinner. At its close, a servant
brought in a box of Monopoly cigars. 'No,' said the Director, 'Mr X
does not smoke those cigars.' Whispered instructions followed and
presently the servant came in with one of X's own particular brand!
'I am sure you would prefer to smoke one of your own cigars,' said
the Director, 'I will send the rest round to you tomorrow.'

Probably the rebuke would have been less tactfully administered if the culprit had filled a more lowly position but, in
general, while smuggling as a trade is severely punished, a more
indulgent attitude used to be adopted towards the offender who
tried to evade the laws on his own account. A year or two ago, a
Chinese pedlar was caught in Osaka selling smuggled cigars. No
doubt under pressure, he gave a list of foreigners to whom he
had sold them. Each foreigner was visited in turn and asked if he
had any smuggled cigars. When they admitted it, not unreasonable fines were imposed and the matter was dropped but none
of them bought smuggled cigars thereafter!

Netherlands Vice-Consul

In addition to my far from arduous duties as British Consul at
Nagasaki, I was in charge of the Netherlands interests, the rou-

tine work of which sometimes occupied more time than did the work for my own Government. I once had the interesting experience of comparing the procedure of the two countries in matters of registration. Two friends – one British and one Dutch – had the sentimental idea of being married on the same day. They attended with their brides together. The British marriage occupied less than five minutes and the Dutch, twenty-five minutes, the reason being that the entry in the Dutch register consisted of a longish record which I had to write out word for word.

My Dutch work had a humorous side. One day a Japanese woman called and explained that she wished to register her child. The father it appeared, was a Dutchman residing in the East Indies. She produced a letter from him stating that she was coming back to Japan to have the child and asking me to register it as his in due course. 'That's quite in order,' I said, 'but have you a medical certificate?' The woman looked blank. 'Haven't you had a doctor to attend to you?' I next asked. 'No, I don't need a doctor.' 'Well,' I said, 'I must have some sort of proof.' The woman began to look more and more dumbfounded. 'What is it – a boy or a girl?' 'I don't know.' 'What! You don't know the sex of your child? What is its name?' 'I haven't decided that yet.' 'If you can't give me any sort of proof and you cannot give me any details, how am I to know you have a child? Where is it?' A smile broke through the woman's bewilderment. 'Here it is,' and she pointed to her person. The child was yet to be born but she had wanted to get the registration over first and then return to her native village away in the country to have it.

Visits of HM Ships

For the most part, life flowed on uneventfully week to week, month to month and year to year. From time to time the monotony would be varied by the arrival of one of HM Ships for a stay of a few days when the small British community would strive to give the officers and men a good time. I had always to warn the captain to put his men on their guard against the spurious whisky sold in the grog-shops. The warning was evidently taken to heart. On one occasion, a skipper lent me a few men to do some plumbing at the Consulate which I had tried in vain to get done properly by local plumbers. The men worked hard all morning and, as it was a hot day, I offered them a drink. 'Which do you prefer – whisky or beer?' 'Beer, if you don't mind Sir. We have been told it is dangerous to drink whisky on shore.'

Local Community

If Nagasaki was dull owing to the absence of work in my time, life was very pleasant. The foreign business community consisted of some thirty households living in old-style bungalows pictur-esquely situated on a bluff, overlooking the harbour. If one met the same people at dinner at each other's houses, that was only to be expected in a small community and Nagasaki hospitality was noted. There was a cleavage between the business and the missionary community living on another bluff just behind the waterfront. My wife and I tried to make a bridge over this gulf but it could not be done. The missionaries, I fear, looked on the business men as dissipated and ungodly and the latter considered the missionaries smug and self-satisfied and to argue against the prejudices of either was a waste of breath.

Unzen

In summer there was excellent bathing down the bay. My wife and family went to Unzen,[77] a hill resort three or four hours off. I used to go up on Saturdays and, as work became slacker and slacker, on Fridays. Out of this fact grew a rumour at headquarters (the Embassy) that I transferred the Consulate to Unzen during the summer months. I only heard the story afterwards but it arose in this way. One Sunday I received a wireless telegram relayed from Nagasaki from which I learnt the Ambassador was due in

---

[77] Mount Unzen is an active volcanic group of several overlapping stratovolcanoes in Nagasaki Prefecture. The volcano was most recently active from 1990 to 1995, and a large eruption in 1991 generated a pyroclastic flow that killed forty-three people, including three volcanologists. Currently its highest peak is 1,486 metres, which emerged in the 1991 eruption.

Nagasaki early on Monday morning. The telegram arrived late in
the afternoon and, as I could not get a conveyance, I had to walk
and run most of the way to the nearest railway station where I just
caught the last train back to Nagasaki. Normally, I returned on
Monday morning, arriving just before noon. I happened to mention to the Ambassador that I had only just managed to get back
in time to greet him. Some time later, the Consul-General in Kobe
complained that he was unable to get leave as the office was under-
staffed. 'Well,' said the Ambassador, 'why don't you do as White
does and transfer the Consulate-General to Rokko (the summer
resort behind Kobe) for the summer?' When I heard this story
years later, my only regret was that I had not spent the summers at
Unzen instead of going up only at week-ends!

Nagasaki Oddities

The foreign community at Nagasaki was a small one but it had
its fair percentage of oddities. There was the Doyen of the Consular Corps. This was the Russian Consul, a dignified gentleman
of the old school appointed in the time of the Czarist regime. His
government had long ceased to exist but he continued to function and, as the Senior Consul at Nagasaki, had become Doyen.
No one was sufficiently interested to upset the arrangement.
I fancy that the Japanese authorities felt that it was up to the
Consuls themselves to arrange a matter of this sort and I had no
wish to take away from this pathetic figure his empty honour.

Another oddity was a miser who used to shuffle round in filthy
clothes, a repulsive looking object. As Secretary of the Nagasaki
Club I once called on him in company with the President of the
Club because we wished to buy from him the compound on
which the Club stood. We found that he lived on the upper floor
of a dilapidated old *godown*.[78] The steps up which we climbed were
crumbling and the floor on which we found ourselves had fallen
away in places. There were a few old broken down chairs on which
we fearfully perched ourselves and the whole place was indescrib-

---

[78]   Godown: in India and East Asia, a warehouse, especially one at a
        dockside.

ably dirty and squalid. And yet the Frenchman we were visiting owned a great deal of property and was, in reality, a rich man.

Then there was the retired Consul, a man who had been a competent officer but had been allowed to retire for the good of himself and the country he represented because he drank like a fish and latterly was rarely sober. His Japanese wife came down quietly to collect his pension. I gave her the title which, legally, was not hers but which she certainly deserved for she had stood by him for years even through his drinking bouts when he threw bottles at her. In my time he had begun to quieten down. He had two bad attacks of delirium tremens and this had scared him so that, in place of spirits, he contented himself with less potent beer.

There was a retired army officer married to a Japanese. Both he and his wife had 'bats in the belfry'. Whenever he called on me he would regale me with long accounts of the battle he was waging with the demons that were striving hard to affect lodgement in his organs. He would chase them out of his lungs, say, only to find them battering at his kidneys. There was a retired sea-dog, a Dane of over eighty, who had spent his entire life on the sea in sailing ships. He was never so happy as when he was asked in what year he had gone to sea: he would triumphantly reply that he hadn't gone to sea because he was born there. There was a Dutch ship's chandler, an enormous man of some three hundred pounds, whose pride was that he could allow anyone to butt him or hit him in the pit of the stomach without being inconvenienced. It used to grieve him that I was of such slight build and he would beseech me to eat plenty of salt fish and wash it down with gallons of beer.

I am not suggesting, of course, that the foreign community of Nagasaki was composed of oddities. Those we had stood out noticeably because the community was a small one. But what it lacked in numbers, the community made up for in hospitality and sociability. The years drifted by pleasantly but, I fear, aimlessly. One opportunity that I let slip when at Nagasaki, was to study the history of early foreign associations. Paske-Smith,[79]

---

79   Montagu Bentley Talbot Paske-Smith (1886–1946). Joined the Japan Consular Service in 1907, and served in several posts, including, Tamsui

who followed me as Consul, made the fullest use of his time and produced very interesting literature on the subject. But then I was not entirely idle. In the years 1920–1923 the children's education occupied all my spare time.

In 1925 the more interesting post of Dairen fell vacant and I was only too delighted to accept it when it was offered to me.

in Taiwan and Manila. He was later minister to Colombia (1936–1941). Like George Sansom, he carried on the scholarly tradition established by earlier members of the service. His major work, *Western Barbarians in Japan and Formosa in Tokugawa Days 1603–1858* (1930), is still widely cited. He also edited much material relating to the East India Company's interests in Japan, as well as a collection of material on the persecution of Japanese Christians at the end of the Tokugawa period, and other works.

Chapter 11

CONSUL AT DAIREN, 1925–1927

ဢ

Brief Outline of Earlier Manchurian History

Note: I wrote this section in 1938. Since that time Japan has run amuck but I leave it as an impression of the state of affairs at that time.

I ARRIVED AT Dairen[80] at an interesting time. Although it was impossible then to predict the outcome, it was obvious that opposing forces were gathering momentum which must result in a clash sooner or later. Manchuria was under the rule of the famous Chang Tso Lin,[81] a typical ex-bandit warlord.

---

[80] Dalian (*Darien* in Japanese, *Dalny* in Russian) is a major city and seaport in the south of *Liaoning* Province, China. It is the southernmost city of *Northeast China* (Manchuria) and China's northernmost warm water port, at the tip of the *Liaodong Peninsula*. Dalian is the province's second largest city after the provincial capital *Shenyang* (Mukden). Greater Dalian includes the port district Lüshunkou, which was previously known as Rhojun to the Japanese and Port Arthur to the Russians. Korea lies across the Yellow Sea to the east.

[81] Zhang Zuolin (Chang Tso-lin) was the warlord of Manchuria from 1916 to 1928. He successfully invaded China proper in October 1924 in the Second Zhili-Fengtian War. He gained control of Beijing, including China's internationally recognized government, in April 1926. The economy of Manchuria, the basis of Zhang's power, was overtaxed by his adventurism and collapsed in the winter of 1927–1928. Zhang was defeated by the Nationalists under Chiang Kai-shek in May 1928. He was killed by a bomb planted by a Japanese Kwantung (Guanndong) Army officer on 4 June 1928. Although Zhang had been Japan's proxy in China, Japanese militarists were infuriated by his failure to stop the advance of the Nationalists. Zhang was fiercely anti-Republican and

Chang Tso Lin had made himself independent of the Chinese Government. But for the presence of the Japanese Army, he would have been absolute master of the country.

I have never been able to feel much sympathy with China over the loss of Manchuria. China lost Manchuria, not on September 18th, 1931, but at the beginning of the century. In 1896 China gave Russia the concession to build a railway across North Manchuria to connect Chita in Siberia to Vladivostock. In 1898 she handed over what is now known as the Kwantung Leased Territory,[82] to Russia – lock, stock and barrel – and extended the railway concession to cover a line subsequently built from Harbin[83] to Port Arthur and Talienwan.[84] During the Boxer rebellion Russia occupied strategic points in Manchuria with her troops and afterwards, while making vague promises of withdrawal, actually refused to budge. I still remember a *Punch* cartoon of the period depicting the Russian bear, tail just leaving one corner of Manchuria and head coming in at another. Russia had come to stay and, though the western powers might bluster,

---

[82] supported the restoration of the Qing dynasty. His nicknames include the 'Old Marshal', 'Rain Marshal' and 'Mukden Tiger'. Gavan McCormack, *Chang Tso-lin in North East China 1914–1928: China, Japan and the Manchurian Idea* (Stanford CA: Stanford University Press, 1977). For the Kwantung army, see note 86, below.

[82] The Kwantung Leased Territory was a territory in the southern part of the Liaodong Peninsula in Manchuria that existed from 1898 to 1945. It was one of the numerous territorial concessions that the Empire of China was compelled to award to foreign countries at the end of the nineteenth century. The territory included the militarily and economically significant ports of Lüshunkou (Port Arthur, Port-Artur in Russian, or Ryojun in Japanese) and Dalian (Dairen in Japanese). Kwantung means 'East of Shanhai Pass'. It originally referred to all of Manchuria but later came to be used more narrowly for the area of the leased territory. The lease was originally held by the Russians, but after the Russo-Japanese War (1904–1905), the Territory was handed over to the Japanese (the victors)

[83] Harbin is the largest City in North-Eastern China (Manchuria). See Fig. 1 for a map showing the North Manchurian railway from Harbin to Dairen.

[84] Dalian Bay (Talianwan), is a bay on the southeast side of the Liaodong Peninsula, open to the Yellow Sea in the east. Downtown Dalian lies along the southern shore of the bay.

they were powerless. Russia was also rapidly getting a strangle-hold on Corea. She had a naval base at Masampo[85] and numerous concessions at other strategic points. It was only a question of time before Russia took Corea also.

Japan then staked her existence on a war with Russia, while her ally, Great Britain, held the ring and pushed the Russians out of South Manchuria. The western powers expected that Japan, having pulled the chestnuts out of the fire, would hand them round for general consumption. On paper they were right but it was expecting a little too much of human nature. All wars are fought in defence of sacred principles, never for selfish ends, and yet, somehow, the winners generally seem to gain material benefits. They have to insist on them, not for selfish ends of course, but to prevent their vanquished trying to disturb the peace again. Right or wrong, Japan considered she had won the right to dominate South Manchuria.

There was one fly in the ointment. Japan could not annex South Manchuria nor yet establish a protectorate since she had been fighting 'to preserve the integrity of China'. She had also fought to preserve the integrity of Corea but, fortunately, the Coreans themselves asked to be annexed, or so the world was told. China was not so reasonable. She even asked that Manchuria should be given back to her. And so, in theory, it was given back. But Japan kept the, renamed, South Manchuria Railway and Russia what remained of the Chinese Eastern Railway. Japan, and also Russia, retained what was of far greater strategic value – the right to maintain railway guards and to administer the railway towns which were growing up at important points.

Thanks mainly to the railways, Manchuria developed out of all recognition in the next twenty years. Russia lost her grip on North Manchuria after the Bolshevik Revolution but Japan had

---

[85]   Generally now known as Masan. In the late nineteenth century Masanhappo-gu (Happo or Masampo in Japanese) in the South of Korea, was 'one of the finest harbours in East Asia, though still only a fishing-village' – see Ian Nish, *The Origins of the Russo-Japanese War*, (London: Longman, 1985) p. 61. It became a treaty port in 1899. It is now part of the city of Changwon.

consolidated her position in South Manchuria. All trade and industry naturally gravitated to the railway towns and the Kwantung Army,[86] through its 'railway guards', could bring decisive influence to bear upon the Chinese administration.

But the latter had also been gaining in power. The industrious Chinese farmer and merchant had made the fullest use of improved transport and, as a combined result of their industry and thoroughly efficient railway management, the population in the interior had increased by leaps and bounds. The South Manchuria Railway constituted a Japanese enclave but, outside the railway, Chang Tso Lin was paramount. If the old bandit warlord had had the interests of Manchuria at heart, he had only to give his people good government and watch Manchuria grow in prosperity. Who knows? With a contented population behind him he might, in due course, have raised the slogan of Manchuria for the Manchurians. Could he have succeeded? Probably not. The Japanese were watching too carefully but, at all events, we should not have watched the pitiful debacle of 1931 when the Kwantung Army contemptuously brushed aside the Chinese administration like a pack of cards.

Chang Tso Lin was not thinking of Manchuria. He was thinking of his own ambitions. He was drawn by the magnet of Peking and the hope of making himself master of China. A greater man than he had been betrayed to his downfall by the same lure. Chang Tso Lin had a trained army that was not to be despised. He had at his beck and call foreign adventurers who would procure arms and ammunition for him and make guns, trench-mortars, shot and shell for him at his Mukden Arsenal. And in the middle twenties, Chang Tso Lin was busily bleeding Manchuria while in pursuance of his insane ambition. He entered into secret

---

86   Following its victory in the Russo-Japanese War (1904–1905), Japan obtained the Kwantung Leased Territory and the areas adjacent to the South Manchurian Railway. The Kwantung Army was formed at this time to guard these new territories and became the largest and most prestigious command in the Imperial Japanese Army. Many of its personnel, such as Chiefs of Staff Seishirō Itagaki and Hideki Tōjō were promoted to high positions in both the military and civil government. It was largely responsible for the creation of the Japanese-dominated 'Empire of Manchukuo' in 1932.

alliance with this and that warlord in north China and, each time that his plans miscarried owing to the defection of his allies and he had to come limping back to Mukden, he would sit down and work out new schemes, new combinations.

Towards the end of 1925 it seemed that his time was up. One of his own generals, Kuo Sung Lin, despatched on some expedition towards China, suddenly raised the standard of revolt and marched back on Mukden. For a time, Kuo Sung Lin carried all before him and shortly he was within striking distance of Mukden. But then the *deus ex machina* suddenly spoke. The Kwantung Army announced that no military operations in the railway zone would be permitted. Since the South Manchuria Railway stood between Kuo Sung Lin and his objective, he was finished. The spirit had gone out of his army and, presently, the mounted warriors of the northern province of Heilongjiang, the governor of which had stood by his chief, cut them to pieces.[87]

In 1926, Chang Tso Lin came down to the Leased Territory and called on the Civil and Military administration. Ostensibly a purely formal visit, it was really a visit to return thanks for assistance. He had not wished to come. To thank the Japanese who were a thorn in his side, was gall and wormwood to him but he had no option.

His near-defeat seems to have brought home to him the decisive power of the railways. He had wished to transport troops from the north by the Chinese Eastern Railway but the management had tactlessly demanded payment in hard cash on the nail. Had the Kwantung Army not intervened, Kung Suo Lin would have struck at Mukden before the northern troops arrived.

From this time dated the Chinese policy of building a network of railways which were to encircle the South Manchuria Railway and the Chinese Eastern Railway. Japan appeared irresolute at this time. She protested vigorously but did not back up the protest with force and the railways were gradually extended in the following years.

---

[87]   Kuo Sung Lin (Guo Songling 1883–1925) was caught and executed in December 1925.

But Chang Tso Lin was to pursue his ambitions until, returning in a hurry from Peking, he met his death under suspicious
circumstances in 1928. During the years I was in Dairen – 1925–
1927 – the value of the fengpiao (Mukden dollar), originally at
par with the yen, came down from fifty yen to several thousand
to the yen. He raised money by buying up crops with freshly-
printed supplies of fengpiao and selling for foreign currency.
When the fengpiao came cascading down, he thought to stop it
by forbidding exchange transactions and, to show he meant business, stood traders up against the wall and shot them.

In 1926 I made a tour of the railways. I was rarely out of the
railway zone but, where I had the opportunity of making com-
parisons, I was struck by the contrast between the neatness and
order of the Japanese towns and the dirt and the disorder of the
Chinese. I came to Mukden again in 1938 after the establish-
ment of the new State and, again, I was impressed by the change.

In considering the 'Manchurian Incident'[88] I have no intention of constituting myself Japan's advocate. Two wrongs do not
make a right and Japan put herself fatally in the wrong, first
by the methods she employed and, second, by the disingenu-
ous account of what happened on September 18th, 1931. But I
have always thought that Japan had a better case than the one
she put forward. China sold her birthright for a mess of pottage.
Without doing a hands-turn she came back and her representatives continued the story of misgovernment. The country grew
in wealth in spite of corruption and inefficiency because of the
blessing of the South Manchuria Railway on which they could

---

[88]   The Mukden Incident, also known as the Manchurian Incident, was
a staged event engineered by the Japanese military as a pretext for the
Japanese invasion of Manchuria in 1931. On 18 September 1931, a small
quantity of dynamite was detonated close to a railway line owned by
Japan's South Manchuria Railway near Mukden. Although the explosion
failed to destroy the track and a train passed over it minutes later, the
Imperial Japanese Army responded with a full invasion that led to the
occupation of Manchuria, in which Japan established its puppet state of
Manchukuo (Manzhouguo) six months later. The ruse was soon exposed
leading Japan to diplomatic isolation and its March 1933 withdrawal
from the League of Nations.

not lay their hands. Instead of trying to put their house in order, they planned to oust the Japanese by intrigue.

If you see an armed robber take possessions of the next-door house and you have good reason to suppose he contemplates taking yours also, you are justified in attacking him. When you have turned him out, you should hand the house back to its owner, but, supposing you know that the moment your back is turned, the robber will come back, what then? Granted that it suited Japan's book to remain in South Manchuria after she had thrown Russia out, it was also the only course she could pursue. By 1931 she had added to the lives she lost on the battle fields, the enormous capital she had poured into development of the railways and industries in the railway zone. Was it reasonable to expect that she would sit down quietly and watch her interest being cleverly undermined by peaceful intrigue when she had the power to strike? So the argument would run. It can be answered of course but there is one point on which I am convinced and that is that China herself asked for the Manchurian débâcle.

Opportunity makes the thief and there 'but for the grace of God walked I'. It is always difficult to say where cool self-interest ends and acquisitiveness begins. I remember a talk with a leading South Manchuria Railways director who was responsible for the running of the railway. There was talk of his retirement and I asked him what he would like to do. He pointed to a map of China and said that he would dearly love to be able to take charge of a Chinese railway and show what could be done with it under thoroughly efficient management. I think that the sight of the misgovernment and mismanagement going on around them in Manchuria irked the Japanese: their hands itched to take hold of it and run it, as they thought, properly. It is wrong of course to meddle with other people's possessions but the temptation is a natural one. Unfortunately, *l'appétit vient en mangeant*. 'Japanese military have no designs on China' – they have told us so, and that in all seriousness, and I think that they really believe it – but they have an irresistible urge to put it in order and, if the Chinese have an invincible dislike to be put in order, then 'they clearly do not understand what is good for them'.

When the military grew tired of civilian diplomacy, they took a duster and wiped out the Chinese administration of Manchuria and said to the civilian, "Here you are, see you make a good job of it, you can arrange the details as you will, provided you carefully eschew the evils of the west – communism, private capitalism, materialism, individualism, self-interest.' Then the military looked over the Great Wall and doubts began to assail them. Here was a breeding-ground of wrong doctrine right at their doors. Better clean it up and, for that matter, the whole of China's northern border was a corridor through which blew the death-dealing wind of communism. Much better to occupy it and close the entrance at the other end. And, presently, the army found itself engaged in a major war with China – all because the Chinese had mistaken ideas about government.

Everyone knows it is dangerous to place the face too near the jaws of the most faithful dog in case they should snap. The dog means no harm: it is an instinct and if he injures you, he will be most distressed. The Japanese is now over-running China and snapping at everyone in his path. He means no harm (at least he has so persuaded himself), he is snapping at these pestilential Reds and you should keep out of the way. He is engaged on a sacred mission. He is reconstructing the Far East. It is a glorious mission and it is strange that western powers should not co-operate. They *must* do so – or take the consequences.

Great Britain once had a sacred mission – the task of shouldering the white man's burden. We learnt the folly of that doctrine years ago. Somehow the other Powers never saw it in the same light. Is it permissible to hope that Japan will come one day to see the folly of her sacred mission – the task of shouldering the yellow man's burden?

One hopes that the time will come but it is not yet. At present Japan thinks somewhat as follows: 'as the scroll of history unfolds before our eyes, the page on which we are inscribing the characters of Japanese influence grows wider and wider, until it seems to embrace almost the destinies of mankind. Truly this is a great, an august and Imperial work that lies before us. I pray the gods we may be equal to the task.' This is a quotation, not from a

Japanese speech, but from one by Lord Curzon in 1896, merely changing 'Japanese' for 'British' and 'gods' for 'God'.

Relations with Local Officials

I have wandered far from the subject of my work at Dairen from 1925 to 1927. It was, in every way, a congenial task. Relations with the Governor, Count Kodama,[89] were excellent. His wife, a daughter of General Terauchi, was a gracious hostess. I was to meet them again later when I was Consul-General at Seoul and Kodama was Civil Administrator of Corea. As a host, Kodama had one pleasing trait which is rare among Japanese: he never depreciated his own goods. At dinner he would say, 'I want you to try that claret. I think it is good myself but I would like your opinion.' Needless to say, it was good. At the end of the evening he would produce a whisky. 'I am told this is good. But I am no judge of whisky. What do you think?' Opinion as to this whisky was divided. Foreigners who had a slight headache the following day were inclined to ascribe it to the whisky but a more likely explanation was that they had done themselves rather too well the night before. Personally, I think it was first class. In fact, I have a shrewd suspicion that it had originally come from a stock ordered out for the Prince of Wales' Garter Mission in 1922. I do know that much greater stocks were bought than could ever have been consumed by the mission. In fact I heard the whole story years later.

> When it was decided that the Prince of Wales was to come to Japan, the Embassy in London was instructed to order supplies. An official made enquiries and found that a special brand of whisky, not sold to the public, would be acceptable. The maker agreed, somewhat reluctantly, to supply it for this special purpose and ample stocks

---

[89]   Count Kodama Hideo (1876–1947) was a Japanese politician and wartime cabinet minister. He was the eldest son of famed Russo-Japanese War general, Kodama Gentarō, and his wife was the daughter of Prime Minister Terauchi Masatake. From 1923 to 1927 Kodama was governor of the Kwantung Leased Territory. In the late 1920s, Kodama was the civilian administrator in Korea under the governor general.

Fig. 1 Map of North-East Asia in the early 1930s
In the 1930s the Japanese Empire included Manchuria and Korea. The map
shows the treaty ports and most important towns with the names as used at the time.
It also shows the key railway lines. The South Manchurian Railway in particular
was a stronghold of the Japanese.

2

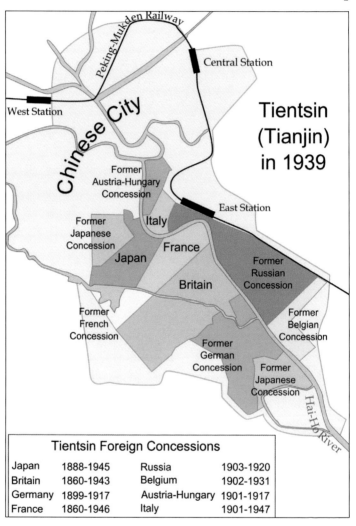

West Station

Central Station

Peking-Mukden Railway

Chinese City

Tientsin (Tianjin) in 1939

Former Austria-Hungary Concession

Italy

East Station

Former Japanese Concession

Japan

France

Former Russian Concession

Britain

Former French Concession

Former Belgian Concession

Former German Concession

Former Japanese Concession

Hai-Ho River

Tientsin Foreign Concessions

Japan	1888-1945	Russia	1903-1920
Britain	1860-1943	Belgium	1902-1931
Germany	1899-1917	Austria-Hungary	1901-1917
France	1860-1946	Italy	1901-1947

Fig. 2 Map of Tientsin (now Tianjin) in 1939, when White took office as Consul-General
At this time only the British, French, Japanese and Italian concessions remained

1

K.Tamoto 北海道写真館
田本製

Traditional Japanese Portrait of Kathleen (left) and Edith Hall, 1895

2

Oswald White's School Photograph in 1900
At Mercers' School in the City of London

3

John Carey Hall when he was Consul-General of Yokohama, circa 1908
At this time Hall was Consul-General of Yokohama as well as Oswald
White's boss and soon-to-be father-in-law

4

Marriage of Oswald White to Kathleen Hall, Yokohama, 15 February 1908

Kathleen White in Japan with her three daughters in 1913

Oswald White (centre) in Nagasaki, circa 1920

Portrait of Oswald White in Nagasaki, 1924

Oswald White at the King's Birthday Celebration, Dairen, 1926

Oswald White with his eldest daughter
Kitty, Dairen, 1927

10

Portrait of Oswald White when he was
Consul-General at Osaka, 1931

11

Oswald White at a British Consul function in Osaka, 1931

12

Portrait of Oswald White, London, 1958 – the year of the publication
of his translation of Shigemitsu's memoirs

13

Four Generations of Whites and Reads in the Hampstead Garden Suburb, London, June 1969
Photo taken at David Read's house, showing Oswald White with his daughter Betty Read
(née White), her son David Read and his sons Fergus and Hugo Read. Taken at
David Read's house in the Hampstead Garden Suburb, London.

were sent out to Japan in advance. Presently a frantic message was received at the Embassy in London asking for more whisky to be sent. The officials of the Department in Japan had sampled it and found it good. Cases were given here and there and presently the stocks had dwindled seriously. For years after, influential hosts who were in an expansive mood would produce a very special whisky and it was always the same brand not to be bought in the market.

The President of the South Manchuria Railway was a scholar, at one time President of a University in Japan. He seemed out of place but the South Manchuria Railway certainly did not suffer. I fancy he merely supervised and left the directors more or less to their own devices so long as results were good. None the less, he could act decisively when the occasion demanded. I was once grossly insulted by a member of the staff of the Governor. While pondering as to the best manner of dealing with the situation without causing too much unpleasantness, I had the happy idea of mentioning the matter to the SMR President. Within a few days, the offending official had called on me and apologised.

I mention this trivial affair as the solitary instance of rudeness to me by a Japanese official. My relations have always been marked with politeness and courtesy. When I came later as Consul-General to Mukden, in 1938, I received exactly the same consideration and courtesy as if I had been duly accredited and was not the representative of a country which refused to recognise Manchukuo. My American and French colleagues received the same treatment. In manners I do not think we can beat the Japanese official (though I cannot say the same for Japanese army officers, many of whom were distinctly offensive in their manner). It was one thing that made my years of service in Japan so pleasant.

To revert to the little incident, the official had at one time been Consul-General at Singapore. Rumour had it that he had become 'unstuck' there. He was one of a limited number of former Consul-Generals whom I have met occupying, what seemed to me, subordinate positions in the Japanese Colonies. It would seem that after a year or two as Consul-General they have either to justify promotion to higher posts in the diplomatic service or

retire. But all government posts are poorly paid and a large proportion of officials seize the first opportunity that offers to enter
the business world. One constantly meets bankers and company
directors who, at one time, have been officials in the Customs, in
Communications or in Prefectural Offices.

The South Manchuria Railway

Prior to the Manchurian incident there were three institutions
controlling Japanese activities in Manchuria from their base in
the Kwantung Leased Territory. First came the Kwantung Army
which was all powerful. Second, in theory, came the Governor
of the Territory with control over Japanese Consuls in Manchuria. But actually the SMR appeared to foreign observers to
rank immediately after the Army. The little incident of which
I have spoken seemed to prove it. Half of its capital was, and
is, owned by the Japanese Government which contented itself
with a smaller dividend than that paid to the private shareholder
in return for the public services rendered by the railway. The
SMR was an imperium in itself. It built, developed and ran the
railway towns, constructed water-works, supplied electricity and
gas, erected hospitals and schools and generally made of the railway towns little oases of tidiness and order. Out of the railways
and collieries grew a host of ancillary undertakings – harbours,
hotels, steamships, iron works, machinery, chemical industries
and so on. No doubt there was room for criticism though I saw
little but, taking it all in all, I think that Japan could justly claim
that the SMR was an instrument which had brought little but
good to Manchuria.

The SMR itself was modelled on Government lines.
The directors supervised their own departments but the actual
work was done by the permanent staff which had grown up in
the service. For the most part, the heads of sections were not anxious to become directors. They were experts at their own job and
not likely to be displaced but a director was liable to be pushed
out by a re-shuffle. The President was a Government nominee
and he usually liked to bring in a few of his protégés. A Director's

position, therefore, was far from secure. The President himself rarely held office for long. A change of Cabinet in Tokyo usually spelt the end of his term. In a smaller concern these constant changes would have caused chaos but while the heads changed, the permanent staff remained and 'carried on'.

In those days, the SMR were refreshingly free from the atmosphere of suspicion and secrecy that now meets the foreign enquirer for information from government and private sources. The directors and heads of departments simply used their discretion in answering questions. Information that might conceivably lead to further trade was freely given. And even on matters that were not, strictly speaking, the concern of a foreign Consul, directors were generally prepared to talk frankly on the understanding that their remarks were treated as confidential. I am sure that they realised that a secretive policy would only raise suspicions as to the policy and motives of the company. In the last ten years the Japanese Government has built a wall round business and industry over which the foreign Consul or business man endeavours to peep at his peril. Instances abound but I will give only one.

Spionitis

A few years ago the National City Bank of New York instructed its Osaka office to send it photos of some of the leading business offices of Osaka. It seems a strange request but there could be no question of spying. The demand could have been filled by cutting out the pictures from the advertisements in periodicals and trade journals. Pictures of different sections of Osaka abound in the advertising literature put out by the Municipality, the Chamber of Commerce and the leading dailies. The manager employed the simplest method. He engaged a local photographer and told him to go round and take a few pictures. The photographer perched himself on a vantage ground in a main street to photograph a building and was immediately pounced upon by the Police. There followed a storm in a teacup, police investigations and scare-lines in the papers. Naturally the excitement died down as quickly as it had arisen: the whole thing was too absurd. It was merely another instance of the spionitis which not only tends to embitter the foreign resident in Japan but also scares away the tourist. All the efforts of the Japan Tourist Bureau, the Imperial Government Railways and the steamship companies to make travel to and in Japan pleasant for the foreigner, count as little compared with the harm done by the anti-spy scare-monger.

Japanese official and business circles have always inclined to reticence but once they had confidence in the discretion of the enquirer, they would 'loosen up'. I am sure my friends in the SMR never had cause to regret their confidence in me. They showed me over their iron works at Anshan[90] and shale-oil plant at Fushun. Having no technical knowledge I was not likely to bring away any information that could have done any harm and a short while later I had forgotten such details as I had assimilated at the time but I still remember the impression I formed of the courage of Japanese engineers in the face of heart-breaking difficulties.

Anshan Iron and Steel Works

An over-enthusiastic engineer began the trouble at Anshan. Finding supplies of good-grade ore in the vicinity, he went ahead too fast and erected plant to treat it. Too late it was discovered that, though there is abundant ore at Anshan, it is nearly all low-grade. That was the least of the difficulty. The technical details were over my head but I gathered that there were two types of ore present – hermatite and magnetite – which separated out in fine grains, the concentration of which was one of exceptional difficulty. Experts were sent abroad to study methods used in treating similar ores. Armed with the experience they had gained, they tackled the problem and, when I visited Anshan, a new plant had just been erected which they were confident would prove satisfactory. I suspect that they were still far from a final solution

---

90   The Anshan steelworks were established in 1916 as the Showa steelworks. It is still in operation.

since it is only in the last few years that Anshan has produced iron and steel in quantity.

Fushun Oil[91]

The story of Fushun oil is also one of early discouragement. The coal at the famous 'open cut' is in thick seams separated by layers of shale and, at an early stage, the possibility of distilling oil from the shale was considered. Samples were sent to Scotland and it was found that the oil was not recoverable in sufficient quantity to make the undertaking payable by processes used in Great Britain. Further enquiries in Germany and elsewhere showed that other processes also were unsuitable. It was, in fact, an entirely new proposition since it was merely because mining costs were nil that it was worth consideration. After study of all known processes, Japanese engineers started to work on a modified process of their own. I was shown the first experimental plant that was erected in 1926. It was only in 1938 (when I came as Consul-General to Mukden), that the experiments were beginning to bear fruit. It is very doubtful whether the process could ever pay in competition with natural petroleum but under the planned economy in which most countries now indulge, it bids fair to be a useful asset to the country.

Tour of Railways

In 1926 I made a tour of part of the railways of Manchuria. There were then three systems – the Chinese Eastern Railway (Russian), the South Manchuria Railway (Japanese) and government lines, some built by the SMR as feeders to their own lines and others built by the government to compete with the SMR. Of the government lines the first class were government only in name. The government never paid for the lines the SMR built for them and no serious attempt was made to collect payment. They were operated by the SMR and, except that the conditions made them more costly to run, they were as good as SMR lines.

---

[91]   Fushan Oil is now part of the PetroChina Company.

As related elsewhere, the Kuo Sung Lin rebellion at the end of 1925 had brought home to Chang Tso Lin his dependence on the railways and his desire to throw off foreign influence had led him to initiate a policy of building lines of his own to encircle the SMR and CER lines. But in 1926 this policy had only just begun and, when I made my trip, one line built nominally for him under a contract made earlier had just been completed joining Ssupingkai[92] on the main SMR with Tsitsihar[93] on the CER line from Manchouli[94] to Harbin. One of the main objects of my tour was to see this new line.

It actually started north at a junction named Chengchiatun on an older line running westward to Tungliao.[95] I went first to this town. It was on the edge of Inner Mongolia. The latter part of the railway ran through desert and its purpose was not apparent unless it was to be carried on westward to the grasslands in competition with the 'ship of the desert'. As a matter of fact, it has never been carried further westward and possibly never will but in 1938 when I continued this trip to Linhsi[96] in the far west of Manchuria, as it is now constituted, I did so over a road of sorts, transported by motor-bus and truck. Chang Tso Lin had, however, his own idea as to a use for this railway as he showed when, shortly afterwards, he built a line from Tungliao south to Tahushan on the Peking-Mukden line and had then the makings of a trunk line from Tahushan to Tsitsihar, if only he could get the section from Chegchiatun to Tsitsihar out of the hands of the SMR. Alas for the best laid schemes; this and other parts of the network he built to freeze out foreign influence have been taken over by the Government of Manchukuo, which is entirely under Japanese influence.

---

92   Siping (Ssupingkai), is a prefecture-level city in the west of Jilin province in Northeastern China

93   Qiqihar (Tsitsihar) is one of the thirteen Larger Municipalities in China, and the second largest city in Heilongjiang province in Northeastern China

94   Manchouli (Manzhouli) is a city in the Inner Mongolia Autonomous Region of China, close to the Mongolian border. It is China's busiest land port of entry.

95   Now Tongliao, a city in Inner Mongolia

96   Lin-hsi (Linxi) is a county of eastern Inner Mongolia, China.

Tungliao was, at that time, generally known as Pa-in-ka-la, the Mongolian name for the district, but the Mongols had, by this time, become absorbed in the Chinese peaceful penetration or had retreated further west and there were few signs of Mongol influence. I was, however, taken to call on a 'living Buddha' residing at a monastery a few miles outside Tungliao. This reverend gentleman was, I gathered, under Japanese patronage. He received me without ceremony in his shirt-sleeves and regaled me with Mongolian tea. He was fat and jovial and I formed an impression, which may of course have been unjustified, that he did not exercise his mind unduly about the spiritual welfare of himself and his flock.

Tungliao itself and Taonan, where I stayed later, were mere collections of mud huts with here and there a few more portentous buildings. The roads were deep in dust and degenerated into quagmires when it rained. For the most part, the country round looked barren and unproductive though the industry of the Chinese farmer succeeds in getting crops to grow in relatively fertile spots. But one needs to go a hundred miles further westward before coming to the grass-land: the intervening area is mainly desert.

When I returned to Chengchiatun and resumed my journey northward, there were cultivated patches interspersed with long stretches of sand. Cultivation lessened as we came to the newly opened section of the line. Stations were not yet built: the train came to a halt and immigrants climbed down, shouldered their bundles and trudged off. It looked as though they were starting off into the unknown but there were, no doubt, settlements in the vicinity for which they were making. I was a spectator of the birth, or possibly the re-birth, of a country. The desert is not irreclaimable. The prevailing west wind blowing over a desiccated country has brought the sand ever eastward. But the opening up of Manchuria by the railways has shown that this land can be won back, though only by unremitting toil. Large sections are, unfortunately, alkaline and here the assistance of the scientist will be necessary.

Since I made my trip, other railways have been built and this section west of the main trunk line is being rapidly colonised.

I joined the CER at Angangchi (station for Tsitsihas) and went to Harbin. The heyday of this city had already past but it was still under Russian control. Foreign residents seemed to like Harbin but on the three occasions I have visited it I have looked at the city with jaundiced eyes. Judging from what one reads, it was a gay, carefree city at the height of its prosperity. But it had fallen on evil days. Even in 1926 it was going rapidly down-hill. At a famous cabaret-restaurant which I visited, there was an air of forced gaiety. I was told by one of the habitués that the average foreigner had not the money to spend on the lavish entertainment that had formerly been the custom and that the rich patrons were, for the most part, Chinese. In 1938 and 1939 when I went to Harbin again, shabby gentility had been replaced by downright poverty and the saddest sight of the city was the crowds of Russian beggars in the streets.

Social Amenities

Life in Dairen in the years 1925–1927 was very pleasant. Though they gave no favours to the foreigner in business, the Japanese, official and mercantile, were, at that time, very well-disposed to them. It was almost entirely due to the support of the SMR and leading Japanese firms that it had been possible to build the Dairen Club. The money required was raised by debentures of which they took the lion's share. When the time came to pay the first interest, some of the Japanese asked what this was for. They had mentally said goodbye to their money when they subscribed it and, but for the fact that there were also foreign debenture-holders who expected to receive the interest they had been promised, the debentures might then and there have been wiped out!

There was a good golf course at Hoshigaura (Star Beach) to which the foreigners belonged. It was run on somewhat autocratic lines by an inner clique of Japanese with one or two foreigners who, however, were heavily outnumbered: I have mentioned elsewhere the nickname 'mining club' given to the Ibaraki Golf Club. There was one hole at Hoshigaura with a bunker designed to catch a drive with a short carry. This bunker shifted backwards and forwards more than once and it was popularly supposed that it varied accordingly as the Captain and President was 'on' or 'off' his drive. Here, as elsewhere, the keenness of the Japanese put the foreigner to shame. Whenever they had time to spare, the Japanese were out practising and, after a long Sunday of three rounds or so, many of them would be found going over again and again the shots they had been missing during the day. If application counts, the Japanese should make the best golfers in the world. Unfortunately, today the game is frowned on by the authorities as a luxury game.

Trade in Narcotics

There was only one motor-road but that a fine one, full of scenic 'beauties', from Dairen to Port Arthur along the coast. This was supposed to have been built out of money derived from opium. I mention the report without expressing any opinion but I am bound to say that the treatment of the problem of narcotics is a blot on the Japanese administration of all the foreign territories they have taken over. When I first went to Corea, the up-country missionaries were commenting bitterly on the growing peddling of narcotics. Their use was growing constantly. In Manchuria the story was the same and in north China. And yet in all these places there were elaborate regulations for the control of the manufacture, sale and consumption of narcotics. Were these regulations merely window-dressing or were they unfortunate results due to inefficiency? I have never been able to make up my mind but I incline to the second reason. It was clear, however, that the junior monopoly officials were venal. The higher officials were either bribable also or, more probably, apathetic. There was one question which I never saw answered. The legitimate needs for medical purposes were fully met from the licensed import. But, side by side with this legitimate import, was a large traffic in smuggled narcotics and, from time to time, large hauls were made. A few of the ring would be tried, found guilty and imprisoned but still the trade went on and fresh hauls would be announced. What became of the confiscated opium, heroin, etc.? No-one knows.

I once assisted at a haul. The manager of a foreign bank informed me that, by chance, he had found two big packages addressed to his comprador, marked to be called for. The comprador promptly disclaimed all knowledge of the parcels. The manager and I therefore opened them. Inside were dozens and dozens of what purported to be tooth-powder but we were suspicious. We called in a monopoly expert and the so-called tooth-powder proved to be heroin, worth twenty to thirty thousand yen.[97]

Foreign Community

The foreign community of Dairen consisted of British, Americans, Germans, Danes and Russians. There were at that time no national barriers of feeling and all sections mingled together amicably at the Dairen Club. I am sorry to have to admit that the only quarrelling was among the British themselves. Small communities are liable to develop friction on petty issues but Dairen was particularly unfortunate. A trumpery little squabble over the question of which rooms in the new club were to be used by the wives of members divided the British community into factions for over a year. One member took the matter so much to heart that he resigned from the Club with the absurd result that when a senior director of his firm came on a visit to Dairen I had to introduce both him and the ex-member to the club. Other members who were aggrieved did not resign but simply stayed away and appeals that they would drop their personal feelings in the interests of British solidarity fell on stony ground. It was over a year before the wound was healed.

---

97   For narcotics in the Japanese Empire, see John M. Jennings, *The Opium Empire: Japanese Imperialism and Drug Trafficking in Asia, 1895–1945* (Westport, Conn.: Praeger, 1977).

Chapter 12

CONSUL-GENERAL AT SEOUL, 1928–1931

ଙ୍କ

Comparison of New Regime with Old

WHILE ON HOME leave from Dairen in 1927, I received my promotion to Consul-General and was appointed to Seoul where I spent those happy but uneventful years from 1928 to 1931. The Corea I came back to was very different from the Corea I had left in 1910. At that time the Coreans were not resigned to their fate and small armed bands of insurgents roamed the country. The official organ daily reported clashes between these bands and Japanese soldiers, gendarmes or police. Outside the big towns it was dangerous for a Japanese to stir out unarmed and still more dangerous armed, for then his arms invited attack. On the main roads, gendarmerie stations were strung out every twelve-and-a-half miles and when I travelled by road from Wŏnsan[98] (Gensan) to Seoul, I made the first seventy-five miles under escort.

Amidst so much tragedy one little incident afforded comic relief. The Salvation Army had just opened up a Corean branch. The news spread round among the Coreans that a British army had arrived – no doubt to deliver them from the Japanese – and when officers of the army proceeded to a provincial town they

---

98   Wŏnsan (Gensan in Japanese) is a port city and naval base now in North Korea, located on the westernmost shore of the Sea of Japan (East Korean Sea). It is the provincial capital of Kangwon Province, which is divided between the two Koreas. The port was opened to foreign trade in the 1880s.

were startled to be met en-route by the local insurgents who wished to join forces with them. Fortunately, the sense of proportion of the Japanese was not so distorted by xenophobia as it is now and the incident did not embitter relations between the Salvation Army and the authorities.

In 1928 the Coreans, though inwardly discontent, had resigned themselves to the new regime and, materially, were far better off as a result of the change. Malcontents flirted with communism and, from time to time, were rounded up and imprisoned. But the mass of the people asked only to be allowed to live in peace. The Japanese, with characteristic energy, had opened up communications, had revolutionised public services and had developed industry and trade. During the three years I was stationed in Seoul I travelled over most of the country in comparative comfort and found law and order everywhere.

Decline in Importance of Chemulpo

Foreign interests in Corea had declined and were approaching vanishing point. In 1909 I had enjoyed my first spell of authority as Acting Consul at Chemulpo for several months. Before the coming of the Japanese, Chemulpo had been the principal port of Corea. It carried on a fairish foreign trade and had a sprinkling of foreign firms. The Blue Funnel line called there and the Vice-Consul had written glowing reports of future prospects of the port. No doubt as a result, the office had been elevated to a Consulate and the officer in question had received his promotion. Only a few years were to run before the Consulate was closed down and replaced by an agency! The officer had seen Chemulpo through rose-coloured spectacles. When I saw it in 1909 I could discern no warrant for optimism. The Consulate is finely situated on a knoll overlooking the harbour. From this point of vantage the Consul had looked down and, in his mind's eye, had pictured a port filled with shipping. But he must have looked only at high tide. Chemulpo has a very high rise and fall. At low water one looked over an expanse of mud. Small coasting vessels came in at high tide and careened in at low, thus saving docking charges. Large vessels had to anchor two miles or more off-shore. So much for 'one of the world's leading sea-ports'. Chemulpo today has a small dock and does a thriving domestic trade but foreign interests are moribund.[99]

Foreign Mining Concessions

Ex pede Herculem. Corean trade has grown considerably but it has been re-orientated: Japan has taken it all and there is no field for the foreign trader. The mines[100] were the last strong-hold of foreign interests. About the beginning of the century, mining engineers tumbled over each other looking for prospects and applying for concessions. It became almost a matter of national pride to have one. Speaking from memory, I can recollect British, American, French, Italian and Belgian concessions. Most of the mines proved holes in the ground and the successes could be numbered on the fingers of one hand. But I doubt if the engineer-promoters lost money. Undeterred by failures, they went on until they found something that looked like a promising mine. Then they floated a company which paid all the expenses they had been put to, retained a portion of the shares and were 'sitting pretty'. I know of one mine on to the cost of which was tacked the cost of another which had been worked for a year only to prove a failure. When friends of the promoters were let in 'on the ground floor', they did not realise that they were buying the basement also. An inauguration dinner to which the prospective share-holders were invited and dined and wined lavishly would, as like as not, be charged up to promoting expenses. Even when the engineer's guess proved correct and the gold was actually there in payable quantities, the company began by being hopelessly watered.

---

[99]   White's predecessor was more prescient than he was. Incheon, which has absorbed Chemulpo, is now South Korea's second largest port, after Busan.

[100]   There is extensive coverage of Western involvement in Korean mining in Donald N. Clark, *Living Dangerously in Korea: The Western Experience 1900–1950* (Norwalk, CT: EastBridge, 2003), while Robert Neff in Seoul is working on a book to be called *Nodaji: The Western Mining Experience in Joseon/Korea*.

The shareholders did not always lose their money. Suan[101] more than paid back its capital within a few years. This was heady wine and when another big company was floated, the ten yen shares almost immediately went to thirty yen, only to drop to nothing when it was discovered that not only was there no gold in the mine, but there never had been! In the meantime, the responsible engineer had left. This was a particularly bad case. I know of no other case in which a mine was salted. But for a good example of buying a pig in a poke one need go no further than investment in gold mines in Corea.

When I went back to Corea only three foreign mines were actually operating. Two employed big staffs but one – Suan – had only two foreign engineers. This mine had a curious history. As just related, it had begun as a tremendous success and then the gold disappeared – I think owing to faulting. It was closed down and abandoned. But a foreign engineer had an idea that he could extract gold and/or copper from the mine dump. It should be explained that owing to technical difficulties in treating the ore the mine operators had been unable to extract the whole content of gold and copper. In order to be at liberty to work the dump, the engineer bought the whole mine for a song. He found that the problem that had baffled the company engineers was beyond him also but, in the meantime, he had stumbled on the missing vein in the mine out of which he proceeded to make a small fortune.

Since I left Corea, I understand that all the foreign mine interests have been sold out to Japanese companies. This presumably involves the closure of the few foreign firms still left in Seoul since most of their business was with the mines and leaves the oil companies as the only business interest in the field.

Missionary Work

One branch of foreign activity remains – the missionary.[102] Since the former Hermit Kingdom has been opened up to the west-

---

[101] Suan gold mine is located in North Hwanghae Province, North Korea.

[102] There is a huge volume of writing on Christianity and missionary work in Korea. White might have been familiar with George L. Paik, *The History of Protestant Missionaries in Korea*, (originally published in 1929, reprinted Seoul: Yonsei University Press, 1970). See also Allen D. Clark,

erner, it has been the centre of intense missionary enterprise. Foreign missions founded churches, schools and hospitals throughout the country. The old Corean government, which did not concern itself with the welfare of the masses, allowed the missions a more or less free hand and, in a country that was pitiably backward, they undoubtedly benefited the Coreans greatly by their labours. But under the Japanese regime their work has become increasingly difficult. It is the Japanese method to order the lives of their subjects meticulously down to the smallest detail and it soon became manifest that, in some respects, missionary teaching ran counter to Japanese ideas. To give one instance of many, the Japanese authorities on ceremonial occasions demand that school students march to the local shrine and bow: the missionary maintains that a Christian student cannot do obeisance at a (heathen) shrine. A way out was offered by the official assurance that it was not a religious, but a national act and many missionaries accepted this solution. Others could not reconcile it with their conscience and serious trouble ensued, usually ending in the closing of the school concerned.

The question is too big to be discussed here. I wish to speak only of my own personal contact with the missionary. In my trips round the country I visited most of the Protestant Missions, American as well as British, and I am perhaps more competent to discuss them than the average layman.

The missionary comes in for a good deal of criticism from the outside world. Some of it is prejudiced. I took note of the standard of living. In no case did it seem high to me and in some cases it struck me as unduly low. Then most missionaries take a month off in the summer and gather at some resort. Personally I think it a very wise provision: when a missionary has been away from his own people for eleven months, it is well that he should relax for a bit in their company in order that he may go back refreshed to his work. The criticism of narrow-mindedness is more serious but, on the whole, I do not think that it can be sustained. I conversed with members of different denominations and concluded

---

A History of the Church In Korea, (Seoul: Christian Literature Society of Korea, 1971) and Kim and Kim, *History of Korean Christianity*.

that, repugnant as were Japanese methods, the missionaries were making a valiant effort to co-operate with the authorities. Before the missionary adjusted himself to the new conditions, friction was constant but it was decreasing and had almost disappeared. But the basic difficulty remains that, unless compromised, Anglo-Saxon ideals are utterly opposed in vital respects to Japanese and the relations between the official and the missionary, though outwardly cordial, maintained an uneasy equilibrium.

One instance of petty-mindedness tended to cause amusement to the layman. The first American missionaries were very strait-laced and taught their converts that it was sinful to smoke tobacco, to drink alcoholic liquors or to play cards. Most of the missions continued to follow this early teaching though, when tackled on the point, the missionary would admit that smoking and drinking in moderation was possibly unwise but not sinful. As a confirmed smoker I found the enforced abstention when staying at their houses, an irksome, if wholesome, discipline. One host begged me to smoke, though he could not do so himself, and confessed that a considerable portion of the funds subscribed to his mission came from tobacco plantations in Virginia. Many families circumvent the ban on cards by using packs on which the familiar four suits are replaced by other designs!

In criticising these little foibles I do not wish to cast doubt on the essential honesty of purpose of the missionary as a class. I had many friends among them whom I regarded with great respect and affection. As a whole, they did fine work and, if occasionally they were the source of trouble, that was because under the existing conditions a missionary needed to be not only a sincere Christian but somewhat of a diplomat as well.

Official Tours

I have mentioned that I travelled over most of Corea during my second term. I had a good excuse for these official tours in that they gave me an opportunity of meeting the British local residents, both mining and missionary, and studying their local problems on the spot and also of seeing the work that the new administration was accomplishing. At the same time I found these trips most interesting and pleasant. In a peaceful world, if we shall ever see one again, Corea could take its place as one of the beauty spots. Far Easterners already know the Diamond Mountains[103] which are like Chinese porcelain landscapes come to life on a grand scale. The setting of the early Kingdom of *Silla*[104] in the south-east is beautiful enough to warrant a visit even without the wonderful relics of the rock-temple near Keishu and the artistic treasures housed in the local museum. Then, for the tourist with a historic or artistic bent, there is Heijo (Pingyang)[105] with its early Tang tombs in the vicinity and also, though rarely visited now, Koshu (Kongju)[106] the centre of another early Corean Kingdom, *Paekche.*[107] The sea-coast is almost uniformly beautiful, deeply indented on the east and south, with the hills running down and ending in cliffs and bluffs overlooking the deep blue sea.

---

[103] Kumgang (Diamond) is a 1,638-metre mountain in Kangwon Province, North Korea. It is about 50 kilometres from the South Korean city of Sokcho in Kangwon – one of the two divided by the divison of Korea. It is one of the best-known mountains in North Korea, located on the east coast of the country, in Mount Kumgang Tourist Region. Mount Kumgang is part of the Taebaek mountain range which runs along the east of the Korean peninsula.

[104] Silla (57 BC – 935 AD) was one of the Three Kingdoms of Korea, along with Goguryeo (Koguryo) and Baekje (Paekche). The Three Kingdoms alternately battled and allied with each other as they expanded control over the whole peninsula, with Silla eventually triumphing, with Tang Chinese help.

[105] Pyongyang (Heijō in Japanese. Literally 'Flat Land' or 'Peaceful Land') is the capital of the North Korea. The area around the city was called Nanglang during the early Three Kingdoms period. In 668, Pyongyang became the capital of the Protectorate General to Pacify the East established by the Tang dynasty of China. Later in the seventh century it was taken by Silla. From 1896 it was the capital of South Pyongan Province.

[106] Gongju, or Kongju, is a city in South Korea, near the West coast. It was the capital of the Baekje Kingdom from AD 475 to 538.

[107] Baekje or Paekche (18 BC – 660 AD) was one of the Three Kingdoms of Korea, located in the South-West of the peninsular. In 660, it was defeated by an alliance of Silla and Chinese Tang Dynasty, submitting to Unified Silla.

Perhaps the most interesting trip I made, in company with Mr Macrae,[108] then Commercial Secretary at the British Embassy at Tokyo, was up the east coast and down the river Yalu.[109] I am afraid I remember the amusing interests better than the scenery. The river was disappointing. At one time thickly wooded, the forests have been cut down and the banks are lined with scrub. But it was an experience to come down in a 'propeller boat', a very shallow boat with a flat bottom designed to shoot the rapids. The power came from an aeroplane engine stationed at the stern, the noise from which was deafening. The trip down took, if I remember rightly, three days as the boat had to tie up at night. Half way down we paid a call on a Chinese governor stationed at Linhsien[110] on the right bank. The governor set himself out to entertain us with true Oriental hospitality. He first plied us with drinks and then with food and when I protested I could eat and drink no more, besought me to lie down for an hour or two before starting in again. Finally, when we succeeded in leaving without hurting his feelings, he piled us into a Peking cart to return to the river side, his last words to the attendant being 'Take great care of that gentleman, he is very tight.'

The attendant I have just spoken of was one of the Japanese policemen who were invariably attached to me by local authorities to see that I came to no harm and, no doubt, also

---

[108]   Herbert Alexander Macrae (1886–1967). Joined the Japan Consular Service 1909, and was acting commercial secretary and later commercial counsellor 1940–1941. He also served at Christiana (now Oslo) in the First World War. Briefly in the Board of Trade after 1945, and wrote *The future development of the Japanese economy and the opportunities for British trade with Japan* (London: HMSO, 1948).

[109]   The Yalu River, in Korean the Amnok, which together with the Tumen River to its east, and a small portion of Paektu Mountain, forms the border between the Korean peninsula and China. The area was heavily involved in military conflicts in the first Sino-Japanese War, the Russo-Japanese War and the Korean War.

[110]   Linjiang (Linkiang or Linhsien) is a city in southern Jilin Province, China, on the right bank of the Yalu river. The city briefly served as the capital of Manchukuo in August 1945.

to see that I got up to no mischief. Though the presence of these unwanted chaperones is never very welcome, I found them extremely useful on occasion as I passed on to them the task of arranging, in advance, my accommodation and transport. They were generally polite and unobtrusive and grateful for little courtesies. But Macrae and I could not resist one little trick. We had decided to vary the monotony of the propeller boat by walking one section. The policeman could not, for the life of him, make out why we wanted to walk when there was transport available but, having at last grasped the fact that the foolish foreigner really liked walking for walking's sake, he valiantly set out with us. It was not a long trek but Macrae and I, being both good walkers, we set a steady, slightly over four miles an hour pace, which we kept up till the noon-day halt and then to our destination at tea-time. At the finish it was all the policeman could do to hobble in. A round or two of beer restored his spirits but I think that he was glad to say goodbye to his eccentric charges.

On this trip I came in for unmerciful ragging from Macrae over the title 'Excellency' with which I was usually addressed by local officials. It is an unfortunate habit of Oriental nations to give honorific titles to which the addressee is not entitled. In recent years it has become customary to use the equivalent of Excellency when speaking to, or of, any official who is in charge of his particular department. Most formal speeches begin, 'Excellencies and Gentlemen' though there may be no higher official than the local Chief of Police present. Having noted that officials en-route addressed me by this title, Macrae himself proceeded to address me as Excellency for the rest of the trip. The system is a bad one as inducing an inflated sense of self-importance but I was in no danger of becoming over-conceited on this journey!

US Consul-General Miller

The record of my second term in Corea would be incomplete without reference to the US Consul-General, Mr R. S. Miller.[111] He had served most of his career in Japan and Corea, was a Japanese scholar and was experienced in Japanese ways. Miller was, in a way, the 'father' of the foreign community. As doyen of the Consular corps he was naturally consulted by his colleagues but also private members of the community constantly went to him for advice. Quiet and unassuming, he was always willing to help anyone who wanted assistance. In one little matter we were in friendly disagreement. Four times a year the Governor-General of Corea held an official reception at which full uniform was the order of the day. Since Miller had no uniform, I maintained that he should go in swallow-tail and white tie! Miller declined to put on this rig at ten in the morning and insisted on going in a morning-coat. Technically wrong, he had common-sense on his side and I confess that, in his place, I should have done exactly the same! Miller's two recreations were golf and poker. At the former he had his own rules; if a first shot off the tee was a dud, then we were allowed a second and sometimes even a third. It wasn't golf but we enjoyed it. At poker I think it was owing to his influence that we played a 'gentlemanly' game. Anyone holding 'four of a kind' or higher was supposed to signal by raising with the smallest counter. Everyone then threw in his hand and the holder was compensated with a 'bonus' from everyone at the table. Again, it wasn't poker according to Hoyle but it worked well and since we played for small stakes, no one could suffer any grievous financial damage. The before-dinner game at the Club was justly popular and I fear was the cause of more than one 'poker-widow'. An extremely lovable man, the whole of the foreign community grieved when Miller was transferred to the State Department at Washington.

---

[111]   Ranford S. Miller served in Korea on several occasions and was later director of the Bureau of East Asia in the State Department. Although he thought that the Japanese takeover was good for Korea, he was condemnatory of Japanese actions in the wake of the March First uprising in 1919. See Clark, *Living Dangerously in Korea*, passim.

Chapter 13

CONSUL-GENERAL AT OSAKA, 1931–1937

෨

IN 1931 I was transferred to Osaka. Since I had left in 1919, the post had gradually grown in importance and was now to be raised to a Consulate-General. The original proposal was that both the Kobe and the Osaka offices should be under the control of the Consul-General but I formed the opinion that it was better that he should devote all his attention to the Osaka office and that Kobe should remain independent under a Consul. My view was accepted but the solution was not popular with the British community in Kobe which was larger and more important than the British community in Osaka. The leaders of the community often voiced their resentment to me but I used to assure them that, since their main interest was the trade of Osaka, I could be of more use to them if I was closely in touch with the business men of Osaka: my services were always at their disposal as I lived in Kobe. But it was undoubtedly unfortunate that Kobe should be only a Consulate while Osaka was a Consulate-General and after I was transferred to Mukden, the original proposal was adopted.

Relations with Japanese: Osaka Club

I made it my business to keep in touch with the leading Japanese business men in Osaka. This proved a simple matter. During my previous spell there I had been made a member of the Osaka Club and I resumed my membership. It is a club composed of the heads of all the major enterprises in Osaka. I frequently went there to lunch and soon had an acquaintance with most of the members. Since foreigners were rarely seen in the Club and there was little of the spirit of aloofness and cliquishness of the western club, it was not necessary to wait round for introductions but as soon as my face became familiar, the members accepted me as one of themselves.

I must say that the members, most of whom were affluent and held important positions in the business world, set a praiseworthy example of simplicity. Lunch was 'table d'hôte' and cost the equivalent of two shillings; practically every one drank water. Long tables were set out in the dining room and members, as they arrived, took the first vacant seat. After lunch a number of members sat in the lounge where conversation of a general nature on topics of the day took place.

In recent years the Japanese have shown a disposition to regard the foreign Consul with suspicion as though he were an authorised spy. This attitude is a foolish one. I never learnt any secrets at the Osaka Club or elsewhere but by mixing with the Japanese I was able to interpret their views and I consider the advantage was as much on their side as mine. We on our side tend to regard any action taken by the Japanese that rouses our ire as being inspired by wilful cussedness. As often as not our reaction is equally incomprehensible to the Japanese. It is essential that we should fight for our own point of view but when we begin by misunderstanding their motives, we start out on the wrong foot. In Osaka I regarded it as much my duty to study the Japanese point of view as to explain ours and I think my Japanese friends appreciated my attitude.

Osaka Rotary Club

Another club to which I was glad to belong was the Rotary Club of Osaka. Foreign members were necessarily limited since a knowledge of Japanese was essential and the foreign business men in Osaka who could speak Japanese and were willing and eligible to join could be numbered on the fingers of one hand. There was a welcome absence of 'hot air' at the meetings though there was the inevitable exchange of goodwill speeches, which sound so well and mean so little, when representatives of Rotary Clubs in other countries visited us.

The second half of the meeting was given up to speeches or talks, generally by members on either their own business or any subject of which they had made a study. Since the Club was a cross-section of all the leading industries, businesses and professions of Osaka, the talks were usually most interesting, ranging as they did over a great variety of topics. When the programme committee failed to produce speakers, one or two skilful talkers could always be prevailed on to step into the breach. The editor of a leading local newspaper, who was one of the wittiest talkers I have ever met, was always ready to discuss topics of the day humorously and yet penetratingly.

To anticipate, in 1940 the Rotary Club in Japan and Manchuria came under the ban against internationalism and, bowing to the wishes of the government, voluntarily dissolved. Foreign well-wishers of Japan can only deplore the growth of intense nationalism. During my time in Osaka, the Chief of Police, the Mayor and a number of municipal officials were members and appeared to enjoy the meetings, nor can I think that they saw anything in the proceedings to cause them concern. Tendentious speech-making was rigidly barred: in Osaka and elsewhere I belonged to three rotary clubs in turn, Seoul, Osaka and Mukden. I derived considerable benefit but it was entirely of an intangible nature. The patriotism of the Japanese members, who comprised all but a negligible portion of the members, was never affected one whit. The sole criticism that the government could justly bring against the movement was that it increased the breadth of mind of its members.[112]

Ibaraki Golf Club

Another point of contact with the Japanese of Osaka was the Ibaraki Golf Club. The desire of the Japanese to excel in everything they take up was manifested in this club. It was popularly known

---

[112]   Rotary began in Japan in 1921. For the briefest mention of the Osaka club, see https://www.rghfhome.org/first100/global/asia/clubs/osaka.htm. (accessed 2 September 2016).

as the mining club because the committee, in its craze for a perfect lay-out, at one time employed an army of workmen to pull down a hill and build it up in a different position. By the time it had been re-laid and each green had been remodelled, a round of the course to me, as one of the world's worst golfers, had become a nightmare. But the members, who practised assiduously, took it in their stride and no doubt the standard of golf improved though the few unfortunate members whose game stood still were left stranded.[113]

Consular Corps

On arrival at Osaka I was elected Doyen of the newly-formed Consular Corps. I think this corps must have been unique. It contained one other career-Consul, the German, two or three foreign merchant-Consuls and about a dozen Japanese merchant-Consuls. The latter had no, or at all events precious little, Consular work to do: it was merely a matter of prestige. The sole activity of the corps was to turn out in its splendour on ceremonial occasions. Certain members clearly loved fine feathers and one, who represented a small Eastern power, covered himself in glory on one occasion by appearing resplendent in an uniform which he was popularly supposed to have designed himself, of white duck faced with gold lace, the whole surmounted by an enormous helmet. The rest of the corps were, by order, in morning coats and the spectacle of those peacock feathers in the midst of our sombre garb was dazzling in the extreme. One of the most respected members of the Corps used to wear more medals (conferred, I understood, by different countries in return for monetary contributions towards the advancement of good friendship between the nations) than I have ever seen worn by one person. In 1938 the Emperor of Japan visited Osaka during army manoeuvres and I applied through the proper channels for an audience. The request was granted but at the last moment I was informed that the corps was expected to line up with a host of officials and bow when His Imperial Majesty passed. This was

---

[113] The Ibaraki Golf Club was founded in 1923 – http://www.reesjonesinc. com/ibaraki/ (accessed 2 September 2016).

not my idea of an audience and I pressed for a separate reception in accordance with usual procedure at the posts. This point was conceded after some discussion but, in the meantime, two members of the corps were so afraid that there would be no audience at all that they used their influence to get themselves included in just such a modified audience as I have described. Their chagrin was great when they learnt that they had thereby missed the opportunity of being present at a special reception. I have said that the Corps had no activities other than ceremonial. I do it an injustice. It secured free passes over several of the tramway systems running round Osaka.

Japan-British Society

During my stay in Osaka I was instrumental in starting the Japan-British Society in Kwansai[114] (a conveniently vague term for the whole area of which Osaka is the centre). There has for many years been such a society in Tokyo and a simpler method would have been to establish an Osaka branch but Osaka has always been a little jealous of Tokyo's predominant position. If Tokyo is the centre of administration, Osaka claims to be the leading business centre of the country. The Osaka society filled a useful function in bringing together the British and the Japanese businessmen of Osaka and Japan. It was never expected that it would materially affect international relations and, in fact, it never did. I am not a great believer in the value of these so-called cultural associations unless there is a background of real friendship between the countries concerned. The goodwill they engender evaporates into thin air the moment there is a conflict of interests. At meetings speakers will declare (I admit to having done it myself!) that there are no questions between the

---

[114]   The Kansai or Kinki region lies in the southern-central region of Japan's main island Honshū. The urban region of Osaka, Kobe and Kyoto (collectively the centre of Kansai) is the second most populated in Japan after the Greater Tokyo Area. For the Japan-British Society, which was revived after the Second World War, see http://www.kansainichiei.jp/e/about_us.html (accessed 2 September 2016).

two countries that cannot be settled by amicable discussion but let India, Canada, South Africa or Australia raise its import tariff against Japan and there is little talk of amicable discussion. The industrial leaders talk instead of retaliation and boycotts and the friendly atmosphere disappears overnight.

Growth of Anti-British Feeling

The years from 1932 onwards marked the growth of anti-British feeling in Japan. Politically we angered the Japanese by our action over the Manchurian question. I have always thought that Great Britain should either have taken a still stronger line or piped down. As a result we did China little good and we showed Japan that the time when we could intervene successfully in the Far East had passed. By ranging ourselves on the side of opposition, we pushed Japan a step further on her way towards Germany. It is only fair to admit, however, that the course on which Japan had embarked was bound to bring her up against Great Britain sooner or later.

Trade Friction

In the economic field also, the drive to capture markets which previously had been dominated by us, caused friction. At the end of 1931 Japan went off the gold standard and the yen was allowed to sink to half (previously 2/0½[115]) before it was pegged at that rate. Orders for Japanese goods poured in and foreign markets were soon flooded with them. Slight tariff raises having proved ineffective, the Indian Government suddenly, without warning, clapped on prohibitive duties against Japanese cotton manufactured goods. The Japanese Cotton Federation retaliated by boycotting Indian cotton.

It was an open secret that the boycott decision was not unanimous and, if it had not been for the resentment aroused by the unexpected nature of the blow, it might not have been adopted.

---

[115] Two shillings and a halfpenny in the pre-decimal British currency. The modern equivalent would be about 10 pence.

As it was, the voice of moderation was stilled and a storm of abuse against Great Britain was raised. No doubt Lancashire had brought pressure to bear but the Japanese insisted that India was merely obeying the behest of the British Government. The Japanese have always refused to believe that the Indian Government has any vestige of power and they poured the vials of their wrath on the home government.

An element of humour was introduced into an otherwise entirely unpleasant situation by the Japanese accusation that, as leading proponents of free trade, we had broken faith by resorting to protection. Japan herself has, for years, been building up her industries by means of an ever-growing tariff wall. And yet the Japanese cotton manufacturer and exporter rent his clothes and called heaven to witness the perfidy of the British.

Our rule in India was abused in scurrilous terms. The sufferings of the unfortunate Indians at the hands of the bloodsucking British were painted in lurid colours. And the Indians were adjured to remember that Codlin was their friend and not Short.[116]

Most of this wild talk was pure propaganda. When feelings were running at fever point, a Japanese friend begged me not to take it to heart. He assured me that the average Japanese realised that British interests should come first in India just as they thought that Japanese rights should come first in Manchuria. When the dispute had ended, a leading cotton magnate who had attacked Great Britain tooth and nail, remarked that he trusted I bore no ill-feelings. He said that when he was engaged in a fight, he used every weapon he could lay hands on. In fact, he was surprised at the moderation we had shown! I gathered that he loved a good fight.

I think my presence at the Rotary Club must have acted as a brake on free expression. The President of the Cotton Federation frequently reported on the position during the negotiations which took place but nothing was said to which I wished to take exception. Only on one occasion a member (who afterwards)

---

[116] 'Codlin is the friend, not Short'. From Charles Dickens' *Old Curiosity Shop*.

became a member of the Cabinet) referred to the Machiavellian tactics of Great Britain. The chairman at once called out the equivalent of 'Order!' and this example of bad manners was never repeated.

After protracted negotiations an agreement was reached between the two governments that Japan would limit her exports to a fixed scale based on the quantity of Indian cotton purchased. Thereafter, similar disputes occurred with Canada and Australia as well as with a number of other countries and it was left to the US to discover the most satisfactory method of dealing with the question. A mission composed of leading American cotton manufacturers and merchants visited Japan and came to an agreement with the Cotton Federation under which the latter voluntarily controlled exports to the US within limits which that country could absorb without difficulty.

Japan's Missed Trade Opportunities

In a sense, the years 1932 to 1935 were, for Japan, a tragedy of lost opportunity. World markets were clamouring for Japanese goods which were good value for the money. Unfortunately, the exporter at one end and the importer at the other, between them killed the goose that laid the golden eggs. The process worked in this way. A, an exporter, books a big order from (a), an importer, at 100 which represents a big profit to A at prices ruling in Japan and also to (a) at prices ruling in his market. Then B books a big order from (b) at 99, C at 98 and so on. For a time no great harm is done; the prices still represent a good profit at both ends. But, by the time the latest arrivals in the trade have taken a hand, X is booking an order from (x) at 70. When all these orders have been filled, the market is badly overstocked and prices slump. Since (x) can sell at 70 (plus expenses), early importers or dealers who have bought from them have to take a heavy loss, the market is thrown into chaos and the government steps in, trade stops for a time and when it is resumed, future purchases will be at 70. But in the meantime the import tariff has been raised and the low price received by the Japanese exporter will not stimulate trade:

the volume will be no greater than could have been done at 100. Moreover, the 70 does not represent a fair return to the manufacturer. The organisation of the weaving industry in Japan is complicated by the presence of the small-scale weaver who, if pushed to it, will work at a return which represents bare subsistence.

The result was that the enormous trade done in these years from 1932 onwards did not bring any great profit to Japan. The exporter displayed marvellous energy in exploiting new markets but in most cases the history was the same – initial success, a flood of orders, a mad rush to get in on the trade, market overstocked, a high tariff wall, and finally, trade much reduced from the peak with profits cut. Control measures, which were adopted later, would, if adopted at the beginning, have retained the early profits of the trade. But the Japanese cotton manufacturer and exporter, instead of taking in a reef, crowded on all sails. They saw Japan dominating every market: in imagination they had the whole world in fee. If they had had the foresight to anticipate the coming storm, they might have averted it. When it fell on them, their resentment knew no bounds and they attributed all their ills to Great Britain, the dog-in-the-manger that grudged them their meal.

Economic Troubles

The second half of my term in Osaka, say from 1935 to 1937, was a time of increasing discomfort for the manufacturer and merchant but now the trouble came from within. Manchuria was proving a costly blessing but it was only a portion of the burden. Her own action in leaving the League of Nations left Japan with a sense of isolation, The military preached a coming emergency and army and naval preparations were pushed on feverishly. The effect on the economic structure of industry and trade was serious. Money was being drained into unproductive channels and, though in the towns there was a fictitious air of prosperity, farmers and fishermen, who at the best of times live on the subsistence line, were impoverished. Externally the balance of trade was going heavily against Japan. The country is dependent on foreign sources for supplies of raw material for her industries and now a large portion of the bill was going towards the manufacture of munitions. Presently, imports had to be restricted by means of exchange control and Japan had set her feet on the path of planned economy.

To a well-wisher of the Japanese people as apart from their government and its policy, the course which the country was taking could not but arouse misgiving. I am convinced that the good people of Osaka were not interested in Japan's self-imposed 'divine mission' as the liberator and leader of Asia. Nor for that matter, have I met a Chinese who admitted that he wished to be led by the Japanese. Comment of the Osaka merchant on the Manchurian experiment was restrained but it was far from enthusiastic. Osaka is the Manchester of Japan and its citizens only ask to be left to their own devices. They have great, perhaps excessive, confidence in their ability to beat their competitors in other markets by peaceful methods. It was galling to them to be hemmed in by the restrictions imposed or caused by the military.

Spionitis

Spionitis became rampant. Every foreigner, official, merchant or missionary was a potential spy. I have mentioned elsewhere the ludicrous case of the manager of the National City Bank who came under suspicion because he hired a Japanese photographer to take pictures of leading offices in Osaka to provide material for an album that his head office was compiling in illustration of the activities of the bank overseas.

The average Japanese manufacturer is no less jealous of his trade-secrets than his competitor in other countries and to extract information is like drawing teeth. He cannot be blamed for this attitude: there is no reason why he should talk about his private business. But now word was passed round by the government that manufacturers and merchants were not to disclose trade information. It is one of the duties of British Consuls to answer enquiries as to output, etc. required by British firms to assist them in the development of their trade. Since the Consul does not know the answer himself, he asks a member of the trade for the information. But it was no longer possible to investigate direct nor to ask a friendly British merchant to do it in case the latter should get into trouble. If it simplified a Consul's task since he could but reply that the required information was unobtainable, it was none the less galling to have to confess one's inability to obtain it. And an atmosphere of suspicion becomes irksome after a time. But I never detected any less cordiality on the part of my friends.

Lack of Contact between Foreigner and Japanese

On the whole, when my second spell at Osaka ended in 1937, I looked back with satisfaction at the five-and-a-half years I had spent there. I could not point to any very tangible results of my term of office but I flattered myself that I had been of service to the British community. It is unfortunate, but inevitable, that there should be a wall between that community and the Japanese owing partly to the language difficulty but mainly to entirely different habits of social life. Another bar to social contact between the British community in Kobe and the members of the Japanese business world is due to the fact that the important Japanese firms are mostly in Osaka. There were, of course, numerous exceptions but the average British merchant never met any Japanese of his own class. It was impossible to break down this wall though the Japan-British Society provided one small meeting ground but, as Consul-General at Osaka, I was able to form a link and I regarded this as one of my principal duties. Side by side with legitimate grievances that the one side had against the other, were quite a number of unreasoning prejudices. Some of these, at least, I was able to remove and I think that when I left, mutual relations were better than when I arrived.

My Wife's Illness

In my own family life the last five years had been the saddest time I had ever experienced. My wife was taken seriously ill shortly after our arrival and, though she rallied, she was stricken down later with a very serious paralysis and, after lingering on between life and death for three years, was mercifully released at the beginning of 1937. Way back in 1906 when he gave his somewhat grudging consent to our engagement, my father-in-law had intimated clearly enough that I was scarcely good enough for Kathleen. After the lapse of thirty years I was not prepared to contest this verdict. Kathleen had stood loyally by my side from the time I was a second assistant, had encouraged me in difficult times, had given me gentle counsel when I needed it and, above all, had set me a standard of unselfishness in her care of me and our three children which I tried in vain to live up to. I recognise in myself a vein of selfishness. In big things I have, I hope, been able to eliminate it but I am far from thinking I have been equally successful in the small things incidental to every-day life.

I think that the best evidence of the happiness of our married life that I can offer is afforded by the fact that I married again towards the end of 1937. I had long admired the character of Margaret ('Peggy') Anderson who was justly universally popular in the foreign communities of Kobe and Yokohama and I count myself lucky that I was able to persuade her to throw in her lot with mine. It has been one of the greatest, if not *the* greatest blessing of my life to have enjoyed the companionship of two perfect women.

Chapter 14

CONSUL-GENERAL AT MUKDEN, 1938–1939

&

Reasons for Taking Post

I RETURNED TO England on leave on May 1937. Towards the end of the year I was asked by the Foreign Office if I would go to Mukden on my return and it was intimated to me that, if I wished, I could refuse. The truth was that Mukden was a thankless task and though an officer would be scarcely likely to refuse it if the appointment meant promotion, he would think twice before accepting if he were already Consul-General. Indeed, a junior of mine had been offered the post and had turned it down while the officer I was being asked to replace on his transfer to another post, was also a junior of mine. None the less, much to the surprise of my friends, I accepted the transfer to Mukden.

I had, of course, my own reasons for so doing. For one thing the Foreign Office had sugared the pill by putting the offer in the form of an appeal and, though I realised this, I did not think it wise to reject it for this reason. As a matter of general principle, I have never made a request for a post or intrigued against a disliked appointment. For this attitude I take no credit: the post that looks attractive from a distance often proves the reverse in actual experience and vice versa. But I think that my main reason for accepting Mukden was the desire to see what I could do in a difficult post. Mukden appealed to the spirit of adventure that is present in all of us. In other words, it was its very difficulties that attracted me: I wanted to see if I could save or salvage some of the vestiges of British interests in Manchuria.

Anomalous Position

Great Britain has never, of course, recognised the existence of the new state of Manchukuo. In theory, Manchuria is still part of China and Consular appointments are notified, if at all, to the Chinese Government. What is sauce for the goose is sauce for the gander: the government of Manchukuo does not recognise British Consuls, who have officially no standing at all. Carried to its logical conclusion, the theory of non-recognition would mean that the non-recognising country would not send Consuls or, if it did, that the ostracised country would not allow them to function. Actually, neither side wished to push matters to this extreme. His Majesty's Government continued to appoint Consuls-General to Mukden and to Harbin who exchanged calls and maintained relations with the Mayors of these cities and with the Governors of the Provinces in which they are situated. Official relations were also maintained with the Japanese Embassy in Hsinking,[117] the capital, and the Japanese Consuls throughout the country.

At first, no relations whatsoever existed with the central administration, all action being taken through the Japanese Embassy on whose good offices the Consul-General had to rely. In the early days this method had apparently worked satisfactorily enough. The infant administration was anxious not to antagonise foreign powers, which it hoped would presently recognise the new regime and had promised to fulfil existing treaty obligations (which included extra-territoriality). But, as time passed, the new administration felt that it had made good and became steadily more and more uncompromising. In the meantime, my predecessor had, wisely I think, established informal relations with the Manchurian Foreign Affairs Bureau, Hsinking being in his Consular district.

---

[117]   Changchun is the capital and largest city of Jilin province, northeast China (Manchuria), in the centre of the Songliao Plain. In 1932 the capital of Manchukuo, a Japan-controlled puppet state in Manchuria, was established and built around Changchun. The city was then renamed Hsinking (Xinjing – new capital). It reverted to being Changchun after the Second World War.

Destruction of Foreign Interests

In the years intervening between 1932 and 1938 the Government had been setting up a form of administration that had spelt ruin to foreign interests in the country. A discussion of the novel form of state socialism introduced would be out of place in this book. It is sufficient to state that a series of monopolies had been instituted. These were entrusted to what were known as 'special companies'. The earliest victims were the foreign oil companies which abandoned the field when the refining, distribution and sale of petroleum products were handed over to a special company and thereafter, though still operating in Dairen, declined to have dealings with the monopoly. In 1936, Japan 'graciously' relinquished extra-territoriality on behalf of her nationals. She could well afford to do so seeing that the administration was controlled by Japanese. But what was unpalatable to the foreign powers was that Manchukuo then proceeded to denounce extra-territoriality. In 1937 financial stringency compelled the government to introduce exchange control similar to that in force in Japan.

Official Representation

Against these successive encroachments on Treaty rights, His Majesty's Government (in common with US, France and other powers) protested unavailingly. The protests were usually made in Tokyo to the Japanese Government, which blandly replied that it was no concern of hers, and in Hsinking to the Foreign Affairs Bureau, which ignored them. It may be asked how could the Mukden Consul-General present a protest to a government which did not recognise him and which his own government did not recognise? The answer is that he called unofficially and left a memorandum after delivering his message verbally. If the whole situation had not been so tragic, it would have been *opéra bouffe*. An official can use various forms of communication varying from the downright 'note' to the informal talk. But the man who starts out by saying that he does not recognise the man he is addressing is surely straining the meaning of the word when he addresses an official complaint in a semi-official manner. A semi-official or an informal communication is not a communication made by a semi-official or an informal official, but a communication made by an official in a semi-official or informal manner. In so saying I am not criticising the Consul-General who had to make the best of conditions he had not himself created. I merely draw attention to the amusing side of the business since it is well to see the humour of a trying situation. Nor am I criticising His Majesty's Government which could not dispose of the Manchurian question as a local problem but had to treat it in accordance with its international, world-wide policy.

None the less I could not help ardently wishing that Manchuria *could* have been handled as a local problem. British vested interests, with one exception, had been driven out and British trade was fast disappearing. Exchange control aimed to balance trade by restricting imports to countries which took Manchurian exports. Moreover, Japan was given first choice since the balance of trade between Manchuria and Japan could be settled by book-entries, the Manchurian yuan at par with the Japanese yen. As a result, no licences were issued for the import of British sugar, chemicals and textiles. Actually, Great Britain did take Manchurian produce – beans and oil-seed, furs and skins, bristles, pheasants – but the British importer bought these articles because he wanted them, not as a consideration for sales of British manufacturers.

Non-recognition – the Stumbling Block

I had more than one interview with the Director of the General Affairs Board on the subject. Mr Hoshino[118] expressed his views

---

[118] This was Hoshino Naoki (1892–1978), who was somewhat economical with the truth about his role. He appears to have been closely involved with the narcotics trade in Manzhouguo and was tried as a war criminal at the end of the war. He was sentenced to life imprisonment but released in 1958. His memoirs, published in 1963, defended the Manzhouguo administration. See Wikipedia entry at https://en.wikipedia.org/wiki/Naoki Hoshino (accessed 11 July 2016).

with considerable frankness. He described himself as, and I think was, a plain business man uninterested in diplomatic formalities. Treatment of British trade was not dictated by political motives. If I could show him that Manchuria would benefit by British trade, he would foster it, recognition or no recognition. But Manchuria could not allow herself the luxury of free trade. She was hard put to it to find the foreign currency needed to buy essential imports. She was bound to buy these in the most favourable market.

The only answer to this was a trade agreement. But this could only be negotiated successfully by a government department and this would amount to recognition. I pointed this out to Mr Hoshino but he replied that, in so far as he was concerned, the question of recognition did not enter into it but that was for us to decide. On this note the discussion ended. His Majesty's Government could not enter into a trade agreement without forswearing its principles. A possible weapon would have been retaliation but I question whether the stoppage of British purchase of Manchurian produce would have had any effect since the British market was not essential to Manchuria.

Mr Kameyama,[119] Director of the Bureau of Foreign Affairs, took a similar line: 'His Majesty's Government cannot recognise Manchukuo? Very well, let's shelve that argument and try to work out a *modus vivendi*. Why cannot His Majesty's Government be more practical? You come to me and ask me to adjust British grievances. I am only too pleased to do my best but so soon as I take up a question with the department concerned, they rejoin, 'Who is the British Consul-General? We do not know him.' Then I argue that this is a question of investigating a complaint of injustice and hitherto I have had some success but

---

[119] Kameyama Kazuji (1895–1980). Japanese foreign ministry bureaucrat, who later became chief of the encoding office at the time of Pearl Harbor. He wrote a book on issues in communications between Japan and the Soviet Union, *Nisso kokkō mondai 1917–1945* (pub. 1973). See David Kahn, *The Codebreakers: The Story of Secret Writing* (New York Signet Books 1973), pp. 31, 43, 44 and https://library.soas.ac.uk/Author/Home?author=%E4%BA%80%E5%B1%B1%E4%B8%80%E4%BA%8C%2C+1895 (accessed 11 July 2016).

latterly departments have been inclined to say that if the British Government will not take a more realistic attitude and recognise the Manchukuo Government, they cannot listen to any more complaints.' Mr Kameyama's suggestion, therefore, was that I should take the title of Trade Commissioner with an office in Hsinking while continuing as Consul-General in Mukden. This would give me a local standing in Hsinking and I was promised that the government would not regard it as recognition.

I am sure that the proposition was made in good faith but His Majesty's Government could not agree to it. It would have implied a weakening of the strong stand that, in common with the US Government, they had taken against what was considered aggression by Japan against China. The League of Nations had done its best to lock, bolt and bar the door against any dealings with Manchukuo and, though certain other countries gradually fell away from this high moral stand, the three principal champions (Great Britain, US and France) stood their ground. A new conception of international relations had taken shape. I am not an expert on international law but I think I am right in saying that formerly the criterion was the *present* standing of the state requesting recognition: its past record might be black but if it appeared genuinely desirous and capable of becoming a decent member of the family of nations, then it could be admitted. The new conception was to outlaw the wrongdoer until he admitted his wrongdoing and redressed the wrong.

I think that the new conception was born before its time. Up to and including 1937, non-recognition had not seriously harmed Manchukuo which, under Japanese control, had steadily gained in strength. But for external events I think that, sooner or later, the Powers would have had to give way. But then Japan made the supreme blunder known as the China Incident[120] and the question of Manchukuo became merged in a larger issue.

---

[120]   The Marco Polo Bridge Incident, also known as the Lugouqiao Incident or the July 7th Incident, was the start of the China Incident. It was a battle between the Republic of China's National Revolutionary Army and the Imperial Japanese Army, often used as the marker for the start of the Second Sino-Japanese War (1937–1945). The eleven-arch granite bridge

Finally, in 1939, the European War and, in 1940, the Tripartite Pact, aligned Japan so definitely against Great Britain that the question of Manchukuo retired definitely into the background.

On the rare occasions on which I met the Japanese Ambassador, he asked me to report to my government what strides Manchukuo had made and how worthy it was of recognition but I was able to turn aside the argument by suggesting that the China Incident should first be settled. The question of recognition was like King Charles' head: sooner or later it cropped up in conversation with Japanese officials. But it was never seriously pressed. It was recognised that a gulf existed which I could not be expected to bridge permanently but I was constantly asked to assist in devising some form of temporary structure that would permit of contact. For the first year of my term of office in Mukden I racked my brains to devise some scheme since it was obvious that British interests were on the verge of extinction but I eventually gave up the problem as insoluble. The problem would have been simple enough if the new state had been merely on probation. It had been definitely outlawed and His Majesty's Government could not agree to any compromise.

On the whole, I think that my appointment to Mukden was a mistake because my Japanese friends heralded it as indicating a change of policy. I did my best to disabuse them of the notion but the wish was father to the thought and, though they did not say so, I am sure that they did not believe my disavowal of any change. If, however, they felt anything in the nature of disappointment when they found that the total impasse continued, Japanese officials never showed any signs of it and I received nothing but courtesy from them during my stay.

This is not intended as an essay on the Manchurian problem but only as an account of my own personal contact with it. I should be sorry to give an impression that the Consul-General in Mukden was all important. There was also a Consul-General of equal rank in Harbin where the business community was much more important than in Mukden. The Consul-General at

---

which gives its name to the incident is an architecturally significant structure, restored by the Kangxi Emperor (1662–1722).

Mukden came at times more prominently into the picture owing to the mere chance that Hsinking, the capital, happened to be just inside his district and problems that could not be settled on the spot had, as a last resort – usually a forlorn hope! – to be referred to the central authority.

Hsinking

A word on the capital may not be out of place. As the name indicates it is a new capital. Formerly there was a railway town known as Changchun[121] covering a small area round the station. This was incorporated in the new city of which it formed a section. The city was laid out on generous, not to say grandiose, proportions. The main thoroughfares were wide and impressive though the buildings were scarcely in keeping. In 1938 the government offices were housed in structures that looked well from the outside but, in many instances, bore evidence inside of their hasty construction. The Bank of Manchuria, however, was a fine building worthy of any capital city. Taken by and large there were grounds of justification for the pride of the citizens in the city that was growing up. In one respect it was an unsatisfactory place to visit. There was only one reasonably comfortable hotel – the SMR Hotel at the station. This was always so crowded that, latterly, I found it impossible to get accommodation and had to travel up on the night train. In winter it was not pleasant

---

[121]   In May 1898, Changchun got its first railway station, located in Kuancheng, part of the railway from Harbin to Lüshun (the southern branch of the Chinese Eastern Railway), constructed by the Russian Empire. After Russia's loss of the southernmost section of this branch as a result of the Russo-Japanese War of 1904–1905, the Kuancheng station became the last Russian station on this branch. The next station just a short distance to the south, the new 'Japanese' Changchun station, became the first station of the South Manchuria Railway, which now owned all the tracks running farther south, to Lüshun, which they re-gauged to the standard gauge. A special Russo-Japanese agreement of 1907 provided that Russian gauge tracks would continue from the 'Russian' Kuancheng Station to the 'Japanese' Changchun Station, and vice versa, standard gauge tracks provided by the South Manchuria Railway would continue from Changchun Station to Kuancheng Station.

to arrive in the early morning in an inadequately heated hotel. But I have to admit that the hotel had one amenity which I appreciated: it had stocks of Guinness and of Bass unobtainable elsewhere! Taxis were almost unobtainable owing to shortage of petrol but the Japanese Embassy or the Foreign Affairs Bureau were good enough to lend me a car when required.

Hsinking had no foreign community and no amusements and the Italian Minister and his staff complained bitterly of the dullness of their life. It was significant that they spent a good deal of their time in Harbin, Dairen and even Tientsin and Peking! In 1929 (sic. 1939) the diplomatic corps was strengthened by the arrival of the new German Minister. Dr Wagner[122] was an old friend of mine, having been a colleague in Osaka. I fancy he was very pleased at his appointment as Minister but he agreed as to the unspeakable dullness of the place. On the other hand there was, at the time, a growing colony of German merchants as a result of the barter agreement between Germany and Manchukuo. Whenever I had to go up to Hsinking I was only too delighted to hurry back to Mukden when my business was done.

Life in Mukden

By comparison, life in Mukden was pleasant. The German community kept to itself but the rest of the foreign community – British, American, with a sprinkling of French and other nationalities – was very socially inclined. The meeting ground was the Mukden Club, a ramshackle building but the scene of many a pleasant function. We had to thank the Japanese for the construction of first-class golf links at Tungling, some ten miles out of Mukden. Then there were the Peiling woods,[123] ten minutes out by car, the walks in which were delightful at all seasons but especially in winter when the ground was carpeted in snow. This about ended the attractions of Mukden though for sportsmen

---

[122]   This appears to be Dr Wilhelm Wagner (1884–??), who was a Doctor of Jurisprudence and held the Iron Cross First Class. Information from various editions of yearbooks, accessed 11 July 2016.

[123]   Peiling (Beiling) was an Imperial Manchu burial ground.

there was excellent shooting for half the year. On the other side of the ledger was the absence of vanity in the life – there was no music, of course no theatres, not even foreign films since the inevitable 'special company' had driven foreign distributors out of the field. Spring months were trying owing to the high winds which raised heavy clouds of dust and dirt and a short period in summer was uncomfortably hot but for the most part of the year the climate was bracing and pleasant. Even in the midst of winter clear skies and a bright sun compensated for the extreme cold. I think the main drawback to life in Mukden was the drabness of much of the countryside which had a depressing effect after a time.

The Problem of Extra-territoriality

To return to my official life, one knotty problem was extra-territoriality. The Manchukuo Government maintained that it was dead, His Majesty's Government maintained that it was alive. The latter was correct as a Treaty right cannot be cancelled by unilateral action but how was the contention to be enforced? The correct procedure was to protest against any extension of jurisdiction to British subjects but there was a danger that the British subject would be the victim if the case went against him by default. At first, vigorous protests had been effective in checking the action of the authorities but the time had passed when they would pay attention to protests. I have never, in any case, been a great believer in the efficacy of protests when the other side has made up its mind. They have frequently the effect of making your opponent more obstinate and closing the door to any possible settlement. I have always tried to find a middle line and only to protest when other methods failed.

Two cases occurred in my district while I was in Mukden. One was a civil case which was likely to be followed, if successful, by a criminal case. It was an action for damages for malfeasance against a missionary doctor. I was satisfied that the doctor had a good defence but he admitted to having made a wrong diagnosis in the first instance. There was grave danger, therefore, that the case would go against him and I breathed a sigh of relief when, with the assistance of the Japanese Consul, I got the case settled out of court. The other case illustrates the extreme naïveté of certain missionaries. This man was working in a very out-of-the-way spot in western Manchuria. He had occasion to make a journey for which he obtained the necessary military permit. On the way he made a detour to a point near the frontier where he presumably had converts. This in itself was asking for trouble and he certainly got it. The day before he arrived at this point some sort of 'scrap' had taken place, the exact nature of which is not known but Japanese soldiers had been killed. On the way he indulged his favourite occupation of surveying and photographing the country. In all these doings of his he was acting in good faith but if he had set out to convince the Japanese military authorities that he was a spy, he could not have done better. To carry a camera in a military zone is to invite trouble but it is a harmless amusement compared with making surveys of the country. All unconscious of his offence, the missionary proceeded to his destination where he was promptly arrested. When, some weeks later, I heard of his predicament, it was just on the eve of my own departure and it fell to my successor to extricate him. I believe that after some months' detention, he was released.

Late in September 1939 I was informed that I had been transferred to Tientsin and I arrived there at the end of October to take over from Mr Jamieson[124] who was going on sick leave.

---

[124]   Edgar George Jamieson (1882–1958). Joined the China Consular Service 1902 and served in numerous China posts. During the First World War he was a temporary captain with the China Labour Corps in France. He retired in 1940. His father was also in the China Consular Service. *Foreign Office List*; Coates *China Consuls* p. 529.

Chapter 15

CONSUL-GENERAL AT TIENTSIN, 1939–1941

℘

Events Leading up to the Tientsin Blockade

THE SITUATION I found in Tientsin was so abnormal that I must devote some space to an outline of the events which had led up to the blockade that was in force when I arrived. I should never have found myself Consul-General in Tientsin but for the China Incident. Until a few years ago, the Consular Service in China, like that in Japan, was a closed one. The Chinese language, again like of Japan, is a life-time study, while the Chinese mentality is sufficiently different from that of other nationalities to make it only understandable after long experience. Finally, extra-territoriality presents problems such as are not met with by Consuls in other countries. Consequently the Consular officer appointed to China remained there throughout his career unless he was translated to higher spheres and all the Consular posts were naturally filled from the China Service.

But in 1937 a local scrap at the Marco Polo Bridge between Chinese troops and the Japanese garrison stationed in North China developed into what was actually war between China and Japan though the latter country, for reasons of its own, never declared war but insisted on calling it an incident – the China Incident. By 1939 Japan had occupied the greater part of China's seaboard and had seized most of China's railways as far inland as Hankow.[125] They had already occupied Tientsin and Peking in the early days of the war and had set up a puppet Chinese regime. This, however, had to obey the orders of the Japanese army and, for all practical purposes, North China (and other occupied territories) was under martial law.

The foreign concessions in Tientsin were enclaves of foreign interest that soon proved obnoxious to the Japanese conqueror. There were still four remaining – the British, the French, the Italian and the Japanese. These concessions had, by Treaty and custom, rights of local self-administration and managed their own domestic affairs. The British concession was administered by a Municipal Council consisting of six British and six Chinese members elected by the rate-payers, the Chairman being British. Its 'constitution' was laid down by the Municipal Regulations, popularly known as the Land Regulations, issued by the British Ambassador under authority from the British Government. To the Council were delegated the duties of maintenance of the roads and public services generally and law and order were maintained by the British Municipal Police. Its powers were, in effect, analogous to those of a small borough.

The autonomy of the concession was, however, limited. The Council had no jurisdiction over the residents, and its police, while it was their duty to arrest those who broke the peace, had no powers to punish. Subjects of such foreign powers as retained the right of extra-territoriality were amenable only to their Consular Courts. Chinese and those foreigners who did not enjoy extra-territoriality were subject to the Chinese Courts. It became the duty, therefore, of the Concession authorities to hand over to the latter all Chinese law-breakers, the actual procedure being that in the case of the British concession the Police handed over the accused only on a warrant from the Chinese Court which had been endorsed by the British Consul-General.

---

[125]   Hankou (Hankow), was one of the three cities whose merging formed modern-day Wuhan, the capital of the Hubei province, China. It stands north of the Han and Yangtzi Rivers where the Han falls into the Yangtzi. Hankou is connected by bridges to its former sister cities Hanyang (between Han and Yangtie) and Wuchang (on the south side of the Yangtze).

Even in normal times there is a possibility of friction here. British legal practice is very different from Chinese and our ideas of justice are also different. This indeed was the origin of extra-territoriality. Concessions in China were set aside by mutual agreement to be occupied by foreigners who would be able to live their own life and manage their own affairs in their own way; it was not originally intended that Chinese should live in them. But as the Concessions expanded, the Chinese poured in until, in the British Concession in Tientsin, they were numeri-cally in the proportion of, say, twenty to one. There can be no doubt that the attraction to the Chinese was the comparative absence of restriction. Fortunately they were, with few excep-tions, law-abiding and good citizens. But at all times there was likely to be a certain proportion who were not *personae gratae* to the Chinese administration, whatever it is at the moment. In the unsettled times that followed the formation of the so-called Chinese Republic, many politicians who had been ousted and were in personal danger took refuge in the foreign conces-sions and a custom of sanctuary grew up.[126] Not that they caused any great trouble since for the most part they brought consider-able funds with them and were content to abandon the political arena and settle down in retirement. But it has to be admitted that the principle, if it can be so called, was an infringement of Chinese sovereignty.

When the Japanese military occupied Tientsin and set up a puppet Municipality in the Chinese city, it was not long before disputes arose between the British (and French) Municipal authorities on the one side and the Japanese Consul-General on the other for the Japanese contended that the concessions had become a base in which emissaries of the Chinese Government could plot in safety against the Japanese army. There was a cer-tain amount of truth in the contention though the Japanese were quite wrong in thinking that the British authorities deliberately connived at the presence of terrorists and agitators. They were just

---

[126]   One of those concerned was China's last emperor, Pu Yi, who fled to the Japanese concession at Tianjin in 1924 when he was expelled from the Forbidden City in Beijing.

as anxious as the Japanese to keep them out of the concession. The crux of the problem was the difference between Japanese and British methods and procedures. The Japanese method is to arrest a suspect and, to put it mildly, 'grill' him. The British method is to examine the preliminary evidence and see if there is a *prima facie* case; mere suspicion is not enough. The difference is radical but could have been straightened out but for the mutual distrust that each side felt for the other. It is a fault of the Japanese to be too secretive. In Tientsin the Japanese authorities were prone to say, baldly, that X was a terrorist and demand his arrest and surrender. The British authorities would ask for some evidence and the Japanese would regard this as an affront and would say, to use an expression frequently in their mouths, that the British authorities were lacking in sincerity. The British, on their side, would have been quicker in responding to requests for arrests if they had not had good reason to believe that suspicion, in most cases, rested on 'King's evidence' obtained under torture and so might well be ill-grounded. In the result, bad feeling between the Japanese and the British authorities gradually rose to a high pitch.

Finally, a high Chinese official was assassinated in a cinemahouse in the British concession. In due course the Japanese Consul-General requested the arrest and surrender of four suspects. The British Consul-General had reason, which at a later stage when the whole case had blown over proved to be only too well-founded, to believe that the evidence, which rested on 'confessions' of other Chinese was false, and, though the men were arrested, they were not immediately surrendered. It is not my purpose to detail the wrangle that followed. It is sufficient to say that the Japanese commander, General Homma,[127] finally

---

[127] Lieutenant General Homma Masaharu (1887–1946). Joined the Imperial Japanese Army in 1907 and spent several years in Britain as a military attaché. In 1917 he went to France with the British forces and was awarded the Military Cross. Commander at Tianjin 1938–1940. In 1942 he was sent to the Philippines where he tried to prevent atrocities. Nevertheless, he was executed in April 1946 after being found guilty of war crimes. See John Toland, *The Rising Sun: The Decline and Fall of the Japanese Empire 1936–1945* (London: Cassell, 1971), passim, and 'Masaharu Homma' on Wikipedia (accessed 12 July 2016).

lost patience and in June 1939 proceeded to isolate the British concession by surrounding it with electrified barbed wire. Entry and exit could then only be made through barriers at which stood Japanese sentries with bayonets who, at their sweet will, allowed those who wished to go through to go into the examining shed or made them wait. Foreigners had to produce passports or identity cards. If these disclosed that the holders belonged to 'friendly' nations e.g. German, they passed through without delay. But woe betides the unhappy holder of a British passport or identity card. In the early days of the blockade, several British subjects of both sexes were subjected to the indignity of stripping down to the bare limits of decency in front of hordes of Chinese coolies. This was pure wanton brutality. From a military point of view stripping served no purpose; it was a deliberate attempt to humiliate the British in the eyes of the Chinese and other races. The British residents, thus insulted, were respected members of the community and their identity was plain from their passports or cards. NO! It is possible to forgive much when you think that the other side has been betrayed by bad temper into action which he afterwards regrets and for which he makes suitable amends. But when protests were made by His Majesty's Government and the practice stopped, General Homma merely remarked that it was nothing to a Japanese to strip in public, he did it every day when he went to a public bath-house. This would have been beside the point even if it had been strictly true but it isn't; Japanese at the public bath-house do not strip in the open but in the dressing-room.

I am sorry to have to criticise General Homma whom I afterwards met and whom I found a cultured gentleman and reasonably broad-minded. It is possible that the isolation of the concession took place on orders from higher up and it is probable that he was not fully cognisant of the rigours with which his subordinates enforced the blockade but, as commanding officer, he must take the responsibility. Viewing the 'isolations' objectively one may say that, arbitrary as the action was, if the Japanese thought that it was necessary from a military point of view to isolate the concession in order to prevent bad Chinese from endangering the safety of the Japanese forces, then it is possible to make out a case for isolation. But in that case as soon as the British authorities took steps, as they did, to co-operate in rounding up terrorists, thus ensuring the safety of the Japanese forces, it was the duty of the Japanese command to raise the blockade. The blockade began in June 1939. Negotiations between the British Ambassador and the Japanese Foreign Office then took place which reached agreement on police matters but broke down on the question of the silver stored in the British concession.[128] None the less the British authorities voluntarily put the police agreement into force but not only did the Japanese military continue the blockade but enforced it, as I shall have to tell, with great severity.

A word is necessary as to the silver. This was stored in the vaults of the building belonging to, and formerly occupied by, the Chinese Bank of Communications. In 1935 the Chinese Government withdrew the silver coinage and made dollar notes legal tender. Part of the silver called in in the North of China was stored in the French and British concessions in Tientsin; there were understood to be the equivalent of £2,000,000 and £1,000,000 in the two concessions respectively. The Japanese Government claimed that the Chinese Government had been replaced by the new administration that had been set up and that therefore this silver belonged to this administration and should be surrendered. The British and French Governments felt that the silver had been left by the owner in their keeping and that it would be a breach of trust to hand it over. So the matter rested when the blockade began and the Japanese Government then made the silver one of the terms of negotiation. To anticipate, when agreement was eventually reached, one-tenth of the silver was taken to be used for relief purposes and the remainder was sealed up.

At the beginning of the blockade the Japanese offered to exclude the French concession from its effects if they were allowed

---

[128]   The ambassador, Sir Robert Craigie, has an account of the negotiations in his book *Behind the Japanese Mask* (London: Hutchinson: N.D. [1945]), pp. 72–8. See also the blog at http://www.cshagen.com/category/tientsin-at-war/ (accessed 12 July 2016), for a more lively account.

to put up their barbed wire between the two concessions where they are contiguous. To their great credit, the French authorities declined the offer and the barbed wire was therefore carried right round the two concessions and the French concession was also blockaded though, since the British were the real 'enemy' the French concession was treated more lightly than the British.[129]

One other calamity that had befallen in 1939 needs a passing reference. During the summer occurred the great flood. Tientsin is the meeting place of a number of rivers that run down from the mountains to the north, north-west, west and south-west. During the monsoon season heavy rains on these ranges frequently cause more water to be brought down than can be carried off to the sea. The country round Tientsin is absolutely flat and in time of flood becomes a vast lake. Dykes had been built round the city which had kept off floods since 1916 but in 1939 they were badly in need of repair and they were not quite high enough. At the end of July the water poured in and the whole area was flooded to a depth varying from three to nine feet. For days, the residents went about in sampans (flat-bottomed boats) until the water had been pumped out. The smell was indescribable but curious to relate, no epidemic resulted, possibly because chemical works had been flooded and the chemicals that were mixed in the water neutralised its insanitary content. Damage to buildings was extensive and walls became so wet that it was months before repairs could be effected. A further embarrassment to the harassed British Municipal Council was the presence of some five thousand refugees from the vicinity and surrounding country who poured into the concession and had to be taken care of.

The British Concession in October 1939

I came, therefore, at the end of October 1939, to a concession scarred by the worst flood in its history and 'isolated' from the

---

[129] This major crisis in Anglo-Japanese relations in the summer of 1939 is now known as the Tianjin Incident. Following its resolution, White received letters from the Foreign Office, from the ambassador to Japan and from Anthony Eden (Foreign Minister and future P.M.) to personally thank him for his handling of the incident.

outside world by a circle of barbed wire. This little borough that the Japanese persisted in treating as though it were a plague spot was, and is, a model settlement. I do not claim that its council were supermen. On the contrary, they were human and made mistakes. But the concession with its cleanliness, its orderliness and its security compares very favourably with the Japanese concession and the Chinese city. As for the presence of terrorists, the British concession had no monopoly for they were present in the whole area as frequent outrages in the area under Japanese control proved only too clearly. With a Chinese population of between seventy and eighty thousand it would be unreasonable to expect that there would be no agitators and 'bad hats' among them but I found that our Chief of Police, Mr Dennis,[130] was co-operating very efficiently in nullifying their activities. This word co-operation may have an ugly sound when it is considered that the agitators were working for a government which was recognised by His Majesty's Government as the *de jure* government of China. But it must be remembered that the methods employed by these agitators were those of the terrorist and gangster. I personally had no compunction in handing over a man who, for instance, had plotted to blow up a cinema. Similarly, in such critical times the secret possession of a gun by an owner who cannot offer any reasonable explanation is suspicious. Our first duty was to the concession. I had no quarrel with the patriot who risked his life for what he considered a sacred cause but he abused the hospitality of the British concession when he made use of it to plot and plan against the Japanese and *de facto* administrators. Incidentally, however

---

[130] Detective Chief Inspector Richard Harry Dennis (1897–1972). He served in the Royal Flying Corps in the First World War and joined the Metropolitan Police about 1919. In 1934, he became head of Tianjin Municipal Police, a post he held until he was detained in 1941. He was later accused of spying and held in solitary confinement until repatriated with other officials in August 1942. Dennis carried out investigations relating to the death of Pamela Werner in Beijing in 1937. See the entry on him at https://en.wikipedia.org/wiki/Richard_Harry_Dennis (accessed 12 July 2016). He also features heavily in Paul French, *Midnight in Peking: The Murder that Haunted the Last Days of Old China* (London: Viking, 2012).

wrong the aggressor may be, assassination cannot be defended on moral grounds and is of questionable value as a practical measure.

Severity of Blockade

The fact, then, that the danger to the Japanese forces, if it ever existed, had been effectively curbed, made the blockade meaningless except as a means of extorting material gains from Great Britain, the exact purpose for which it came to be used, and made absolutely indefensible the extreme severity with which it was enforced. This was not war between two opposing armies but ruthless power used against inoffensive civilians. I have always had friendly feelings towards the Japanese people and I can look back to nothing but kindness to myself at their hands during my long career in Japan. I still like individual Japanese and I regret more than I can say that Japan should, as I think, have taken the wrong path in the last decade but Tientsin cured me of any lingering sentiment as regards Japan as a nation.

Not that it would have paid to give way to my feelings of disgust at the doings of the Japanese army. It was, above all, necessary to keep calm and collected. It was up to me to do all that was possible to moderate the severity of the blockade and to ward off dangers to the residents of the concession. More than that was impossible since there is no effective answer to force except more force and that was out of the question in this case.

Examination at the Barriers

The first abuse of their powers was the harshness of the examination at the barriers. Many British residing in the concession worked outside and had to go in and out of the barriers every working day. On arriving at the barriers they would be told to wait. Shortly after I arrived, the time of waiting began to lengthen out from twenty minutes until it became two hours. We had now entered the winter months and a wait at the International Bridge, the most important barrier, of two hours in a biting wind was a serious ordeal. On my protest, made through the Japanese Consul-General, the delay was considerably decreased – for a time. Presently the time lengthened out again. I noted that the change occurred immediately after Japan had been incensed over the action taken by Great Britain in stopping the *Asama Maru*[131] just outside Japanese territorial waters. Another protest resulted in a shortening of the delay time and so it went on for the next eight months – temporary alleviation followed by stiffening whenever some international incident annoyed Japan. I thought at first that it was due merely to bad temper on the part of the sentries but it became fairly clear that action at the barriers depended on instructions from the staff officer responsible, for sentries would refer to their watches and when a certain time was up would let the waiters through.

Persons who had to go through the barriers carried identity cards, bearing their national flag, which were stamped by their Consulate and by the Japanese Consulate. As a rule, the sentries could not read foreign languages and relied on the flag for their decision. Since the British flag meant a longer or shorter hold-up some British subjects resorted to ruses to get through. One actually picked up a card which he found lying around in the examination tent and used this for a time. Others gave themselves out as Irish, Australian, etc. and this sometimes worked. One man used a driv-

131   The *Asama Maru* was a Japanese ocean liner launched in 1929. It was built by Mitsubishi Shipbuilding & Engineering Co. at Nagasaki, Japan. Built for the trans-Pacific Orient-California fortnightly service, she was characterized as 'The Queen of the Sea'. Principal ports-of-call included Hong Kong, Shanghai, Kobe, Yokohama, Honolulu, Los Angeles and San Francisco. On her fourth voyage from Yokohama to San Francisco, the speed of the ship's crossing surpassed the previous record. Before Japan's entry into the Second World War she was intercepted by the Royal Navy 56 km from the coast of Niijima on 21 January 1940. Alerted to reports that Axis sailors in the United States were preparing to arrange transport to Germany, the Royal Navy removed twenty-one of the ship's passengers believed to be survivors of the scuttled German liner *Columbus*. The Government of Japan condemned it as an abuse of belligerent rights and formally protested the action, which further escalated tensions between the two countries. For an account of the incident, see the paper by Chester G. Dunham, 'The *Asama Maru* Incident of January 21, 1940', presented at the Thirteenth Annual Ohio Valley History Conference, October 1997. PDF available on line, accessed 12 July 2016.

ing licence and got away with it once or twice! Incidentally, there were no registered members of the Irish Free State in the concession but there were a number of Irish born in that part of Ireland. I confess to have connived at the use of a limited number of Irish Free State cards by those who had business outside the concession. Unfortunately I had to discontinue the issue of these cards since the number was rapidly growing and I feared the sentries would become suspicious and I was not in a position to answer a direct enquiry on the point from the Japanese Consulate.

I was in constant fear that a British subject would lose his temper at his treatment at the barriers and strike a sentry. This could only have ended in his injury and possible death. But right through the blockade the whole community showed a restraint that was commendable beyond words. There was one near-incident. A British subject one day presented himself at the barrier and the Chinese policeman there waved him inside, though there was a considerable crowd waiting. He professed afterwards to have mistaken this for permission to go right through the enclosure without going into the examination shed. He walked rapidly through, regardless of the shouting he heard behind him and had got through the barrier and on to the International Bridge when the pursuing Japanese sentry jumped in front of him. He foolishly struck up the sentry's rifle and was pinioned from behind by a Chinese policeman. He was then led back to the enclosure and from there to gendarmerie headquarters. At the end of the day, as a result of representations of a member of my staff, he was released and, on the whole, he was lucky to have got off so lightly.

Examination of Shipping

A second annoying feature of the blockade was the examination of British shipping making use of the River Peiho[132] on which

---

132   The Hai River (Bai He or Pei Ho), flows through Beijing and Tianjin before emptying into the Yellow Sea at the Bohai Gulf. The Hai River at Tianjin is formed by the confluence of five waterways: the Southern Canal, the Ziya River, the Daqing River, the Yongding River and the Northern Canal. The southern and northern canals are parts of the

the British concession faces. Ships or boats coming to or leaving the British bank were compelled to call at the DKK[133] wharf in the ex-German concession just below it. Here the Chinese crew and Chinese passengers were lined up on the wharf and examined one by one, both their bodies and their possessions. The ship itself would be examined from bow to stern. Supposing the examination to be satisfactory, it would take at least three hours, frequently an entire day. But if any suspicious document or smuggled goods or money were found, then the ship would be held-up, it might be for three days or more while members of the crew or passengers were examined in the hope of finding the culprit. It was nothing to the gendarmes that a day's hold-up of a passenger ship represents very serious loss to the owners. They professed to hold the owners responsible though I defy anyone to devise a method of eliminating smuggling by a Chinese crew. It is in their blood and on the China coast it is well-known that a few years ago a big haul of opium was made at Hankow from a British gun-boat. Constant representations would after, say, three days' hold-up, result in the release of the unfortunate ship. A year later when in San Francisco I called on Mr Muto,[134] the Japanese Consul-General who had previously been in Tientsin, and I could not resist commenting on a case of opium smuggling which had just been discovered on a large Japanese liner at San Francisco.

Japanese Consul-General

This is a suitable occasion to refer to Mr Muto. My difficulties in Tientsin would have been far greater but for his presence there. I could not have wished for a better official to deal with. He was courteous, reasonable and helpful. His powers were of course limited for the decisions were made by the Japanese Military Headquarters but I knew that he put forward the British case

---

Grand Canal. At Tianjin, through the Grand Canal, the Hai connects with the Yellow and Yangtze rivers. See Fig. 2 for a map of Tientsin with the waterways.

[133]   DKK Line (Dairen Kisen Kaisha) was a shipping company

[134]   This appears to be Muto Yoshito, who took up his post in San Francisco in 1940. No further details.

fairly. It would have been foolish to ask too much of him. I could not go direct to the Commanding Officer, General Homma. At the outset I had made an attempt to make the acquaintance of this officer but received a polite refusal to meet me. I gathered, though not told so in so many words, that communications having been cut when the concession was 'isolated', the General could not meet me without weakening the stand he had taken. In any case the Japanese Consul-General was the correct channel of communication.

Other Authorities Concerned

There are obvious objections to 'shadow boxing'. When my representations on a particular subject failed I could never be certain of the grounds of the refusal since I could not meet the principals. As time went on it was possible, by piecing together information from various sources, to know that certain members of the General's Staff were violently prejudiced against the British and whenever they had the power would use it to harass the British concession. I judged from my experience in Tientsin that subordinate Japanese officers have far too much power to interpret general instructions in any way they think fit. Even when I had been informed that orders had been issued in some particular sense it was usually a matter of two or three days before I could get them carried out because the officer actually responsible would say that he had received no instructions or would carry them out in a way that nullified the original intention. One would have thought that it should be merely a matter of a few moments' telephoning to check up but it never worked that way. The officer would refuse to take any action and it became necessary to start again at the beginning through the Japanese Consulate-General who would ring up Headquarters and confirm that the orders had been issued so that was fine – the orders were there but were not being carried out. Eventually when the officer concerned had held out for a day or two he would either relent and carry out the orders or, frequently enough, would think up reasons why they could not be carried out and refer back to Headquarters and so the pleasant little game of baiting the British concession would continue.

As if this were not enough, there was another authority which had a word to say in most negotiations and that was the Special Military Mission. I have never been entirely clear as to the exact scope of the duties of these military missions in Tientsin and elsewhere but they were usually brought into discussions in which foreign interests were concerned. I had no quarrel with the mission at Tientsin; its directors were straightforward and on occasion helpful, but it was one more hurdle to cross.

Even this does not conclude the catalogue of 'hurdles'. The DKK Wharf was under the control of the Hirota unit and starting across the river on the north bank by the Kato unit and finally passage of goods by land was controlled by the Shimidzu unit (units named after the Colonels in charge). Few questions arose on which one or more of these units had not a say. Technically, under General Homma, they were independent in action and could and did passively obstruct for days at a time.

The difficulties of negotiating through the Japanese Consulate General will be realised. It was a case of Box and Cox all the time. When the main negotiations had been concluded, then the fun began. First the unit concerned had never heard of the subject, then there had been a misunderstanding, then the unit would carry out the undertaking but there were conditions to be observed and so the game went on. How much of it was pure obstruction I could never determine but for the most part I think that it was due to the system. There was far too much decentralisation and each little Jack-in-Office carried on regardless of others until, by patience, he was brought into line.

I am afraid I have wandered into the side-lines from the main struggle of the blockade but it was necessary in order to make it clear that, as Consul-General, I had to set myself limited objectives. An attempt to obtain redress from all the troubles to which the concession was unfairly subjected would have been hopeless. I should have had to sit in the office of the Japanese Consul-General all day and every day and should have accomplished nothing. The only line of action was to concentrate on the big things: the small things could be tackled as they came along but could not be pressed.

Coal Supplies Stopped

A big question did occur shortly after my arrival. From the inception of the blockade coal for the British and French concessions had been brought up the river by barge from Tangku[135] at the mouth of the river. The Hirota unit suddenly stopped the passage of these barges at the DKK wharf. Orders were obtained for their release but at the end of a week the barges were still at the wharf. 'Oh no,' said the unit, 'we are not stopping the barges but all merchandise coming through here needs to be examined so the coal in the barges must be unloaded.' This was pure subterfuge. There was no space on the wharf to begin with and unloading and then reloading under supervision of gendarmes would have taken days. The true inwardness of the unit's action had then become clear. Its object was to starve the concessions of coal. It was significant that similar action had not been taken during the summer and it was initiated just at the onset of winter. The danger of the situation was that, not only would the community freeze but it would have no lighting and no water, since the water supply comes from artesian wells and is pumped up by electricity.

Vigorous representations by the French Consul[136] and me resulted in a compromise. We were asked to state our needs for

---

[135] Tanggu was a district in the Tianjin municipality China and is now part of the newly formed district of Binhai. It is on the Hai River where it enters the Bohai Sea, and is a port for Tianjin, which is about 50 km upriver. Now known as Tianjin Port, it is the largest in Northern China and the fifth largest in the world (as of 2015), acting as the main maritime gateway for Beijing. The Tanggu Truce, or Tangku Truce, was a cease-fire signed between Republic of China and Empire of Japan in Tanggu on 31 May 1933, formally ending the Japanese invasion of Manchuria which had begun two years earlier.

[136] This was probably Charles Jean Lépissier (1882–1975). Born in Cantion where his father was in the Chinese Customs Service, he was French consul at Tianjin 1931–1935 and again from 1938. At some point he became the minister 1943. See http://www.famille-li.com/

the coming winter and after endless discussion, the Japanese military graciously agreed to a quota to be brought in by barges from the opposite bank of the river (Hedong, formerly the Russian concession) at the rate of seven hundred tons a day. Further delays then occurred while the Kato unit shroffed[137] photos of the crews to be employed and when the barges started working the concession was almost denuded of coal.

The quota was barely sufficient for the needs of the concession in the early winter. But normally householders have a few days' supply and the supplier has stocks. The supplier was the Kailan Mining Administration[138] (a combine of British and Chinese interests which owns the principal soft coal mines at Tongshan[139] near Tientsin). It had no stocks left and householders had used up all their coal. It was impossible to distribute one day's supply to every consumer every day. The KMA was compelled, therefore, to distribute a few days' supply to consumers in rotation and those who were low down on the list had to go without coal for days and days. In addition, the poorer Chinese had hitherto used coal balls made from anthracite dust, supplies of which had also been blocked by the Japanese military. They turned to the KMA soft coal. So the two concessions struggled on for two or three weeks. As fast as the coal came in, it went out. During most of that time, about half the concession went without coal. I sat in my office in coat,

---

[137]   A verb and noun, to *schroff*, especially in the Far East, is to examine (especially money) and separate real from fake. A schroff is someone who schroffs!

[138]   The Kailan Mining Administration was formed to oversee the coal mines of the Chinese Engineering and Mining Company and the Lanchow Mining Company, which were producing about 4.5 million tons annually during the 1920s. The company's activities were halted by the victory of the Communists in the Chinese Civil War and it was finally dissolved in 1984.

[139]   Tangshan (Tongshan) is a largely industrial city in northeastern Hebei province, China. It has become known for the 1976 Tangshan earthquake which measured 7.8 on the Richter scale and killed at least 255,000 residents, believed to be the largest earthquake of the twentieth century by death toll. The city has since been rebuilt and has become a tourist attraction. It has been a coal-mining centre since the 1870s.

muffler and hat and had great pleasure in receiving Japanese officials in that garb.

Eventually something like equilibrium was restored and everyone was getting a little coal but it was obvious that when the coldest period came in January and February there would be a near-famine. Fortunately, as a result of endless representations and discussions, an increase to one thousand tons a day was obtained and with this quota we were able to negotiate the rest of the winter.

It is fair to state that there was a serious shortage of coal in the Japanese concession and the Chinese city but the Japanese themselves were responsible. Most of the KMA coal was going to Japan but there were still sufficient supplies left to satisfy the Tientsin area. While the struggle was going on there were ample stocks belonging to the KMA lying at Hedong. There was never any attempt to hold back supplies from the rest of the area. All that we asked was that we should be allowed to bring in enough of our own coal to supply the two concessions. At the finish we got it but only as the result of a heart-breaking struggle.

Flour Problem

In the early part of 1940 a serious shortage of flour occurred in North China, Peking being the principal sufferer. Half of the area had been flooded in the summer of 1939 and had produced no food-stuffs. Moreover, the principal towns were packed with refugees, some of whom had obtained employment but most of whom were living in camps, dependent on the authorities for food. As stocks dwindled, the price of flour soared. The authorities tried price control but this was worse than useless for richer Chinese got their flour by hole-and-corner methods and stocks disappeared faster than ever. Then the authorities came to the French Consul and me and asked us to commandeer flour stocks in the two concessions. There were indeed stocks far in excess of our requirements and it would have been criminal to allow them to lie there while people at our doors were starving. My colleague and I were only too willing to take steps to see that the supplies were made available but I had watched the measures adopted by the Japanese in Manchuria to secure rationed distribution of short supplies. I had seen how these measures had failed and I was sure that they were unsound. Also there was a technical difficulty. The flour did not belong to the concession authorities but to private owners.

Why did not the owners sell the stocks they owned seeing that they had bought them at a time when flour was cheap? For a variety of reasons. The flour was an investment. The value of the dollar had dropped from ½ to 9d. and from 9d. to 4d. and might go further. Paper money might be worth anything or nothing whereas flour represented something tangible the price of which would go up as the dollar went down. Moreover, the price fixed by the authorities was below replacement costs and importers were unwilling to import fresh supplies if they thought they would have to sell at a loss. But worse were the arbitrary methods of the authorities. Dealers who had moved their stocks out found them seized and paid for at any price the authorities thought fit to pay.

To end the deadlock I arranged a meeting of representatives of the authorities and of the principal merchants at which I ascertained what daily supplies from the British concession would be regarded as sufficient. At the same time I begged the Mayor to cancel the fixed price. Finally, various emergency orders were issued calling on holders of flour to register their stocks and the flour guild were told plainly that if they did not themselves get the stocks moving, they would run in to trouble. I did not specify the trouble but if necessary I proposed, if the Municipal Council agreed, to get an order issued that any flour not sold by a certain date must be sold to the Council. But no further measures were required. The Mayor removed the price control and prices, instead of rising, immediately dropped. The flour guild had been alarmed just sufficiently to see that, if they did not co-operate, they would lose out. The flour began to move out of the concession at the desired rate. New orders were placed abroad and the situation righted itself.

Stoppage of Fresh Foodstuffs

Life in the concession was never without excitement. In the early spring prices in the fresh food markets suddenly began to jump without apparent reason. Enquiry showed that food trucks were being held up at the barrier. They were not being stopped, Oh, no! They merely waited their turn for examination and that was very thorough; a sack of potatoes, for instance, would have to be emptied in the road and then repacked. This by the bye was a favourite method. In the early days of the blockade milk receptacles would be opened and kept for a couple of hours until the milk turned in the hot summer sun. Well, this trouble was straightened out and the Municipal Council was allowed to send two large trucks a day to bring in food-stuffs and the trucks were passed without delay – except when the guard was disgruntled and held a truck up on some frivolous pretext. Meanwhile the blockade carried on its weary way.

Examination of Goods

This examination of goods at the barriers, though only a source of danger in the instances I have mentioned, was the cause of irritation and serious loss to merchants. Imagine how wearisome Customs examination proves on occasion, even when the Customs officer is as anxious as you are to get it over. But imagine how far more vexatious if it were his constant aim and endeavour to prevent you taking in anything that would be of use to you and you will get an idea of the intolerable burden of the barriers. Most of the produce arriving from the interior at Tientsin for export has to be carefully inspected and sorted or processed before it can be exported. None of this produce was allowed to pass the barrier. Complaints were useless; they would, after endless delays, be passed on to the military who would, several weeks later, reply that such and such an article was not being stopped but it was subject to control and a special permit was necessary in each case to move it. When the permit was applied for, it was not forthcoming: the officer in charge of that section was in Peking and it was not certain when he would be back; the form of application had been wrongly made out; a prior permit from another section was necessary and so on and so forth. To such lengths were these embargoes carried out that a bag of oranges would be confiscated, a piece of cloth would be taboo because textiles were on the control list, etc., etc.

Bribery at Barriers

At barriers at which trucks could enter, a line stretched for half to a mile and a half. The drivers frequently jacked up the wheels to save the tyres and left them for days at a time. And yet goods came through – at a price. As the blockade continued, a 'racket' grew up. Newspapers abroad reported it and questions were asked in the House of Commons. The Japanese authorities indignantly denied it and the whole question became a source of embarrassment to me. Whenever accusations were made abroad, the military took it out on the hide of the unfortunate British resident (I have mentioned earlier that the severity of the system increased whenever something occurred to arouse the ire of our gaolers). The only thing I could do was to soft-pedal publicity. Why anger the Japanese military by exposing a situation which would not be remedied and would in fact be made worse since military headquarters maintained that there was no bribery and corruption and reacted violently to any statement that there was? Unfortunately, though I am absolutely convinced that it existed, it was in the nature of things impossible to produce proof.

The racket was worked in the following manner. I have referred to the line of trucks outside the barriers. It was esti-mated that ten to twenty days were required to reach the barrier and even then there was no guarantee that the truck's contents would be allowed through. But some truck companies would make a bargain with their clients: if the client would pay ten day's demurrage at fifteen dollars a day, then the company would carry the loss if the truck were held up more than ten days while the client, in return, would not ask for any portion of his one hundred and fifty dollars if the truck came through in less than ten days. On the face of it, this was a legitimate business risk, legal and above-board. Actually the terms of the contract were pure subterfuge. The client knew that if he paid his hundred and fifty dollars (or more in the case of a valuable cargo), his goods would come through in a few days. How did this happen? There could be only one explanation. The so-called demurrage money was used in bribing those who had it in their power to stop the goods coming through.

It was impossible to produce proof. Those who paid the money admitted doing so but were naturally unwilling to come forward and give evidence nor would it have availed if they had done so. The contract was never committed to paper and the system was worked entirely by Chinese brokers who took the money on a verbal understanding. Exactly who got it is uncertain. The most likely supposition is that it was paid to the Chinese policemen who worked under the Japanese soldiers at the barriers. It is incredible, however, that the latter did not get their share for the policemen had no powers to pass the trucks; that was entirely under the control of the soldiers. Nor does it seem probable that those higher up were ignorant of what was going on. How high the corruption went it is impossible to say. The public generally were inclined to think that the whole system was organised by the Japanese army to secure funds to meet its enormous expenses. For myself, I do not believe this. I think that the money went into private pockets and that it was organised by officers directly responsible for the barrier posts or that the Chinese, who worked the racket, suggested the scheme and the Japanese concerned found the temptation irresistible.

In small matters a bribe of one or two dollars to the Chinese policemen generally worked. Tientsin residents who had been up to Peking for the week-end would put the money at the top of their suit-case. When their car got into the compound, they would get out and the cars and the luggage would be examined. In a few minutes the car would be passed and they would proceed home but the money would be no longer in the suit-case. Similarly, Chinese would stroll along the line of waiting Chinese outside the barriers: a few dollars would ensure rapid promotion in the queue.

During the height of the coal shortage it was possible to buy a limited quantity of coal in the French concession from a certain merchant at one hundred dollars a ton (the correct price being about twenty dollars). The merchant himself was quite open about it when I discussed the subject with him later. The difference of eighty dollars went in bribes to the right quarter. He maintained that the greater part of the money went to a certain military unit. I had no means of checking the statement and had no desire to do so. I know from his own lips that he got the coal and I knew persons who had bought or had had the opportunity of buying the coal.

Raising of Barriers

While the British concession was enduring the blockade with what patience it could muster, negotiations were proceeding between the British and Japanese Government. It is not for me to discuss these negotiations which were conducted on our behalf with the greatest skill, resource and courage by Sir Robert Craigie, our Ambassador in Tokyo. One of the causes of the long delay in reaching a final agreement was the necessity of obtaining the consent of the Chungking[140] Government to the silver compromise. This was finally obtained and on June 20th, 1940, the blockade was raised.

There had been a number of false rumours since the end of 1939 that the barriers were going and when they actually went, British and Chinese residents were inclined to be sceptical, the more so since the Tokyo agreement was bilateral and the published sections contained no actual guarantee that the barriers would be lifted. I have said some hard things about the Japanese army in the preceding pages and it is pleasant to give a word of praise. There were no half measures about the raising of the blockade. Punctually at 6 p.m. the barriers went down and, what

---

[140]   Chungking (Chongqing) is a major city in Southwest China and one of the five national central cities in China. During the Second Sino-Japanese War (1937–1945) it was Generalissimo Chiang Kai-shek's provisional capital.

was just as important, the examination at the DKK was ended though details of the examination at the British bund by British officials with the co-operation of Japanese gendarmes, as provided in the agreement, had yet to be worked out. Reluctance on the part of the Japanese army to bind itself down to a fixed time within which to remove the barbed wire had also aroused some suspicion but work was started immediately and the wires disappeared entirely in a few days. Thereafter the presence at the former Japanese Consulate General on Victoria Road of Japanese gendarmes, charged with the duty of assisting the British Municipal Police when raids were required and their tendency to carry out unauthorised intelligence work in the concession as well as to usurp the duties of the Customs officers in ships' inspection at the Bund caused hitches from time to time, but it is fair to state that the Japanese army carried out the terms of the agreement not only in the letter but also in the spirit.

The blockade had been a tragic blunder. It is easy to be wise after the event but there can be little doubt that the Japanese would never have instituted it if the concessions which were made later by the British Government had been made earlier. The quarrel arose over the demand for surrender of the four accused men but once the blockade started the Japanese increased their demands and in particular made it a condition that the silver should be surrendered but owing to patience and skilful negotiation these demands were whittled down and the claim that the whole of the silver should be handed over was replaced by the compromise that one tenth should be used for relief purposes, a solution to which the Chinese Government consented, though grudgingly. It is remarkable to say, therefore, that the British Government gained nothing by refusing to compromise at the beginning and the Japanese Government gained nothing by resorting to military tactics. If we concede the one hundred thousand pounds from the silver in the British concession and a similar amount (two hundred thousand pounds) from the French concession as a gain, we have to count on the debit side the cost of maintaining the blockade for a whole year, not to speak of the gigantic loss to North China for it is impossible to disrupt and disorganise the economic system of a province by isolating a principal section of that system without causing loss all round.

Appreciation of British Community

The unfortunate residents of the British concession were forced to suffer through no fault of their own. For a whole year British and Chinese were only allowed to go in and out under humiliating conditions, their necessities of life were obtained on sufferance and more than once they were on the brink of disaster, their trade was stopped and they were subjected to the mental strain of being cooped up like birds in a cage. But the British community never faltered in their philosophic acceptance of the situation. They took the hard knocks that were coming to them and stood up for more without murmuring and without complaining. I had the privilege of holding the post of Consul-General during eight months of the blockade and I have nothing but admiration for the spirit shown by the Tientsin British. The local Chinese accepted the situation with their usual stoicism. The American community were spared the humiliations imposed on the British subjects at the barriers but for the rest they had to put up with the same restrictions. Incensed as they were at the restrictions which we all had to endure, they co-operated wholeheartedly in the measures taken by the British authorities. There were also other nationals in fair number in the British concession – French, Belgian, Dutch. I think that they all recognised the difficulties that we were up against and only asked that they should be treated as well as the other residents, which of course they were. If the blockade had its melancholy side, it leaves in my mind a pleasant memory of a public-spirited, high-minded community facing adversity with courage and common-sense.

Sealing up the Silver

It fell to me to put into effect, in collaboration with Mr Muto, the silver agreement. This provided that the silver was to be sealed up after the equivalent of one hundred thousand pounds had been taken out, to be used for purposes of relief. It was unfortunate that a definite number of dollars had not been mentioned. The silver dollar was no longer current and had no fixed value. Its value depended on the silver content and the price that the silver would command at a given moment. The silver content of different issues was known but the silver stored in the British concession had not been sorted and no one knew how many dollars of each particular issue there were. To add to the difficulty, the term 'equivalent of one hundred thousand pounds' could be variously interpreted. The Chungking Government, naturally anxious to conserve as much as possible of its silver reserves, wished to read it as meaning silver to the value of a hundred thousand pounds *in Tientsin*. But it was the clear intention of the agreement that sufficient silver should be taken to buy a hundred thousand pounds of supplies for purposes of flood relief. There was no market in Tientsin and it was logical, therefore, to read the agreement as meaning sufficient silver to produce a hundred thousand pounds at some place where there was a market, in this case Bombay. This meant that allowance must be made for shipping, insurance and other charges. This was the view taken by the British Government and was the interpretation that I, therefore, adopted. It did not, of course, settle the vexed question of the exact quantity but on my suggestion an approximate equivalent (1,500,000 dollars) was taken, the exact amount to be calculated and adjusted later. The manager of the Chinese Bank of Communications, in whose vaults the silver was stored, agreed to this compromise and we proceeded with the work.

The silver was stored below the offices of the British Consulate. This was a pure coincidence due to the fact that the Consulate had rented the ground floor of the premises belonging to, and formerly occupied by, the Bank of Communications but it gave me a curious feeling of being responsible for the silver. What if it had been spirited away? Common sense replied that it was far too bulky to be moved out secretly but one or two hauls of silver made by our police from would-be smugglers kept my uneasiness alive. However, the silver was there all right as we found.

On the appointed day there was a formidable array of officials. The manager of the Bank of Communications was present with his staff. Next came Mr Muto. By arrangement he and I had appointed the Managers of the Yokohama Specie Bank[141] and the Chartered Bank[142] to advise us in working out details and to attend to the actual operation and here I wish to record my gratitude to Mr Hyslop whose loyal co-operation, experience and ability guided me through the many pitfalls awaiting the layman who dabbles in banking problems. The bankers were assisted by shroffs and coolies and, of course, gendarmes and police were in full force.

The silver was stored in two inner vaults in the basement. We were able to see into the smaller one as the wooden grill left a space open at the top. Originally the silver had been packed in thousands in gunny bags. We could see that those at the bottom had rotted in the flood and spilled their contents on to the floor but bags on top were intact and we hoped to get fifteen hundred of these bags which would give us the 1,500,000 dollars required. The vault was therefore opened up and the coolies started bringing out the bags. But our hopes of an early solution faded when the supply of intact bags gave out. We then decided to try our luck with the other vault. This was closed by a heavy iron door so there was no means of telling in what state the bags were inside. The lock had rusted up and a locksmith had to be obtained to open it. It opened inwards or should have done but it had to be forced with a battering-ram. Finally enough space was opened to enable me to squeeze inside. There an amazing sight met my eyes. Flood damage here was far more serious and practically all the bags had rotted. Such of the gunny as remained had sprouted fungus and interspersed with the silver dollars, which had cascaded over the floor, were growths of what looked like wool. As the others joined me we climbed over a crumbling hill of dollars worth the best part of a million pounds.

---

[141] Yokohama Specie Bank was founded in Yokohama, Japan in 1880. It became The Bank of Tokyo, Ltd. in 1947. The bank played a significant role in Japanese trade with China.

[142] Now the Standard Chartered Bank.

Our hopes of getting fifteen hundred bags had gone and we decided to close up this vault. A coolie had to be summoned to shovel away the dollars that had flowed down round the door, no light task since as fast as the coins were cleared at any spot, fresh coins would come sliding down. It was a curious sight to see this coolie, working at wages of a dollar a day at the outside, nonchalantly throwing aside shovelfuls of, say, five hundred dollars at a time for all the world like a navvy throwing mud and dirt out of a trench that he is excavating.

Short cuts had proved impossible and we adopted the only other alternative. The coins in the smaller vault were loaded into trays, carried into a room in the basement, counted into hundreds and packed into cases made for the purpose which were then taken and stored temporarily in the vaults of the Chartered Bank. The operation took the best part of a fortnight. Then early one morning the cases were loaded on a lighter which was escorted down the river to Tangku where the cases were transhipped to a Japanese Bombay liner. I heaved a sigh of relief when I heard the silver had actually been received in Bombay. The proceeds were used to buy Australian flour which was used as relief of sufferers from flood and drought but that is another story into which I do not propose to enter here.

Life in Tientsin

After the barriers were lifted, life in Tientsin settled down to something approaching normal. Compared with Mukden we found Tientsin ideal. It boasts a moderately good climate. High winds, particularly in the spring, are trying, whisking along clouds of local dust and of sand brought from the Gobi desert, so that after a gale from the north-west the air is impregnated with fine particles of dust; it has even been known to rain or sleet mud. The summer is unpleasantly hot until the latter part of August and those who can manage to get away dash off to the seaside resort of Peitaibo,[143] about four hours distant by train.

---

[143]   Peitaiho (Beidaihe) is a popular beach resort on China's Bohai Sea coast. It has a coastline of 22.5 km and is also known as a birding haven.

But for the rest the climate is bright and sunny and even in the winter, which is severe, the sun on a still day compensates for the cold. Most of the sport at Tientsin is concentrated at the combined Race and Country Club when, according to the season and to your inclination, you can get riding, polo, tennis, bowling, badminton, rowing, swimming, walking and skating. The grounds are lovely but the flood in 1939 killed off the flowering trees and temporarily converted them into a wilderness which, however, a few years should see restored to its former beauty. The Tientsin community is a very friendly one and I believe that in normal times life is very gay for those that like social entertainment but in 1940 we felt that this was no time for wild gaiety and concentrated on our local war effort. The British Women's Association, presided over by my wife, worked hard at knitting and preparing comforts for the fighting forces and bombed-out victims at home and the men rallied round the various drives to raise funds, first for the Lord Mayor's Fund and later for the China War Fund centred in Shanghai.

Administration of British Concession

Although the excitement of the barriers was removed, Consular work remained interesting. In internal matters the Municipal Council has full powers but since the concession is only one part of Greater Tientsin, its administration is bound to affect the other administrative areas and since external relations are in the hands of the Consul-General, few important matters could be decided without reference to the latter. The powers of the Consul-General are not clearly defined but are inherent in the constitution of the concession, itself a growth partly of Treaty right and partly of circumstances that have modified with the course of years. He is, or should be, the guide, philosopher and friend of the Council, able to influence it for what he considers its good but with no actual power to initiate action. The system has its defects as well as its qualities. When the Consul-General and the Council see eye to eye, the system is at its best but the former is, as it were, a divided personality. In external matters he is the representative of the Council but as a Consular official he is under the orders of the Ambassador to China and of the Foreign Office and situations may arise, and indeed had arisen in recent times, where action that seemed locally to be in the best interests of the concession would have run counter, or seemed to run counter, to British interests elsewhere. I think myself that where the Council wished to act within the scope of the powers that it is supposed to enjoy, it should have been allowed to do so. It is true that its powers have been given to it by the British Government under King's Regulations and that those powers could be modified or abolished by new regulations but just as it is foolish to give power to an attorney and then to interfere with his use of it, so it is dangerous to give autonomy to a community and then to veto action that it wishes to take in the exercise of the power given to it. There, in a nut-shell, is the cause of the final split with local authorities that ended in the blockade. I am harking back to history past before my time but the lesson is a useful one for the future. I was fortunate enough to find the local authorities in a more conciliatory frame of mind and once they had realised that it was not my aim merely to oppose them but to co-operate whenever the interests of Tientsin seemed to require co-operation, friction was reduced to a minimum.

I should like to record my gratitude to many leading British residents for their whole-hearted support but if I started to make a list I should fear to leave out names worthy of mention. It may not be invidious however to mention three names. When I arrived in Tientsin, Mr A. E. Tipper CBE[144] was Chairman of the Council and had been so for a number of years. A retired business man who public-spiritedly laboured for the good of the community, Mr Tipper is justly beloved not only for his public

---

144   A. E. Tipper had been in Tianjin since at least 1912 and worked in insurance before his retirement. In June 1939 he gave an interview on Japanese-induced food shortages in the city to Reuters that was published in the Singapore *Straits Times* 21 June 1939. See http://eresources.nlb. gov.sg/newspapers/Digitised/Article/straitstimes19390621-1.2.34.aspx (accessed 13 July 2016). See also entries in various yearbooks 1912–1939.

services but for his character also. Shrewd, level-headed, unemotional but candid and outspoken, Mr Tipper led the council through a number of troubled years and earned the respect of the whole community. He was succeeded in 1940 by Mr Turner.[145] Also a business man, he has a profound insight into oriental psychology and, to my mind, tackled the problems that arose that year, notably the police strike, tactfully and wisely. The third name is that of Mr P. H. B. Kent, OBE MC.[146] One of the oldest residents of Tientsin, a lawyer by profession, Mr Kent early interested himself in public matters. For years he has been Chairman of the China Association Tientsin Branch and of the Associated British Committee. Without axe to grind, he has proved himself an able, disinterested and hard-working servant of the public, whose name should rank high in the annals of the concession.

Volunteers and Auxiliaries

I should mention also the Tientsin Volunteers and Auxiliaries. The Volunteers did yeoman service in assisting the regulars in the defence of Tientsin against the Boxers in 1900 and it was a volunteer, the late James Watts, who made the historic ride to Taku through the Boxer lines in order to bring word to the allied forces at the mouth of the river of the dire straits of the beleaguered Tientsin community. Thereafter in times of stress the volunteers have come forward for the maintenance of law and order. When, in the summer of 1940, the last detachment of British soldiers in Tientsin was withdrawn, it was clear that an added responsibility had been thrust on the shoulders of the

---

[145] No trace found.

[146] Percy Horace Braund Kent (1876–1963). He was educated at Rugby and Oxford. Called to the Bar, he practised law at Tianjin before the First World War. He was in the Scots Guards in the First World War and retired as a captain in 1920. He then returned to Tianjin and worked for the law firm of Kent and Mounsey. As well as being active in the local Branch of the China Association, he wrote a number of books about China. Supplement to the *London Gazette*, 19 August 1920, p. 8589; Obituary, *Journal of the Royal Central Asian Society,* vol. 50, no. 2 (1963), pp. 210–11.

volunteers. Then also we had the auxiliaries to turn to in time of need. This corps is formed of the senior men who are somewhat too old for the more strenuous work but make up in experience for anything they may lack in powers of physical endurance. A large proportion had served through the Great War and many of them had held high rank. Between them the volunteers with their youth and excellent training and the auxiliaries with their grit and experience formed two fine corps that mutually supplemented the other. In numbers they were small – a little over two hundred all told – but at a conference held early in 1940 it was recognised that the corps could not be used against regular troops. Their role was to maintain order in time of emergency and in order to fulfil this duty the auxiliaries were re-organized as special constables.

Police Strike

It was well that provisional arrangements had been made for the call came suddenly one evening in the autumn of 1940 when our Chinese police went on strike without previous warning. At 5 p.m. when one section went off duty, the incoming section refused to go on duty and in a short time the streets were empty of police. Both the volunteers and the auxiliaries were at once mobilised, the volunteers on hand at their barracks to quell any rioting that might take place and the auxiliaries to take over police duties. When I made a tour of the concession after dinner I found the auxiliaries manning all key points and as far as their numbers would permit, patrolling all important streets. The measures taken were sufficient to impress the Chinese populace and the concession was quiet and peaceful all night. In the meantime, Mr Turner and the Vice-Chairman, Mr Chwang,[147]

---

[147]   Probably the J. S. Chwang listed as a member of the council in 1937. His Chinese name was Zhuang Yuefeng but he was also known as Zhuangren Song (1973–1949), which in the Wade-Giles transliteration would have been Jungren Sung. Before the 1911 Revolution, he was a local government foreign affairs officer in Tianjin, and later a businessman and Rotarian, Chinese Wikipedia entry (accessed 13 July 2016).

had met the strikers, had listened to their grievances and had promised to give them sympathetic consideration. In the morning the police returned to duty.

Though the strike was inexcusable, the Chinese police had grounds for discontent; the cost of living had gone up and wages had not kept pace. The Council were already studying the question but they had perhaps been a little slow and they had tackled charges of corruption separately instead of treating the question as one whole. This problem of corruption is a thorny one. Chinese police expect presents on special occasions – New Year, weddings, festivals and, in general, any occasion where they are called on to perform duties outside their routine duties. Most leading citizens pay these 'cumshaws' gladly, not as a bribe to cover wrongdoing but as a reward for extra zeal. It is, however, difficult to draw the line and there is a tendency on the part of the police to demand presents, a tendency which if unchecked grows rapidly into serious exactions. At the time of the strike, the police were uneasy at the prospect of their outside 'earnings' being stopped at a time when they felt that they had no certainty of higher wages. The Council now acted promptly and offered a new scale of wages which was accepted and there was no more talk of strike.

In the nature of the case the principal burden had fallen on the auxiliaries. The efficiency they showed reflects credit on their commanding officer, Mr Capstick,[148] and his staff. From the manner in which the specials went on duty and maintained order one might have thought they did it every day of their lives instead of sitting at their office desks. There can be no doubt that their quiet efficiency played a great part in inducing a more reasonable attitude of the strikers and in restraining members of the populace that might otherwise have seen an excellent oppor-

---

[148]   A. E. Capstick, educated at Manchester Grammar School. He was a member of the Territorial Army and went to Tianjin before 1914. During the First World War, he was an officer in the Manchester Regiment, reaching the rank of captian and being mentioned in despatches. www.worldwar1schoolarchives.org/wp-content/.../ULULA_1915_02.pdf and www.worldwar1schoolarchives.org/wp-content/.../ULULA_1918_10.pdf (accessed 13 July 2016).

tunity of looting. In the background were the volunteers ready to step in if necessary. Both these corps, the volunteers under Mr Ridler[149] and the auxiliaries under Mr Capstick, had deserved well of the community and it is a pleasure to me to add my little word of appreciation.

Thoughts on the Future of the Concession

A frequent reason for the decay of human institutions is the failure of those responsible for their operation to adapt them to changing conditions. The prime cause of the troubles recently encountered by the foreign concessions and settlements in China has been the iconoclasm of the Japanese army, impatient as it is of the least restraint on its liberty of action. But the impact of the collision would have been less severe if reforms that were overdue had been adopted in good time. I had actual experience only of the British concession at Tientsin but the lessons to be gained from the crisis that it weathered were plain to read.

There had been times when the policy it followed in regard to matters affecting the whole area was not merely in direct opposition to that of the Japanese authorities – that was probably inevitable – but was also at variance with that of the French concession whose interests were identical with those of the British concession. Thus a black-out requested by the Japanese military authorities was agreed to by the French authorities but not by the British so that while the rest of the area was blacked out, the British municipal area remained brilliantly lit up. The reason given for this refusal to co-operate – that hostile airmen who had no quarrel with the foreign concessions would be enabled to avoid damaging them – was logical but it betrayed what to my mind is a wrong conception of the duties of a foreign concession.

A foreign concession in China is not an independent unit. It is an area of Chinese soil the *internal* administration of which has been delegated to a foreign power, the government of which

---

[149] Possibly W. Ridler, who attended a council meeting in 1937. No further details.

has, in turn, transferred it to the local municipal council of the area. To say so is to enunciate a platitude and yet, in practice, this obvious principle was frequently ignored. The practice of affording asylum to political refugees, while it was in accord with British ideals, was a clear infringement of Chinese sovereignty. The tendency to consider problems that arose, such as that of the black-out just quoted, not in their bearing on the interests of the whole area but solely in their effect on the supposed interests of the concession, betrayed forgetfulness of the fact that the concession was not an independent unit existing *in vacuo* but part and parcel of the whole administrative area. Finally, refusal to have any truck with the puppet administration set up locally, on the ground that it was not the *de jure* administration, could only have been successfully maintained if the concession had actually been a sovereign power since the *de jure* government had been forced to abandon the whole of north China.

A pause must be made here to clear up one point. The foregoing remarks may seem to suggest that Great Britain, in common with other foreign powers, had wantonly usurped Chinese rights. Such was not the case. Sovereignty must be not only just but effective and the Chinese central government, while satisfying the first requisite, had not satisfied the second. Even before the overthrow of the Manchu dynasty, the control over provincial governments weakened in proportion to their distance from Peking but after the revolution China temporarily split up into a number of petty kingdoms seized by petty war-lords whose allegiance to Peking was purely nominal. The central government also was at the mercy of the soldier and was seized again and again by those who were temporarily in the ascendant and fancied their turn had come to swoop down on Peking and snatch the reins of government. During the troubled years between the formation of the so-called Republic[150] and the rise of Chiang Kai Shek the country was in chaos and local administrations were

---

[150]   The last imperial dynasty of China, the *Qing* (Manchu dynasty), ruled from 1644 to 1912. This multi-cultural empire formed the territorial base for the modern Chinese state. Its collapse was followed by the Republic of China, lasting from 1912 to 1949. Chiang Kai-shek was the leader of the Republic from 1928.

forced to act by the law of expediency since abstract theories would not have worked; it was all very well to say that rights of sovereignty rested in the Chinese government but if the Chinese government was recognisable, its fiat did not run.

Rights assumed, then, by the concessions were not justified by treaty but were forced on them by circumstances. It is one thing for a settled government to demand the surrender of a refugee fleeing from justice. It is another thing when he is fleeing from the results of a military *coup-d'état*, itself liable to be overturned tomorrow by the next military combination. Government had degenerated into a game of war and temporary dictators toppled over almost as soon as they had set themselves up. The concessions at such times were recognised by all sides as sanctuaries; if the refugee reached them, he was safe.

A second problem was, and is, the presence in the concession of large number of Chinese residents. This was never intended in the original treaties for the concessions were areas set apart by the Chinese government for the exclusive use of the, to them undesirable, foreigner. But the early concessions proved inadequate and adjacent land was added. The resulting area was, in reality, no longer a concession but a 'municipal area'. Chinese flocked in to take up residence until the Chinese residents far outnumbered the foreigner. Their presence soon gave rise to many delicate problems. The Chinese residents were under Chinese jurisdiction but the machinery for enforcing this jurisdiction was wanting. To allow Chinese government servants – police, taxation officials, etc. – to operate would not only create endless confusion but would undermine rights of self-government. A compromise was adopted under which Chinese accused of crime by their courts would be arrested by the municipal police and handed over for trial. Strictly speaking, such surrender should have been unconditional since the accused were Chinese subjects and it is not the business of other authorities to enquire whether their laws are just or have been actually contravened in a particular case. But, here again, to hand over without question any and every Chinese 'wanted' by Chinese authorities would have opened the door to abuse and made a farce of the self-government of the municipal area. So by established usage accused were surrendered only after the warrant issued by the Chinese court had been scrutinised and counter-signed by the Consul. Such scrutiny must, in the nature of things, be perfunctory but it proved a check of sorts on mischievous abuse of municipal rights. (It may be added in parenthesis that Chinese residents discovered by the municipal police breaking the peace were also handed over to the Chinese courts for trial.)

Other instances could be given of infringements of Chinese sovereignty but enough has been said to show that they were not due to any arrogant usurpation of rights but arose inevitably out of the anomaly of foreign concessions and extra-territoriality which are themselves an infringement of Chinese sovereignty. But though friction arose, the system worked well enough until the Japanese army overran Chinese territory. The machinery devised to meet one set of conditions then proved unsuitable to meet the requirements of an entirely new set. For all its ineffi-ciency Chinese administration received the willing acquiescence of the people. I will not say their support for the Chinese private citizen is apathetic. But the Japanese army was in the midst of an inwardly-hostile populace whose sympathies were entirely with any anti-Japanese activities.

The duty of the British Municipal Authorities at such a time was clear. It was, as far as possible normally, to carry on the inter-nal administration and to maintain law and order in the area. Since the municipal area had no sovereign rights, its authori-ties were not concerned in the question who should administer Tientsin city itself. It was not for them to say to the new mayor of the city, 'You were not put there by the rightful Chinese gov-ernment, you are merely a puppet show set up by an aggressor, for us you do not exist.' To do it justice, the British Municipal Council did nothing so foolish. Its attitude was perfectly correct: it did not concern itself with politics. But as events proved, it was between two fires.

Theoretically, the duties of the council are entirely domes-tic. Actually, they are not. To use a common analogy, just as an organ in the human body draws its life's blood from outside and has to confirm its functions to the needs of the whole body, so the life of the concession was bound up with that of the whole Tientsin area. The solution of any problem affecting its internal administration either directly concerned the administration of Tientsin or indirectly would react on it in the immediate future. This was where the trouble lay, for the council was not a free agent. Its external relations were in the hands of the British Consul-General, who acted under the instructions of the British Ambassador, himself in turn under the instructions of the British Government. The Council might, for instance, wish to hand over an accused Chinese to his Court of Justice but the actual transfer needed the sanction of the British Consul-General and, if he withheld sanction, it could not take place. Even if the Council wished to solve the dilemma by expelling the Chinese it could hardly do so in the face of the expressed disapproval of the Consul. The fact is that, though autonomous in name, the municipal area was under the control of the British Government.

The system under which the British Government passed on to the Council the powers of self-government and then interfered in the Council's use of them no doubt had its merits in normal times since the Council is likely to be swayed by local considerations and by its actions to embarrass the British Ambassador in his relations with the Chinese Government. But in the peculiar situation that had arisen, *it was precisely the local considerations that should have been the determining factor* since the Government to which the Ambassador was accredited, though the rightful government, was not at the moment the *de facto* government of the area. No sooner was the Ambassador brought into a question than political considerations would come into play. The Chinese Government would demand that no action should be taken by the British concession that was calculated to assist the Japanese aggressor in consolidating his position. What locally was a matter of maintaining law and order became, when viewed in Chungking, a matter of collaborating with, aiding and abetting, the aggressor.

That was the main cause of the trouble that ensued. A less obvious cause, however, added to the friction that laid the train of the explosion. This was the lack of cohesion between the foreign concessions. It was not to be expected that the British, French and Italian concession authorities would see eye to eye with the Japanese concession authorities but unity between the first three in the days before the outbreak of the present war was not outside the range of possibility. And yet I have mentioned one instance in which the British concession was out of step even with its immediate neighbour the French concession. Though it was apparently not realised by the British authorities at the time, the black-out incident caused the bitterest resentment among the Japanese and the fact that the British alone stood out in opposition while the other two concessions, whose interests were identical, co-operated convinced the Japanese that the British opposition was deliberate obstruction. This conviction grew until, at the finish, the unreasoning fury of the Japanese was directed almost entirely against the British.

I cannot resist the conclusion that this tendency to independent action may be traced to a gradual forgetting of the essential inter-dependence of all the units – foreign concessions and the Chinese municipality – that go to make up Tientsin. Reliance when in doubt, on the guidance of the British Ambassador was an essential part of the system but it obscured a clear view of the equally great need of unity of action among the foreign concessions and ultimately led to the isolation of the British concession.

The remedy, to my mind, lies in the discarding, wherever it proves necessary, of usages which were not guaranteed by treaty but were an outgrowth of conditions that have passed and in a recognition of the principle that the administrative units of the area must 'hang together or be hanged separately', in other words, that problems affecting the whole area must be treated not from the selfish point of view of the supposed interests of one concession but from the broader view point of the interests of the whole area. This attitude involves a good deal of give and take but it does not involve any ignoble surrender of rights. It means that the units should be equal partners in a common enterprise and if the good of the whole community calls for some small sacrifice by one in the interests of all, then the sacrifice may well be made. During my tenure of the post of Consul-General at Tientsin it was my constant, and I think not unsuccessful, ambition to prove that a concession could be administered in such a way that it was not a stumbling block in the eyes of the superior authorities but an asset, a source of profit to the country in which it was situated.

Chapter 16

ANGLO-JAPANESE RELATIONS

ॐ

Note: I wrote this chapter in the summer of 1941 while on leave in Canada. Now that we are at war with Japan, it is out of date but I leave it as my own impression of the conditions that led up to the war. It is true that the first blow was struck against the US and that we ourselves then declared war but until it became clear that the US and Great Britain were going to stand shoulder-to-shoulder in opposing Japan, it was the latter that Japan regarded as the main stumbling-block in the path of her progress.

HAVING SERVED THE whole of my official life in Japan or in territories under her dominion or control, I may be forgiven for holding very definite opinions on the subject of Anglo-Japanese relations and the manner in which we have handled them in recent years. The views I have formed are not, I believe, generally held and since I am not so conceited as to think everyone is blind except myself, I put them forward with some diffidence as a contribution, shall we say, to a study of the problem.

I begin with certain quotations from Sir Austen Chamberlain:[151]

It seems that we are becoming the scold of Europe. We run about shaking our fists in people's faces, screaming that this must be altered and that that must stop. We get ourselves disliked and distrusted and misunderstood, and in the end we achieve nothing and relapse

---

[151] British politician – see D. J. Dutton, 'Chamberlain, Sir (Joseph) Austen (1863–1937)', *Oxford Dictionary of National Biography*, Oxford University Press, 2004; online edn, September 2013. http://www.oxforddnb.com/view/article/32351 (accessed 13 July 2016)

into humiliated silence or laboriously explain how pleased we are. Curzon is convinced that all is well if he delivers an oration or pens a 'superior' despatch.

Do not repeat in this matter the mistake of the Curzon despatch – a great opening, a pause and then nothing.

(Extracts from letters written by Austen to Neville Chamberlain in September and October 1923, quoted in *The Life and Letters of the Rt Hon Sir Austen Chamberlain* by Petrie, pp. 227 and 229).

We decide the practical questions of daily life by instinct rather than by any careful process of reasoning, by rule of thumb rather than by systematic logic. The Frenchman, trusting thought, endeavours to foresee every case and to regulate every action in advance; the Englishman, distrusting the purely intellectual and more conscious of the many accidents of winds and tide, trusts to his experience to inspire the right act at the critical moment and varies his course with the shifting of the winds.

(Extract from an address at Chatham House on 'Great Britain as a European Power', ibid. p. 373).

The two letters from which I have quoted were written during Sir Austen's temporary retirement when he was able to look on the political scene from the outside. I think perhaps that he did not realise that it was not only in that particular period of our history that we were earning unpopularity by our methods but that the faults on which he laid his finger have appeared all too often and that in fact they are the necessary result of the proneness to trust to rule of thumb rather than to logic to which he referred in his Chatham House speech.

In the Far East we have, I think, been displaying the defects as well as the qualities of our system for a long time past.

When they refer to Great Britain the Japanese newspapers usually prefix an adjective for which there is no satisfactory one-word translation. It means, roughly, old and cunning. Great Britain apparently has acquired from long experience a technique of her own in world politics. She uses other nations to further

her own selfish ends. Her support of China is dictated not by any love of that country but by the desire to get her to oppose Japan. She plays off one country against another, allies herself with Japan to weaken Russia and to safeguard her interests in the Far East then, at the bidding of the United States, flings aside Japan like a worn-out glove, stirs up Poland and, through that country, France, to fight Germany and then callously stands aside and watches them defeated. Now that Germany directs her might against Great Britain she turns to the United States and trusts to the latter to save her from her doom. In a word, she is a past-master in the arts of Machiavelli, prefers to let other countries fight her battles for her, whether diplomatic or military but sooner or later will pay the penalty for her misdeeds and will go down in ruins.

This is not entirely a newspaper cliché. I have referred elsewhere to a Japanese, afterwards a Cabinet Minister, who was called to order at a Rotary meting for attacking Great Britain. He used just this adjective of which I am speaking. In fact it has come to be almost a part of our title, just as the French use to speak of 'perfidious Albion' and as we speak of our 'gallant forces', the 'silent service', and used to speak of the 'unspeakable Turk'. There is a note also of unwilling admiration in it as who should say, 'Why cannot Japanese diplomats display similar skill and craft?'

To an Englishman, compelled to read such a curious travesty of British motives and tactics, all this makes disconcerting reading. How do we come to acquire this unsavoury reputation? I think that in a way we are ourselves to blame. Japan, and no doubt other nations, refuse to believe that it is the British habit to take problems as they come and endeavour to settle them on their own merits. When they find Great Britain backing one country one day and blocking it the next, they cannot credit the fact that in the first case we supported the country because we thought her in the right, and in the second withstood her because we thought her in the wrong or judged that she was misusing our support. Our old doctrine of the balance of power, our opportunism, our tendency to range ourselves in recent years on the side of lost causes and then regretfully watch them go under, all give the impression to outsiders that we are unprincipled.

When Japan withdrew from the League of Nations there was a distinct air of nervous tension in the country. Though British and American outspoken disapproval of the Manchurian incident had ended in words, the Japanese were still a little bit afraid that Great Britain might take action. When Italy attacked Ethiopia and Great Britain moved a strong fleet into the Mediterranean, Japan sat up and took notice. Great Britain at last was going to fight. Then followed the Hoare-Laval[152] fiasco and Japan decided that Great Britain was only bluffing. Over the China incident Great Britain has spoken out strongly but Japan has found that deeds have never followed words. Believing, curiously enough, in the justice of her cause, she has been irritated by British opposition but has never allowed it to cause her to swerve from her course.

I am not qualified to speak on our world policy but long residence in the Far East gives me some claim to discuss our actions there. I think that we have shown lack of foresight. We have drifted with the current, oblivious of the rocks ahead until they have loomed up right on our course. Only then have we improvised measures to avoid them. We have a policy, a very simple one, to maintain our established rights but no definite plans, no strategy and, as a result, the tactics we have devised at the eleventh hour have not been wisely chosen.

We have been slow to adapt ourselves to changing conditions. Our policy seems reasonable enough. We have no desire to encroach on other people's preserves but merely to retain our own. Unfortunately time never stands still. What we hold is exactly what others covet. In the Far East Japan wishes to take

---

152   The Hoare-Laval Pact was a December 1935 proposal by British Foreign Secretary Samuel Hoare and French Prime Minister Pierre Laval for ending the Second Italo-Abyssinian War. Italy had wanted to seize the independent nation of Abyssinia (Ethiopia) and to avenge an 1896 humiliating defeat. The Pact offered to partition Abyssinia, and thus achieve Italian dictator Benito Mussolini's goal of making Abyssinia an Italian colony. The proposal met hostile reaction in Britain and France, and never went into effect.

control and her ambitions strike right across British interests. Ever since the Great War it has been clear that our interests clashed and that we had to decide how best to meet the Japanese challenge.

Several courses were open to us. We might decide to oppose Japanese encroachment tooth and nail but in that case we had to decide what steps to take if, as was certain, Japan persisted. We might, for instance, have made common cause with the United States, whose interests were similarly threatened, laid our plans, possibly, for economic war with the proviso that, if this method failed, we must, if needs be, take up arms. If the United States were reluctant to commit themselves to this line of action, we had to decide whether we were strong enough to carry it out successfully alone. If not, then it would have been wiser to decide on compromise. I do not mean that we should have tried to make a bargain with Japan; I do not think that it would have worked. But, when Japan invaded China it was high time to take stock, to realise the weakness of our position and to decide what we could and what we could not preserve. Instead, we carried on as though we were still living in the good old days when a protest backed with a threat of action could carry the day. We continued to protest at each and every infringement of our vested rights and when our protests were brushed aside, we took it 'lying down'.

A good poker player does not make a habit of betting on busted flushes. He builds up a reputation of having the goods and only occasionally puts one across. But, watching our action in the Far East one could not resist the belief that we never look ahead. It is bad tactics to enter an emphatic protest unless one is prepared to take drastic action if it is rejected. The Tientsin incident is a case in point. We refused to hand over the 'four just men' and then, after the Japanese had established the blockade, we handed them over with the face-saving explanation that new evidence had come to light. But the Japanese on their side did not believe that we had at last been convinced that there was a prima facie case against the men. They believed that we had given way to a display of force and they concluded that the time was ripe for a settlement not only of this particular case but of all the local grievances that they nourished against us.

There is some truth in the criticism that we never forget and we never learn. Over the question of Tientsin His Majesty's Government took up a false position at the start. It maintained that the Japanese army was not an army in occupation since Japan herself had declared that she was not making war on China. It took action which implied the right to give sanctuary in the British concession to political refugees. The first contention was technically correct. The right of sanctuary was not tenable. (I have discussed this question in the last chapter.)

In the result we climbed down all along the line. A formula was devised that admitted the right of the Japanese army to take measures to ensure its safety and the principle of sanctuary was tacitly abandoned. We had gone out of our way to present a test case and exposed the essential weakness of our hand. How much better never to have forced the issue! That we did so was, I think, because we had allowed matters to drift and had not faced up to realities in good time. Similar events occurred in other parts of China and by 1940 we had seen a great part of the British heritage destroyed. I do not maintain that we could have maintained it indefinitely but we ourselves hastened the pace by refusing all compromise at the start.

At no time in the last thirty years has there been room for doubt as to Japan's aims. There have been times when she wavered but in the main she has been consistent. The Russo-Japanese War was fought, or so we were told at the time, to preserve the integrity of Corea and China. A few years after the war Japan annexed Corea. It is true that the Corean Government signed away their own independence but the men who made that treaty were the tools of the Japanese, the Quislings of those days. In South Manchuria, Japan set herself to develop the country by means of the South Manchuria Railway but she blocked all attempts of Great Britain and the United States to take a hand in the development of industry and trade. Japan's influence or control, call it what you will, was to be not only paramount but exclusive. All this was inevitable but it did not exactly square with Japan's protestations.

During the Great War Japan attempted to take another step forward. She seized the opportunity when the Powers' hands were tied to press the eleven demands on China[153] which would have put that country under her tutelage. She failed at that time because her proposals raised such an uproar that she judged it wiser to desist but thenceforward there could no longer be any doubt as to her aims. At Washington in 1921–1922, Japan was apparently checkmated. Tsingtao to which she had succeeded as a result of Germany's defeat was given back to China, the Anglo-Japanese Alliance was replaced by the fine-sounding but meaningless Four Power Pact and she had to agree to the 3-5-5 Navy.

Great Britain could not feel too happy about that transaction. Japan was only asked to do the right thing by China and she bowed her head to the display of superior force but she might be excused for thinking that Tsingtao was included in the price to be paid her for the part she had played in the war – a somewhat sordid bargain perhaps but Great Britain had been only too glad to accept Japan's assistance, particularly that of her Navy, in the early days of the war. And it gave one a feeling of discomfort that Great Britain should discard an alliance when its disadvantages

---

[153] In fact, Twenty-One Demands were sent to the Republic of China on 18 January 1915 by the Japanese. They would have greatly extended Japanese control of Manchuria and of the Chinese economy, and were opposed by Britain and the United States. The Chinese responded with a nationwide boycott of Japanese goods; Japan's exports to China fell 40%. Nevertheless Britain (and the United States) forced Japan to drop the fifth set of demands that would have given Japan a large measure of control over the entire Chinese economy and ended the Open Door Policy. Japan obtained its first four sets of goals (11 demands) in a treaty with China on 25 May 1915. This confirmed Japan's recent seizure of German ports and operations in Shandong Province, and expanded Japan's sphere of influence over the railways, coasts and major cities of the province. It extended the lease on Japan's South Manchuria Railway Zone, for ninety-nine years and expanded Japan's sphere of influence in southern Manchuria and eastern Inner Mongolia, to include rights of settlement and extraterritoriality, appointment of financial and administrative officials to the government and priority for Japanese investments in those areas. It also barred China from giving any further concessions to foreign powers except for Japan.

began to outweigh its advantages though a few years earlier a suggestion that Japan should drop the alliance would have been distinctly unwelcome.

But this was not the whole picture. The Japanese, when criticising our action, stress the benefit we had derived in the past from the alliance. But Japan had gained equally. It was no small matter that during her life and death struggle with Russia she had had Great Britain by her side to ensure that she got fair play. During the alliance she had risen to a position of importance in the world and part of the credit should be paid to the alliance. So that the suggestion that Great Britain used Japan as her cat's-paw is untrue.

Great Britain also was not without grounds for complaint. Japan never showed any particular consideration for British interests. It was significant that wherever she gained control, British trade faded out of the picture. To a great extent it was natural that Japan which was making great strides in industry and trade should displace Great Britain in near markets but the measures that the Japanese Government took were calculated to hasten the process – her navigation laws, the annexation of Corea and its conversion into a closed market, the blocking of railway construction in South Manchuria, etc. But what most shook confidence in Japan's goodwill was the attempt to obtain a stranglehold on China during the Great War.

It is possible to argue on both sides. I for one think that Great Britain's decision was a wise one – but only if she looked ahead and foresaw the consequences, for from that time the clash of interests became inevitable. History has shown that the only treaty that stands a chance of success is one into which the participating parties enter voluntarily. Japan considered herself outvoted at Washington. Consider the effect on Japan. She gave up Tsingtao, she agreed to limit her navy to three-fifths of that of Great Britain or the United States, she lost the Anglo-Japanese Alliance and was given in its place the Four Power and Nine Power Pact which she did not want.[154] There was little likelihood

---

[154]   For background, see W. G. Beasley, *The Modern History of Japan* (London: Weidenfeld & Nicholson, 1963), pp. 210–12.

of any country attacking Japan while she herself cherished the
ambition of advancing her position in East Asia. It is true that
she has always disclaimed territorial ambitions but this is mere
juggling with words. She has in succession absorbed Corea and
then Manchuria and if she had her way she would take all China
under her wing.

It was obvious to everyone that knew Japan that the results
of the Washington Conference were a great blow to her and it
should have been obvious in 1922 that the decisions there would
come to be valueless unless Great Britain and/or the United
States were prepared to prevent any infringement. But it would
seem to have been thought that the various treaties and pacts had
settled the trouble and that finis could be written to the story.

It is well to guard against the mistake of regarding Japan as
the villain of the play. It is probable that many Japanese were
not satisfied in their heart of hearts as to the rectitude of some
of the methods employed but as to the essential justice of her
cause no Japanese is in doubt. If you wish to get a great painting
in correct perspective it is necessary to choose the right point of
view. To the Japanese, western diplomacy is suspect. If he has a
long memory, he remembers that Japan was robbed of part of the
fruits of the China-Japan War by a combination of powers which
afterwards stood aside and allowed Russia to occupy Manchuria.
He remembers, what was to him, the humiliation of the Washington Conference. He is standing too close to the painting and
details that, at a slight distance, would blend into the picture
appear crude and repellent to him. (If you told him so, he would
probably retort that you are making the same mistake!) The truth
is that the Japanese is too much of a realist at heart to believe
in Christian doctrines of the rights of the weaker. He sees the
weaker race as a menace to his own safety. He uses the language
of diplomacy because it is the correct thing to do so, but to him
it is the sword that is mightier than the pen and prating to the
contrary is smug and hypocritical – at least when the language
is used by his opponents! It is folly to induce Japan to sign non-
aggression treaties and pacts outlawing war. The Japanese is very
self-centred. When the time comes that another nation blocks

what he considers his natural expansion then to him it is the other nation that is the aggressor!

Anglo-Japanese relations reached the parting of the ways in 1931 when the Japanese Army overthrew the Chinese adminis- tration of Manchuria. It was obvious that the terms aggression, war, independence, territorial integrity, conveyed a different meaning to the Japanese from that which they conveyed to the Anglo-Saxon. The wise thing then would have been to discard them and to try a more realistic approach. It is a waste of time debating the ethics of fox-hunting with a man who believes that the fox enjoys a thrill when hunted while you yourself believe that he suffers agonies of fear. Arguments merely end in mutual annoyance. If you are convinced that you are right, take steps to prevent him but otherwise leave him alone. And yet for the best part of ten years Great Britain and the United States continued to use language which meant nothing to Japan and to protest against each successive invasion of our rights and this in spite of the fact that Japan denied the original premises on which the protests were based.

Much the same thing occurred in Anglo-Japanese trade rela- tions. I have related elsewhere that the new government set up in Manchuria proceeded to strangle British trade both by control of trade and exchange and by a system of monopolies. In occupied China they used the same tactics and produced a still further argument – military necessity.

While governments handle theories, the business man deals with the practice but for the most part is bound to conform to the pattern set by his government. In most cases the British banker and merchant in Manchuria and China resorted to pas- sive resistance. He could not very well co-operate in the forging of chains to bind himself. He stood on his rights and looked to his government to protect him when they were infringed. But when its protests were unheeded, then he had to watch those rights being extinguished. It was not only that he was no longer able to trade; his assets disappeared. The British stake in China and Manchuria was a very big one. Capital had been invested in industry and trade development, in shipping, lightering and

stevedorage, in distribution and in selling organisations, in ware-
houses and processing establishments not only in the ports and
up-country. The value of a capital investment lies not in the
amount of capital sunk in it but in the return that it will make.
The British merchant had had his reverses in the past but he had
stuck to his guns in the lean years and had built up an organisation that worked well under the old order in China. Then Japan
marched in and set to work to inaugurate the 'new order' which
revolutionised everything, set aside the old machinery and proceeded to build anew. What the outcome will be no one can tell,
but the immediate result was chaos. Trade functioned only in fet-
ters and the whole British investment in China was endangered.
The British merchant may be pardoned for feeling embittered
and for demanding assistance from his government. Unfortunately there was little that could be done for him.

In its attempt to defend British interests His Majesty's Government faced two alternatives. It could adopt either a passive
or an active role. In the former case it would accept the actual
position, e.g. in Manchuria that, whatever the rights and wrongs,
Japan was in effective control and the government it had set up
was the *de facto* government. Without going so far as officially
to recognise the Manchukuo Government, British officials stationed there would be instructed to handle problems from the
standpoint that they were dealing with a (*de facto*) government.

This attitude had serious disadvantages. Great Britain was
bound by its commitments to the League of Nations and also
did not wish to embarrass the United States to both of which
the new state was anathema. Moreover, any appearance of com-
pounding the rape of Manchuria was bound to cause complaints
from the Chinese Government whose cause we had espoused.

On the other hand, while a passive role would have required
the greatest tact and diplomacy to prevent its degenerating into
abject surrender or developing into co-operation with the wrongdoer, a middle line would have been possible. It was a matter
of the method of approach. To base arguments on international
law, rights under treaties with China and duties under the various international pacts was poor tactics since for the Japanese to

admit the justice of this reasoning would have been tantamount to admitting that they were in the wrong to be in Manchuria and China in armed force. It was flogging a dead horse. But leaving these arguments aside, the British merchant had still a good case on grounds of elementary justice. He had built up his business in good faith and had invested his capital in it. If he was to be dispossessed, he was at the very least entitled to compensation.

Unfortunately, the political aspects of the question were kept so prominently to the fore that the merits of the case were scarcely given a hearing. The British merchant became the symbol of a system that could not live side by side with the Japanese and so Japanese opinion crystallised into the view that he must be destroyed root and branch.

Would more conciliatory tactics have worked? Since it was never tried, it is impossible to say. The Japanese, as I have hinted more than once, do not readily see the other man's point of view. But in Manchuria, Japanese officials constantly asked me to work for a *modus vivendi* and in Tientsin, so long as I kept controversial matters firmly in the background, it was possible to obtain concessions, not all that I wished but substantial none the less. If it had been possible, I think the method was worth a trial. But I am looking at the question of a Consul's point of view and it is admittedly difficult for a government to put aside political considerations. Moreover, an almost negative attitude had the two further objections that it is liable to be converted from a standstill position into a retrograde movement and that it is derogatory to the prestige of a great nation. And so we come to the alternative.

An active attitude would have involved first energetic protest and then retaliation. The disadvantage of retaliation is that it is, at best, a clumsy weapon. It usually rouses counter-retaliation in the first place. The immediate sufferer is the British merchant on the spot whose activities are still more drastically curtailed and even if the war of retaliation ends successfully, he is not likely to be indemnified for his losses while it was proceeding. Finally, His Majesty's Government has never been in a position to devote its whole attention to Far Eastern problems since its hands have been tied by the constantly recurring crises in Europe. On the other side, retaliation as a weapon has one solid advantage. It is positive and shows that the party employing it means business and is not merely bluffing. If it does not succeed in its main object, it may at least deter the other party from proceeding to further outrages.

So there are, in my opinion, the two alternatives. Personally, I should have liked to see the passive attitude given a fair trial and, if it failed, the gloss to have been taken off and an active method adopted.

In its conduct of Far Eastern affairs in the decade from 1930 to 1940 Great Britain fell between two stools. Its tactics were either too strong or not strong enough. It scolded Japan in season and out of season for its doings in China but it merely succeeded in infuriating her. Protests carried sufficient weight to check the rate of progress at first but not sufficient to stop it. After each check Japan came on again and resorted to ever stronger measures until she cast all prudence to the winds. In the good old melodramas the temporary set-backs suffered by the villain only rouse him to greater wickedness until ultimately the hero wakes to the seriousness of the situation and knocks him out. We resorted to pin-pricks when we should either have resorted to the big stick or decided that we could not fight China's battles for her and had better make the best of a bad job. British merchants would have had a thin time but they would scarcely have suffered such staggering blows in quick succession from a government that had been rendered thoroughly hostile to them. If Japan has become convinced that she cannot rest quiet while any British interests remain in the Far east, we must take some responsibility for turning her thoughts in that direction. We had a difficult hand to play, one which conceivably might have proved impossible, but we did not play it well.

I cannot help thinking that we carry too far our inclination to 'decide the practical questions of daily life by instinct rather than by systematic logic': certainly we have done so in the Far East. In Europe our problems are at our door-step and we can see, or should be able to see, whither they are tending. But the

Far East is too distant; we do not see the rocks until we are right upon them. Moreover, if it is allowable to say so, the tendency to trust to inspiration at the critical moment is apt to result in British officials at different posts pulling in different ways at just that time with disastrous results. This is the price we pay for our contempt of 'systematic logic'.

Index

ℰ∂